Details in Menswear

-The perfect book for a perfectionist-

Ivan M.C. Chen, Ph.D.

This book can be ordered through amazon, createspace.com, other websites, or any bookseller worldwide.

Dedication

In the movie, *Bobby Jones: Stroke of Genius*, Bobby Jones alerted the officials in the middle of the U.S. Open that he (accidentally) caused the ball to move. The officials talked to one another and concluded that no one saw the ball move. Jones insisted that he did. By doing so, he called one stroke penalty upon himself. The chief officer commented, "You are to be congratulated, son." He said so to praise Jones' honesty and sportsmanship. Surprisingly, Jones was not flattered by the kind words. He replied, "Sir, it is like congratulating a man for not robbing the bank. I don't know how else to play the game." Bobby Jones lost that championship game by one stroke.

I have sold men's clothing for two decades and have been stunned by how little consumers know about the clothes they wear every day. Most men buy the wrong size clothing, especially dress shirts and suits. Every time I tried to correct customers, I often got scolded with insulting words. They said that they had worn the same size shirts or suits before I was born, that they had just been measured or just tried on the garments, and so on. Most customers were kind and willing to listen to my explanations. They changed their mind and made necessary adjustment. Some customers would not give me a chance to talk. A few of them refused to buy anything from me. Others complained to the supervisors. Consequently, I was pressured by the management to withhold information or lie to customers in order to make sales.

Over the years, I have endured countless insults, back-stabbing and other unfair treatments. I have lost sales to few customers because of telling the truth. On the other hand, I have also made much more sales and earned great respects from many customers because of telling the same truth. I don't know how else to sell clothes.

This book collects many details that change the mind of tens of thousands of customers about men's clothing. Alan Flusser said, "Selling quality is a craft; doing it well requires an artist's passion and pride." I therefore dedicate this book to those honest and proud salespersons who pay attention to details, take pride in doing their jobs and are not afraid of telling the truth.

Contents

Prince Albert, Consort of the Queen Victoria of the United Kingdom

"A gentleman will take care that his clothes are of the best quality, well-made and suitable to his rank and position."

Introduction

Mark Twain once said, "Clothes make the man. Naked people have little or no influence on society." Despite the importance of clothing, most men do not spend much of their time and effort studying how to dress. Unlike women's dresses, contemporary men's clothing is very uniform. Most men learn about clothing by observing how other men dress. They do not believe it is difficult to buy and wear men's clothing. If they have problems, they think they can always rely on those professionals who sell men's clothing. They rarely realize that salesmen in today's market are often not well trained. John T. Molloy, the author of *Dress for Success*, suggested five reasons for businessmen's dressing for failure. One of the reasons is that they let their favorite salesclerks choose clothing for them. Mortimer Levitt, a custom shirt maker, once sent his executives to several of the better men's stores in New York City to have their collar size verified. He then declared, "Salesmen in the country's best stores do not know how to take a measurement for collar size."

Some men do not trust salespersons; they bring along their spouse, other family members or friends when shopping. Some shoppers do not bring any one, but they may grab any man or woman, who happens to be nearby, and ask for their "male" or "female" opinions. Some men hire image consultants or fashion professionals to shop for them. John T. Molloy believed this is another reason that today's men dress for failure. I once heard a consultant tell her client to choose neckties according to his eye color. Still, some other men are very particular. They have their own opinions and listen to nobody.

Screenshot, fair use.

In the movie, My First Mister, a customer was told that a blue suit will be "totally groovy" with his blue eyes. Nonsense such as this has been carried out on the selling floor everywhere.

I have sold men's clothing for two decades and have met a wide variety of shoppers. Regardless of the type of shoppers, the result is all similar. Most men buy and wear the wrong size or style of clothing. Alan Flusser, a prominent fashion designer and author, claimed that a stunning 90% of all men wear their jacket sleeves too long. The jacket sleeve is one of the most visible parts of an ensemble. If a man can err on his sleeve length, do you not think he is going to make mistakes on other parts of his outfit? What is worse is that most men do not even realize that they know little about the clothes they wear every day. This reminds me of one of the Parkinson's laws.

Parkinson's Law of Meetings (also known as Parkinson's Law of Triviality) states that the time spent in a meeting on an item is inversely proportional to its value. This happens because most people would avoid high-value decisions, which tend to be complex and risky, and few people understand the issues involved. People would rather contribute to the meeting by giving opinions on the subjects they think they understand better: the low-value, low-risk decisions.

Dirty Harry said, "Opinion is like asshole; everybody has one." It is no wonder that many men and women have fallen foul of Parkinson's Law. They constantly argue on the obvious and pay little attention to details. To notice differences in details often requires specific knowledge and keen insights. Most people lack expertise to discuss men's clothing in details, but they surely have a lot of personal experiences to comment on opinionative issues such as whether a shirt, jacket or a pair of pants fits the body, and whether a tie coordinates with a particular outfit.

Most men, including fashion experts, believe whether a pair of pants should be cuffed or not is a personal choice. They do not realize that the bottom finish of these two types of pants should be cut differently and the finish has a significant impact on how the pair of pants looks. Many men prefer cuffed pants but they have their pants cuffed at the wrong width—the best way to cheapen a pair of pants indeed.

Many men spend considerable amount of time, effort and money to shop for ties that they think will go well with their outfits. Then, they tie their ties with a sloppy knot or at the wrong length. They do not understand Oscar Wilde's famous words, "A well-tied tie is the first serious step in life." Every man should tie his tie properly regardless of the look, style or quality of the tie. A well-tied tie should have a forward arch beneath the knot. Billions of men wear ties, but few men can arch out their ties effortlessly.

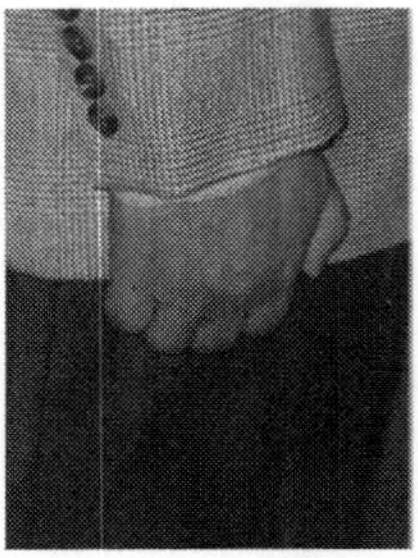

Almost every man cups his fingers to determine the length of a suit jacket. They do not realize that the proper length of the jacket has more to do with the length of torso than to do with the length of arm. The conventional wisdom is to recommend a man who is six feet to wear a long size jacket, and six feet four inches an extra-long size jacket. This may be unwise. The reason that a man is tall is likely because his legs are long. Since the jacket does not cover the legs, the man may not need a long or extra-long jacket. The proper length of a jacket should follow the ideal human figure, which has a torso of two head-lengths, a pelvis of one head-length, and a pair of lower limbs of three and half to four head-lengths.

Fashion experts suggest that the collar of a dress shirt should fit the neck snugly, but no one seems to know how tight the collar should be. Most men prefer a loose collar because they feel it is more comfortable this way. They do not realize there are four dimensions of the shirt collar. Few men ever think about the consequences of wearing a loose collar. No one knows that the sleeve length of a barrel cuff shirt should be different from that of a French cuff shirt. Many men wish to dress well by wearing fancy suits, shirts and ties. But, they choose the button-down collar without knowing that the style is the lease dressy one. Fashion experts believe that the spread collar is dressier than the point and the button-down collar. Nevertheless, no other author can explain why.

Many men like to dress up. They use accessories such as pocket squares and tie clips, but they do not know how to use accessories properly. Most of them mistakenly think that pocket square must match the tie. Alan Flusser complained that matching pocket square and tie is the sure sign of an unsure dresser. Few men know where to place the tie clip or tie tack. They put it on the tie randomly. When I told customers that the best locations to place a tie clip, tie tack or tie chain are the first and second balance points, everybody was stunned and asked "What are you talking about?" Most men prefer two-button jackets to three-button jackets simply because the former is more popular. After I explained to customers that the front V opening of a three-button jacket tends to correspond to the first balance point of the face, many customers changed their mind immediately.

The above are just a few examples to demonstrate that small details can play an important role on how a man dresses and looks. Some details, such as the bottom finish of pants have dramatic impacts. Other details, such as the position of jacket sleeve buttons, may be less important. Because contemporary men's clothing lacks variety, even a small detail can and will make difference to a simple outfit.

In recent years, I have written 12 books on major articles of men's clothing, such as shirts, ties and suits. The books contain detailed information that few authors have ever reported. After writing so many books, I am still learning something new every day. Once in a while I have discovered new facts, ideas and documents that support my theories, thoughts and wisdom. Instead of updating each of the books frequently, I found it appropriate to write a new book to present these new findings. This book was therefore created.

As the title implies, this book focuses on some details of men's clothing that most people neglect. This book is definitely a treasure for those men who like to dress up, especially for those fastidious men who strike for perfection in wearing men's clothing. The book is designed for readers who have had basic understanding of men's clothing. For those who are unfamiliar with men's clothing and need fundamental information on the subject, I recommend them read my other books in addition to this one.

Part One:

Clothes make the man

Screenshot, fair use.

Mark Twain said, "Clothes make the man. Naked people have little or no influence on society." Clothes make the man, but there are good clothes and bad clothes. Often, it is the fine details that distinguish the good clothes. Most men worry much about the obvious but pay little or no attention to details. They wear fancy suits but cannot get their sleeve length right. They prefer cuffed to non-cuffed pants but have their pants cuffed at the wrong width. They wear expensive ties with a sloppy knot or at the wrong length, and are incapable of arching out their ties. They wear dress shirt collars that are far larger than their neck. And, they wear their pants so long that multiple breaks form at the bottom back of the pants. The minute wrong detailing can spoil a good outfit. Hence, treat the details right!

Like most men, Elephant man looked decent in a properly fitted suit.

screenshot, fair use.

One of the most insulting words that I have ever heard is what Meg Ryan said to Tom Hanks in the movie, <u>You've got mail</u>, "You are nothing but a suit." The words were so hurtful that Hanks went silent for a couple of minutes. Billions of men wear suits. Many of them do not wear good suits or the right suits.

James Stewart swam in a large suit.

Fair use.

1. *The art of arching out a tie*

There is no other saying about ties that is more widely quoted than Oscar Wilde's words: "A well-tied tie is the first serious step in life." Every author uses Wilde's words to emphasize the importance of the tie to a man's ensemble or image. Yet, every author misses the key words in Wilde's saying. Most men spend considerable amount of time and effort worrying about whether the tie they wear is of good quality and whether the tie complements what they wear. They miss the point. Wilde did not mention that a pretty tie, an upper-class tie, a quality tie or any other kind of ties is the first serious step in life. He simply said, "A well-tied tie." This echoes my position that a man ought to pay attention to how he ties his tie. A man who owns a good tie but does not know how to tie the tie correctly does not deserve the tie. Just as a man should try to dress well no matter if it is a good day or bad day, a man ought to tie his tie well no matter what he wears is a good tie or bad tie, a right tie or wrong tie.

1-1. What is a well-tied tie?

Fashion experts believe that a well-tied tie should have a forward arch beneath the tie knot, but they have no clear idea how to accomplish this goal. All they can suggest is to pull the tie firmly against the collar. Alan Flusser said, "The necktie should be pulled up into the collar so that it is tight enough to arch out slightly from the neck." Thomas Fink and Yong Mao, the authors of *The 85 Ways to Tie a Tie*, wrote, "A properly executed knot causes the tie to protrude slightly from the neck, forming a hollow before it returns to the chest. This effect may be achieved by gently tightening the tie around the neck and pulling the knot up into the collar."

1-2. An arch beneath the tie knot

It is unthinkable less than a century ago that any well-dressed man would not attempt to arch out his tie. Old photos show that it was common for men to arch out their ties. What methods did these men use? They used a collar pin or a buttoned vest or jacket to support a pulled out tie. These methods do not always work. As collar pins and vests become endangered species these days, most men wear a flat tie that falls straight down from under the collar, producing a dejected look like the branch of a willow. The arching of the tie becomes a lost art.

1-3. Why can't men arch out their ties?

Fashion experts blame everything on the making and construction of the ties. Fink and Mao wrote, "The extent to which a knot will cooperate depends on its backing, the bulk of material in the back of the knot." In truth, whether a tie can arch out or not has a great deal to do with the type of tie knots. Every fashion expert promotes the three most popular tie knots in the world, the four-in-hand, half Windsor, and Windsor. These three knots are the main reasons that billions of men cannot arch out their ties.

In the movie, Mr. Lucky, Laraine Day called Cary Grant's four-in-hand tie knot the "stingy little nub of nothing." She tried to persuade him to switch to the Windsor knot. Grant rejected the idea at first but soon gave up simply because he loved the girl.

by Carl Van Vechten

Senator Huey Long

Congressman David Lewis

by Carl Van Vechten

It is unthinkable less than a century ago that any well-dressed man would not attempt to arch out his tie.

Even a child knows how to pull out his tie so that the tie will not lie flat and lifeless.

Screenshots, fair use.

1-4. Arch out the tie naturally.

"**Ideally** the tie should arch slightly away from the shirt front rather than laying flat and lifeless," wrote Susan Bixler and Nancy Nix-Rice, authors of *The New Professional Image.* They said "ideally" perhaps because it is rare that a man is able to

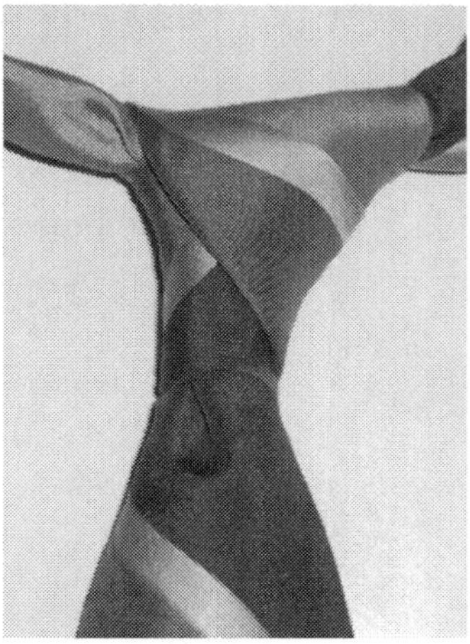

arch out his tie without any special support. In 2008, I published a book, ***The Art of Arching out a Tie***, which revolutionizes the way men tie their ties. The book examines the very factors that influence the arch of a knotted tie. Now you can arch out your tie effortlessly without using any artificial device regardless of the quality of the tie. The method can even turn the most unusual diagonal knot into an arched knot.

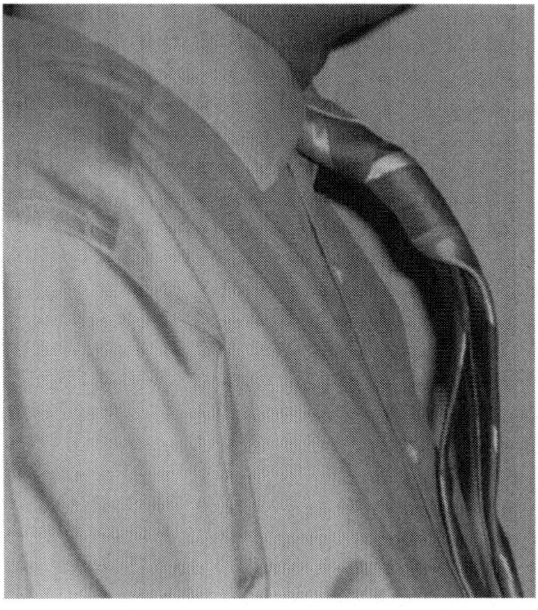

A well-tied tie should have a forward arch beneath the tie knot.

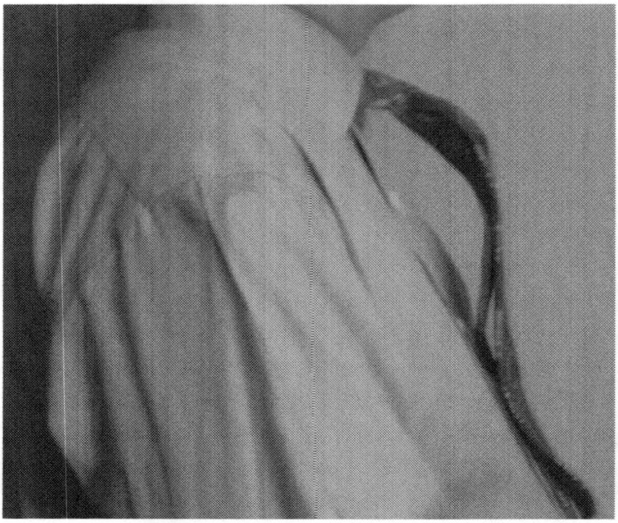

Billions of men live on earth. Few men can arch out the tie without the support of a collar pin, a collar tab, or a vest. The above picture shows the author of this book arches out his tie without using any device. The picture beneath shows the author wears the same shirt and tie, but the tie is weeping. The key secret is in the--tie knot. There are about 100 tie knots. Some knots are more effective in arching out the tie. The two pictures show the stunning difference between the world's simplest knot, the Oriental (above), and the second simplest knot, the four-in-hand (right).

1-5. Type-A vs. type-B knots

In my revolutionary book, *the Art of Arching out a Tie,* I divide tie knots into two groups based on the first move of the knots. When tying a knot, only the large end (or the front end) of the tie is moving around. The large end is called the active end while the narrow end the passive end. To begin a tie knot, we have two choices. We either place the active end **a**bove the passive end (Type-A), or place the active end **b**eneath the passive end (Type-B). I have found Type-B knots help arch out the tie whereas Type-A knots do not. To explain the difference, let me call it the "root", which is the location where both the active and passive end first meet. When the active end is pulled tight in the last move of the knotting process, the pulling force reaches to the root and pulls a Type-B knot outward because the active end is behind the knot. In a Type-A knot, the pulling force works in the opposite direction and pushes the knot inward or downward.

The most common knots are the four-in-hand, half Windsor, and Windsor. They are all Type-A knots. Some men use the Windsor knot to produce a larger knot or to shorten the length of the tie. Alan Flusser and Francois Chaille, the author of *The Book of Ties,* favor the Prince Albert knot over the Windsor because the Albert can produce a similar large knot with a more cylindrical and fashionable shape that fits into more collars than the broader Windsor. The Albert knot is an extension of the four-in-hand, in which the wide end makes a second revolution around the narrow end before finishing to the center. The Prince Albert knot is also a Type-A knot. No wonder that few men can arch out their ties these days because every popular tie knot is a wrong type of knots.

Examples of Type-B knots are the Oriental, Kelvin, Nicky, and Pratt (also known as the Shelby). If you wish to arch out your tie, try one of these knots. If a man has been using one of these knots, he may have accomplished something without knowing it. Fashion experts or image consultants like to call it, "accidentally looking great."

If you use Type-A knots, I suggest that you replace them with Type-B knots. The comparable Type-B knots to several Type-A knots are listed in Table 1.

Screenshot, fair use.

Jesse Watters wore a $950 Bijan tie on the O'Reilly Factor on February 24, 2012. The high price of the tie does not guarantee a good knot.

Table 1

Replacing Type-A with comparable Type-B Knots

Type-A Knot	Type-B Knot
Four-in-hand	Oriental
Half Windsor	Pratt (Shelby), Nicky
Windsor	Plattsburgh
Prince Albert/Victoria	Aaron/Kelvin
Mosconi Diagonal	Ivan Chen Diagonal

Choose the Right Knot

- **For thick ties**
  - Use: Oriental
- **For medium thick ties**
  - Use: Kelvin, Aaron, Pratt, Nicky
- **For thin ties**
  - Use: Kristina
- **For smooth ties**
  - Use: Kelvin, Aaron, Pratt, Nicky
  - Avoid: Oriental
- **For textured ties**
  - Use: Oriental, Kelvin, Aaron
- **For firm (stiff) ties**
  - Use: Oriental, Kelvin, Aaron
- **For soft ties**
  - Use: Kelvin, Aaron, Pratt, Nicky, Kristina
- **To achieve a slim or asymmetrical knot**
  - Use: Oriental, Kelvin, Aaron, Kristina
- **To achieve a triangular or symmetrical knot**
  - Use: Pratt, Nicky

How to tie the Oriental knot

a) ***Cross the ends with the wide end inside-out under the narrow end.***

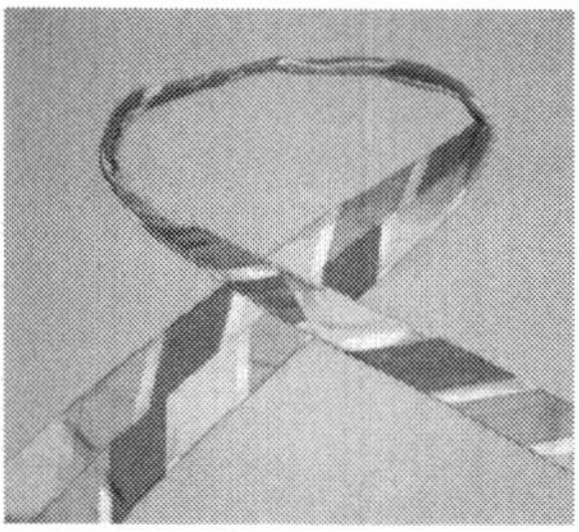

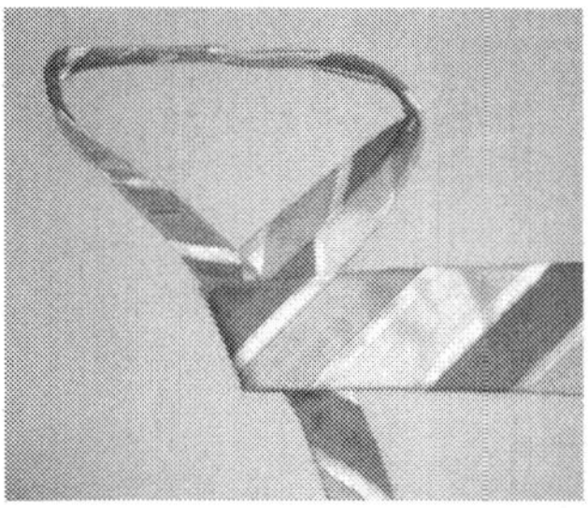

b) ***Fold the wide end horizontally over the narrow end.***

c) ***Bring the wide end up through the neck loop.***

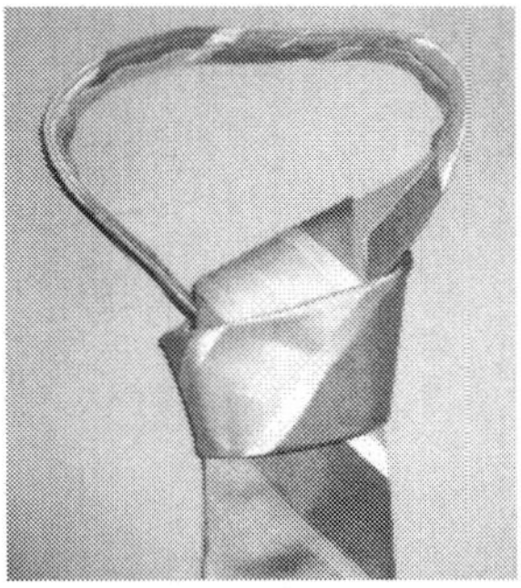

d) ***Tuck the wide end down through the just-created front loop. Tighten the knot and shape it at the collar.***

<u>*How to tie the Kelvin knot*</u>

The Kelvin is an extension of the Oriental. To knot the Kelvin, you simply wrap the wide end a second time around the small end before you bring the wide end up through the neck loop.

e) ***Following the moves in step (a) and (b), now comes the double wrapping. The wide end is wrapped behind the narrow end, pointing to the other side.***

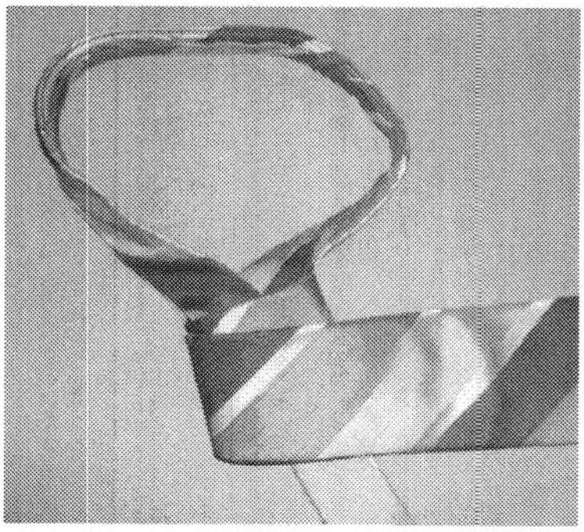

f) ***Fold the wide end over the front again.***

Complete the knot by following the step (c) and (d). The sequence of knotting the Kelvin is (a), (b), (e), (f), (c), and (d).

How to tie the Aaron knot

Because of the double wraps in the Kelvin, you may have difficulty pulling the large end tight enough to form a solid knot. In this case, try a new knot called the Aaron knot, which is a derivative of Kelvin. The Aaron knot differs from the Kelvin at the final move. To complete the Kelvin knot, the wide end is pulled down behind the second wrap. If you tuck the wide end down behind both the second and the first wrap, you will create a new knot. There has been no name for this knot. I call it Aaron in honor of my teenage boy, who asked me to teach him how to tie a necktie for his high school homecoming party. Since it was Aaron's first serious step in life, I gave him the best method that would guarantee him a well-arched tie. The relationship between the Kelvin (left photo) and the Aaron (right photo) is the same as that between the Victoria and the Prince Albert knot.

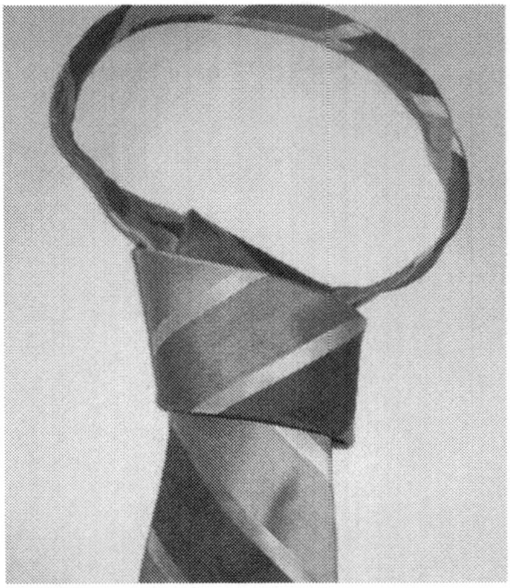

<u>***How to tie the Kristina knot***</u>

It is my firm belief that too much twisting and wrapping not only makes it more easily to damage the tie, but also makes it more difficult to pull the knot tightly. A tight knot is often required for an arched tie. If a large knot is desired, it is preferred to achieve such knot by using a thick or wide tie with a simple knot, instead of a thin or narrow tie with a complicated knot. The great majority of contemporary ties are made using the method invented by Jesse Langsdorf in 1924. The volume or body of the tie is given partly by the weight of the shell fabric but mainly by the bulk of interlining. Many ties, especially the inexpensive ones, may have a thin body owing to the lack of sufficient interlining. It is difficult to create a firm knot without substantial amount of fabric. If you use thin ties, you may have to give one or more rounds of wrapping. I recommend the Kristina, which is the name of my daughter. She often rescues me when I have problems with my computer.

To tie the Kristina knot, you simply tie a Kelvin knot but wrap the wide end around the small end one more revolution before you bring the wide end up through the neck loop.

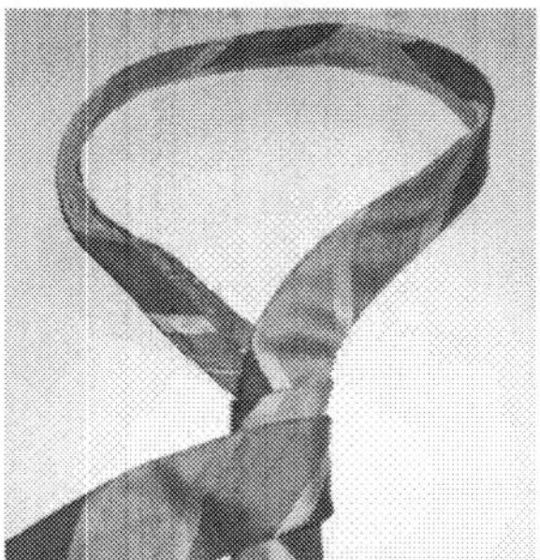

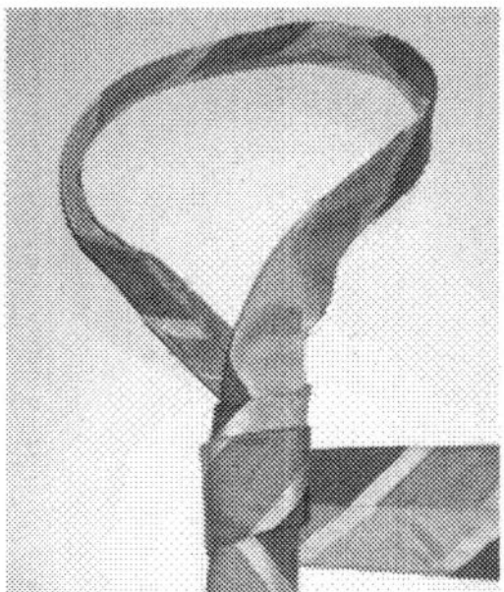

Kelvin ***Kristina***

How to tie the Pratt knot

To tie the Pratt knot, you add two more moves between step (a) and (b).

g) ***Following the move in step (a), bring the wide end forward, up, and over the neck loop.***

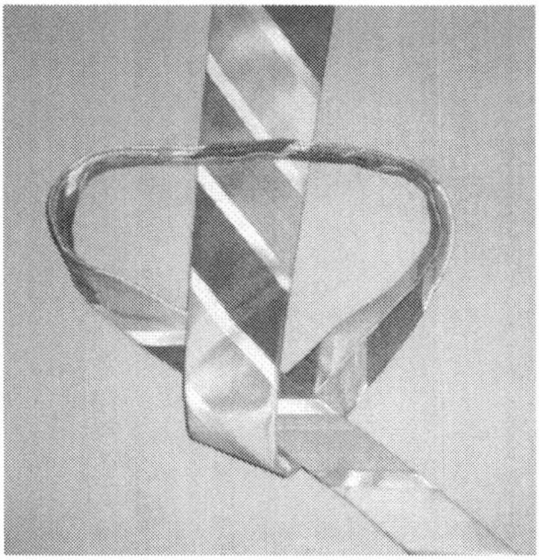

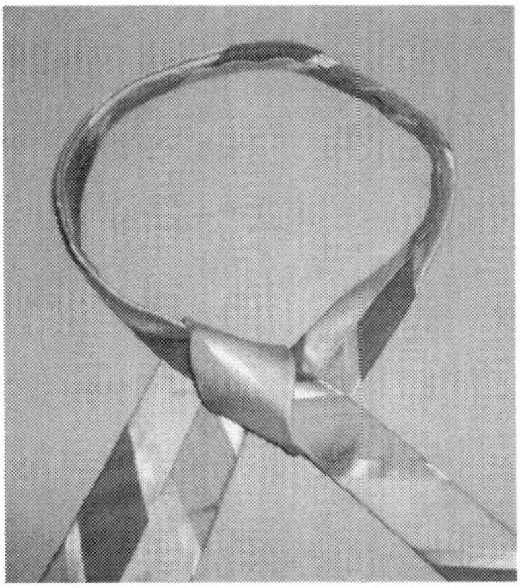

h) ***Pull the wide end down with the back seam showing and draw this wrapping tight.***

Complete the knot by following the step (b), (c) and (d). The sequence of knotting the Pratt is (a), (g), (h), (b), (c), and (d).

How to tie the Nicky knot

If you pull the wide end down to the other side following step (g), the knot becomes the Nicky knot. Both the Nicky and Pratt knots are similar in size and shape. The advantage of the Nicky over the Pratt is that it is a self-releasing knot. It unties itself when the narrow end is removed.

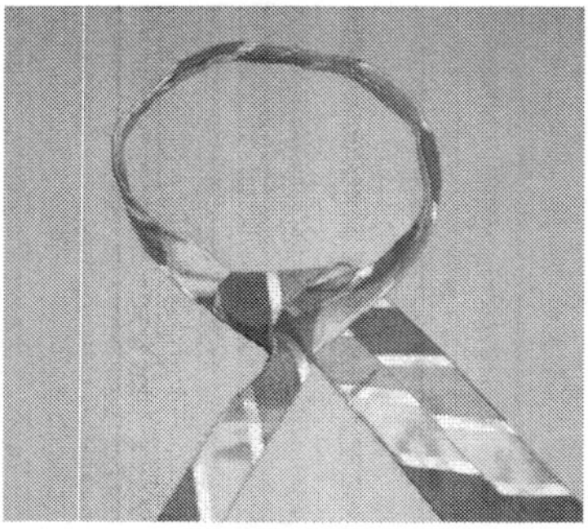

i) Following step (g), pull the wide end down to the other side instead of (h).

j) Fold the wide end horizontally over the narrow end.

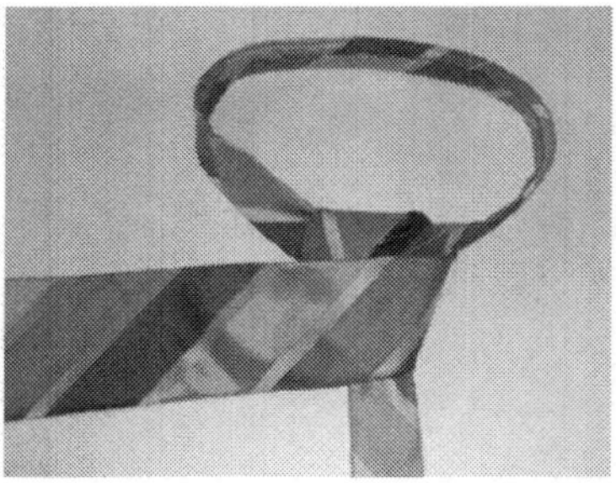

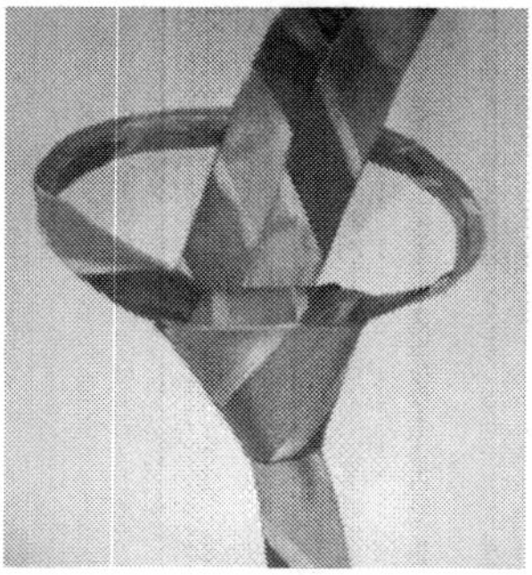

k) Bring the wide end up through the neck loop.

The sequence of knotting the Nicky is (a), (g), (i), (j), (k), and (d).

2. *Better to choke than to be vulgar*

Lincoln wearing a sloppy loose collar and a crooked bowtie.

2-1. Few men know how to measure the collar width correctly.

Many men do not know their collar size. They often have to ask a salesperson for measurement. It is difficult these days to find a salesperson who knows how to measure correctly. Mortimer Levitt, a custom shirt maker, once sent his executives to several of the better men's stores in New York City to have their collar size verified. He then declared, **"Salesmen in the country's best stores do not know how to take a measurement for collar size."** It is even more difficult to find a salesperson who knows how to convert neck size into collar size.

Many fashion publications suggest that the tape must be placed against the Adam's apple when taking the measurement. I doubt the accuracy of this assessment. Not every man has a prominent Adam's apple. Besides, the shirt collar may not sit at the same location as the Adam's apple. No man will enjoy wearing a stiff collar over the Adam's apple.

Most authors also recommend that the collar width is half an inch bigger than the neck size. This is terribly wrong. Many men buy a larger collar for fear that the shirt may shrink. Manufacturers already anticipated the potential shrinkage and added half an inch or more allowance when they made the shirt. A 16 ½" collar on a brand new shirt is actually a 17". As technology improves, manufacturers these days are able to produce shirt collars that guarantee little or no shrinkage. When a collar becomes too tight, it is probably because the man has gained weight, not because the collar has shrunk too much. If a man changes his weight frequently, don't you think the man is better off to own a few shirts of different sizes so that he will always have the correct size shirts to wear?

2-2. Dress shirt collars should fit the neck snuggly.

Many men wear the wrong collar size even though they know their correct neck size. It surprises me that a great majority of men wish to wear a collar size that is bigger, in many cases far bigger, than their actual neck size. Many people, including women, believe that they need extra room around their neck so that they will feel more comfortable and be able to breathe. When the collar is too tight, a man can recognize the problem right away because he can hardly fasten the top button of the shirt. But when the collar is loose, a man may not realize the consequences of wearing a collar that is too big for the neck.

First, the collar of the shirt will find a place to rest on the neck. When it is tight, the collar rises up and parallels the chin line. When it is too loose, the collar sinks down not only leaving a big hole at the bottom of the front neck, but also ruining the parallel between the collar line and the chin line.

Second, a raised collar will show a beautiful side-view of the collar wings standing erect on the chest.

Third, the necktie worn on the collar needs to arch out. To arch out a tie, the tie must hug the neck tightly. When the tie is pulled tighter than the collar band, unsightly wrinkles will appear in the collar and shirtfronts. A sunken collar will push down the tie and make it impossible for the tie to erect.

Bill Gates' collar was so large that it sank down and left a big hole at the bottom of the front neck.

Source: The Archive of the Chancellery of the President of the Republic of Poland, (GNU).

Gregory Peck and Leslie Howard in a tight collar.

By Hans Lachmann, CC-BY 3.0.

Unsightly wrinkles appear when a loose collar is fastened or squeezed by a tightened necktie.

A tight collar is required for an arched tie.

Fourth, the chest and waist size of a readymade shirt is cut according to its collar width. The bigger the collar width, the larger the chest and waist size is. By wearing a collar that is larger than necessary, the body size of the shirt can be overwhelming for the wearer unless the wearer has a relatively large body.

The body size of a dress shirt is made according to the collar width. For each inch increase in the collar, the body size grows about four inches.

Fifth, a large collar diminishes the head.

by Caroline Bonarde Ucci

Sixth, when a man grows older, his neck begins to wrinkle and needs a tall and tight collar front to cover the wrinkles.

By Army.mil, CC-By 2.0.

Finally, the collar of a fine dress shirt is intentionally made to be stiff--which means not to be comfortable. So, why wear a stiff collar shirt and expect it to be comfortable? This reminds me of the conversation between the young Irish girl, Shannon, and her mother in the movie, *Far and Away*. Shannon unfastened the top button of her shirt. Her mother yelled, “Shannon, what is your collar doing?” Shannon replied, “It is choking me.” “Well, do it up,” said the mother, “Better to choke than to be vulgar.”

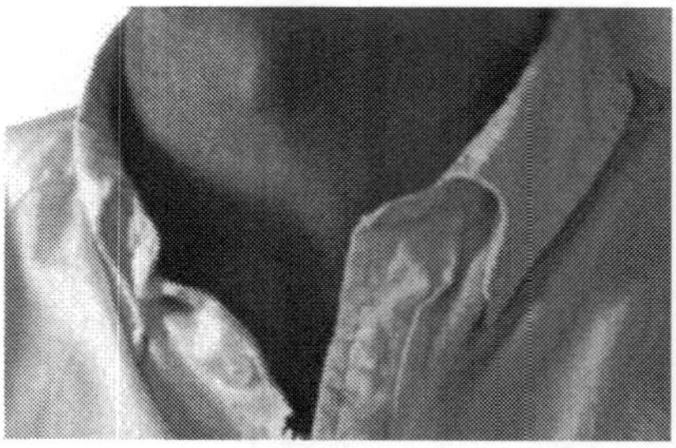

A key difference between a dress and a sport shirt is that the dress shirt has a stiffer collar.

Many men do not fasten the top shirt button, so they think it is irrelevant whether they wear a larger collar. As explained earlier, dress shirts often have a stiff collar. When the top button is unfastened, the collar tends to spring out. The larger the collar is, the farther it will spring out. A customer came to our store to buy dress shirts. I teased him that his collar puckered and looked like the one worn by Nobel laureate, Thomas Cech. I told him that he could make all the dents and wrinkles in his collar disappear. He asked me how. I let him try on a shirt with a collar that was ½" smaller than what he had asked for. He was amazed to notice that his collar became perfectly smooth without any wrinkle or fold. Every time I showed customers the photo of Kobe Bryant, they just could not stop laughing.

by Anthony Chu, CC-BY 2.5

There is an ancient Chinese story. Two soldiers ran away from a fight during a battle. One retreated 50 steps, the other 100 steps. The 50-step turned around and laughed at the 100-step, "You, coward." It is ridiculous to think that a 17" collar is more comfortable to wear than a 16" collar if the man only has a neck of 15". Many men do not even button the collar when wearing a dress shirt. Why do so many men want to wear a collar that is much bigger than their neck? I think the desire for a larger collar size is mainly psychological.

Over a decade, I have met thousands of customers who came to the store to buy dress shirts. I asked them what size they had in mind. Many customers gave a vague answer, such as "16 or 16 ½ inch." This cannot be right. A half inch makes a big difference. Shirt experts believe that every other man needs a quarter size collars. The collars of readymade dress shirts in today's market are fitted to the half-inch instead of the quarter-inch. This means that many men are forced to wear a collar size that is imperfect. When a man says that he wears both 16" and 16 ½" collars, there is a fair chance that neither size is correct.

2-3. The collar is a good fit for a new shirt if the wearer can slip one or two fingers into the gap between the collar and the neck.

It is not always easy to attain the correct collar size by measuring a person's neck with a measuring tape. The neck is somewhat like a cone, in that it gets smaller toward the head. When you measure a person's neck, you may not measure at the same place where the shirt collar will sit. In addition, the slope of the collar can vary among different patterns, styles, brands or makers of the dress shirts. Still, the angle, at which the neck sits on the body, can also vary among different individuals. Since no one can tell how well the collar will rest on a person's neck until the person puts the shirt on, the best way of determining the collar size is to put the shirt on. The collar is a good fit for a new shirt if you can just slip one or two of your fingers (depending on the size of your fingers) into the gap between the collar and your neck. As technologies progress rapidly, manufacturers these days are able to produce collars that guarantee no shrinkage. With no-shrinkage collars, you may want to choose a smaller collar size.

It does not look flattering when shirt collar stands away from the neck, showing a large gap.

A loose shirt collar not only looks unattractive but also pushes the jacket collar away from the neck.

Ryan Pierse / Getty Images, Fair use.

This photo should convince every man why they want to have their neck covered.

The more the neck is covered, the more the face is shown.

And, the more the attention is given to the face, the more powerful the face will appear.

Photo credit:
Middle and bottom left by Georges Biard.
The other three by Nicolas Genin.

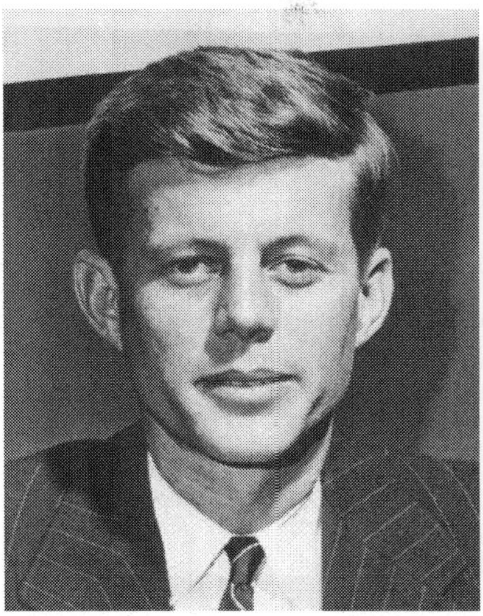

The art of demonstrating power: show more of your face by reducing the exposure of your neck.

The stunning beauty of a tall firm-fitting collar

3. Control your sleeve cuffs!

3-1. There are two types of sleeves: tapered and non-tapered.

A great number of American working class men do not know their proper sleeve length. Most men, especially the elders, like to wear their sleeves short. Consequently, the sleeves pull back whenever their arms stretch or bend.

From the beginning of ancient civilizations, shirtsleeves were cut straight with a wide opening at the end of the sleeves. Ancient men had to wear their sleeves short so that the fabric would not fall over the hands. Today, dress shirt sleeves are tapered and finished at the end with a band called barrel cuff or buttoned cuff, or finished with a fold called French cuff.

by Alan Light

3-2. The sleeve length of a barrel cuff shirt should be longer than the arm.

To wear a barrel cuff shirt correctly, the shirt cuff should fit snugly around the wrist to keep sleeve length from falling over the hand. Because the tight fit around the wrist will restrict arm movement, additional sleeve length must be added to the sleeve to allow the arm to stretch or bend without pulling the cuff. This additional sleeve length will hang above the wrist area and is called "drape". When the cuff fits snugly and the sleeve is long enough, the arm will be able to move in any direction without affecting how the cuff sits on top of the wrist. Thus, the shirt cuff and hand will move as a unit.

The proper sleeve length is affected by the width of the cuff. If you can find a barrel cuff that fits your wrist snugly, add one inch to your correct arm length for "drape." This will give you the sleeve length. If you have a built chest, you may want to add another ½" because the large chest will lift the shirt's armhole up into the armpit. If you wear a suit or sport coat, you may also consider wearing a slightly longer sleeve because the jacket may sometimes hold up the sleeve.

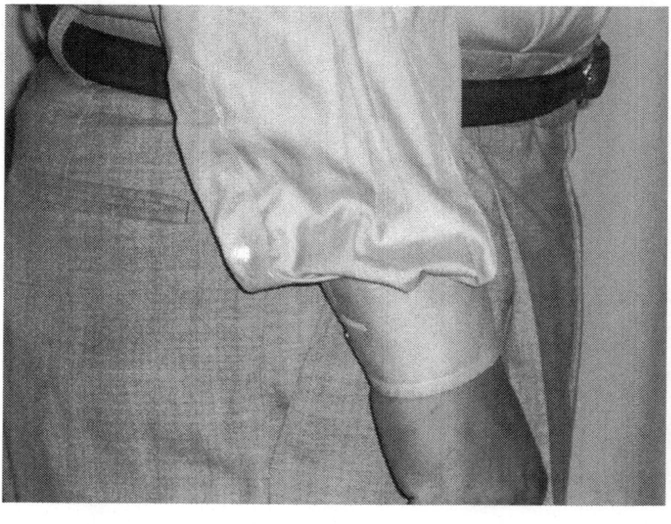

If worn correctly, a barrel cuff will not retreat with the jacket sleeve when the arm stretches or bends.

3-3. The sleeve length of a French cuff shirt is different from that of a barrel cuff shirt.

A French cuff is made differently from the barrel cuff. The French cuff usually has a large opening and requires a cufflink to close the opening. When you wear a barrel cuff sleeve, the extra sleeve length will drape right above the wrist area owing to the tight fit of the cuff. But if you wear a French cuff sleeve and if the sleeve is long, the extra sleeve length will fall over the hand because of the wide opening at the cuff. That is why you should always wear the French cuff sleeve shorter than the barrel cuff sleeve. Nevertheless, I have never met any customer who buys different sleeve lengths for these two different cuff shirts.

Most men prefer a barrel cuff to a French cuff shirt. A barrel cuff can be closed simply by fastening the button already sewn on the cuff, but a French cuff requires a cufflink to fasten it.

The French cuff looks elegant if it is worn with a suit or sport coat. The French cuff fills the gap between the coat sleeve and the hand with the wide and bulky cuff. On the other hand, the barrel cuff leaves a large gap between the coat sleeve and the shirtsleeve because of the narrow opening of the barrel cuff. When you wear a suit or sport coat, your shirtsleeve should extend beyond the end of the coat sleeve about ¼" to ½". As the arm stretches, the barrel cuff shirtsleeve stays at the wrist but the coat sleeve retreats, exposing several inches of the shirtsleeve--which is unbecoming. If you wear a French cuff without drape and if you stretch your arm, the shirt cuff will retreat along with the coat sleeve and maintains its ¼" to ½" extension beyond the coat sleeve.

If you desire a French cuff shirt, wear the sleeves short without drape. Otherwise, the opening of the cuffs will soon wear out or get marked with sweat stain because the cuffs rub against hands constantly. Some manufacturers market average sleeve length French cuff shirts. Unlike an average sleeve length barrel cuff shirt that has two horizontal buttons, an average sleeve length French cuff shirt will have two vertical buttonholes on the inner layer of the cuff. The manufacturers expect the wearer to adjust sleeve length by using one of these two buttonholes. Nevertheless, the distance between the two holes hardly ever exceeds ½".

Many men wear both barrel and French cuff shirts. Few of them know that the proper sleeve length of a French cuff shirt is different from that of a barrel cuff shirt. Some men have a bizarre idea that the sleeve length of a French cuff should be longer than that of a barrel cuff. Alan Flusser claimed that 90%

of all men wear their jacket sleeves too long. This makes it impossible or difficult for the barrel cuff sleeves to show. Some men believe that the French cuff shirt is dressier than the barrel cuff shirt; therefore, they wear longer French cuff sleeves so that the shirt sleeves can stick out under the jacket sleeves. They fail to realize that both barrel and French cuff sleeves should extend beyond the jacket sleeves and no shirt sleeve should fall beyond the wrist. The correct way is to cut short the jacket sleeves.

In order for the French cuff sleeve to function correctly, it should be worn short.

3-4. The proper sleeve length is based on the type of cuffs.

The shirtsleeve is designed to cover the arm, not the hand. In any condition, you should never allow the shirtsleeve to extend beyond the wrist--where the hand and arm meet.

During the latter half of the 19th century, men's readymade shirts came in a single (extra-long) sleeve length. Men used sleeve garters to customize sleeve lengths and keep the cuffs from becoming soiled while working. Readymade dress shirts these days come in different lengths. Men buy shirts with a proper sleeve length and use the buttoned cuff to keep the sleeve from falling over the hand. Today, sleeve garters are seen only in certain professions, such as musicians and poker dealers.

By Tammy Green, CC-BY-SA 2.0

A barbershop quartet at Walt Disney World, wearing sleeve garters

At one time, dress shirts were made in the tailor shop. A tailor would measure a person's wrist width and determined how big the cuff should be. In today's market, shirts are made not to fit an average person but to fit most consumers. Hence, the width of the barrel cuff in most readymade dress shirts tends to be too large for an average person. I have observed that the barrel cuff in some fashion designers' brands is sometimes cut so large that it loses the purpose of having a cuff. A large cuff will cause the additional sleeve length to fall over the hand and hinder the hand movement if the sleeve is long.

Readymade dress shirts are sold in stores according to the collar size and sleeve length. Every man buys dress shirts according to his neck size and arm length. I have never met a man who will give any thought about the cuff width. Many men fear that the shirtsleeve will fall over the hand if the sleeve is longer than the arm length. Instead of dealing with the problem correctly by controlling the cuff width, they wear sleeves short without drape.

If you choose a barrel cuff, you should wear a sleeve length that is at least one inch longer than your arm length to allow your arm to stretch without pulling the cuff. The key is to fit the cuff snugly around your wrist to prevent the sleeve from falling over your hand. If you can slide your hand through the cuff opening without first unfastening the button, the cuff is too large and the additional sleeve length will definitely hang over your hand.

If you cannot find a shirt cuff that fits your wrist snugly, consider sending the shirt to a tailor to have the cuff altered. Or, you can simply move the button yourself to make the cuff fit. If you are unwilling to try either option, you may have to wear a shorter sleeve length.

If you wear a wristwatch or bracelet, consider the watch or the jewel a part of your wrist and adjust your cuff width accordingly. Some people wear the watch or bracelet outside the shirt cuff instead of hiding the jewel under the sleeve. It is showy and may damage the sleeve or jewel by friction.

Bill Gates' sleeves retreat because the cuffs are too large, the sleeves are too short or both.

by Mathieu Scroussi, CC-BY-SA 3.0

4. Which is worse, a larger collar or shorter sleeve?

Frequently, I meet men with a small neck and long arms. These men should have their dress shirts custom made but most of them would rather buy readymade shirts because custom shirts are much more expensive and take time to produce. Most men do not know how precisely a dress shirt should fit. They often wear wrong size shirts without noticing the problem. It is common that a man with a 15" neck wears a 16 ½" or 17" collar because he is unable to find a 15" collar with a 36" or 37" sleeve length to cover his long arms.

Which is worse between a shirt with a larger collar, perfect sleeves and a shirt with a perfect collar, shorter sleeves? Fashion experts suggest that the collar is the most important part of a shirt. When the top button of the shirt is fastened, the collar frames the wearer's face. Despite this advice, almost every man and woman, whom I encountered, preferred a wrong collar with a correct sleeve length to a correct collar with a wrong sleeve length. It is understandable why they would rather err on the side of longer sleeves. It is noticeable when the sleeves are too short but it is not immediately obvious when the collar is too large.

As explained previously, the ideal length of a barrel cuff sleeve should be one or two inches longer than the length of the arm. The extra length is called "drape." The purpose of the drape is to prevent the sleeve cuff from retreating when the arm bends or stretches. Because a man does not bend or stretch his arms most of the time, the extra length can be forsaken. In other words, a man can wear his barrel cuff sleeves slightly short without drape, the same way he wears his French cuff sleeves. A man, who needs a 15" collar and 34" sleeves, may be better off to choose a shirt with a 15" collar and 33" sleeves instead of a shirt with a 15 ½" collar and 34" sleeves if the correct size is unavailable. Between the collar and sleeves, it may be wise to sacrifice the sleeves as long as the sleeves are not two inches or more too short.

Like Tiger Woods, many men never realize their collar is too large.

by Allan Warren, CC-BY-SA 3.0

from Ednortongfdl.PNG, GNU

A risen shirt collar (top photos) brings the beauty of the jacket to the fore whereas a sunken shirt collar (bottom photos) does not. It may be better to have a perfect shirt collar, imperfect sleeves than to have an imperfect collar, perfect sleeves.

by Kristin Dos Santos, CC-BY 2.0

Most men worry about their shirt sleeves' being too short. In truth, a slightly shorter sleeve may not look worse than a larger collar.

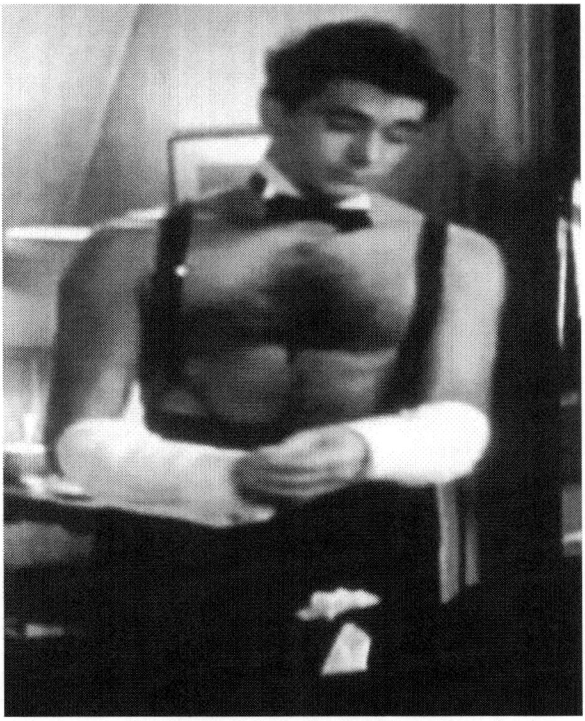

Screenshots from *At Long Last Love*, fair use.

Some men have difficulty finding the right size dress shirts because they have a very small neck with long arms and cannot afford custom shirts. The man found a solution. He wore fake sleeves.

5. How much linen to show?

Traditionally, a well-dressed man has his shirt collar shown ¼" to ½" above the jacket collar. If a tall collar formal shirt is worn, the shirt collar should stick out ¾" instead of the normal ½".

Dress shirt collar should stick out of jacket collar ¼" to ½".

A tall collar formal dress shirt should peek out of the jacket collar ¾".

The collar of the overcoat should be tall enough to cover both the shirt and jacket collars.

Prince Charles' shirt collar was shown above the overcoat collar.

By andibrunt, CC-BY-SA 2.0.

Prince Phillip's coat collar was too low either.

Screenshot, fair use.

During the Fox news show, the Five, on January 2, 2012, Greg Gutfeld complained that he did not like showing a large band of shirt linen under his jacket sleeve. He did not know if his

shirt sleeves were too long or his jacket sleeves were too short. Other photos indicate that Gutfeld wore jacket sleeves that are too long. It appears that on January 2 his shirt cuffs were too loose and sleeves were too long. If he does not want his shirt sleeves to stick out too much, he should wear French cuff sleeves with a shorter length so the sleeves can retreat along with the jacket sleeves.

Most men know that shirt sleeves, when properly dressed, should extend ¼" to ½" beneath the jacket sleeves, but they have no clear ideas how to achieve this goal. According to Alan Flusser, 90% of all men wear their jacket sleeve too long. Consequently, most men hide their shirt sleeves under the jacket sleeves or wear shirt sleeves that are even longer than their jacket sleeves, which are already too long. I have encountered many men, who bought new jackets and wanted the sleeves to be lengthened even though the jacket sleeves were already too long. Readymade shirt sleeve cuffs tend to be too large for the wrists of most men. Too large the cuff causes the shirt sleeve to fall over the hand without drape. Too long the shirt sleeve makes the jacket sleeve look relatively short. Hence, many men, such as Greg Gutfeld, mistakenly wear their jacket sleeves too long to cater to the extra length of their shirt sleeves.

It is silly to wear a certain length of jacket sleeves based on the relative length of shirt sleeves, or vice versa. The proper lengths of the jacket sleeves and shirt sleeves should be based on the arm length and the types of cuffs.

A man should not fear that the jacket sleeves retreat when the arms bend or stretch. The armholes of a jacket tend to be cut large in order to accommodate more customers. When the armpits are cut low, the jacket tends to shake a lot while the arms are moving. It is normal for jacket sleeves to retreat. The jacket has to protect itself by allowing the sleeves to withdraw in order to absorb the stress when the arms are moving, or the jacket will be torn somewhere under the arms.

Most men do not know the proper lengths of jacket and shirt sleeves. I have invented the idea of using the three lines on the wrist to determine the correct lengths of dress shirt, jacket and overcoat sleeves.

If you bend your hand outward, you may notice the three lines on your wrist. Place the end of your jacket sleeve on the first line (away from your hand), shirt sleeve on the second line, and the overcoat on the third.

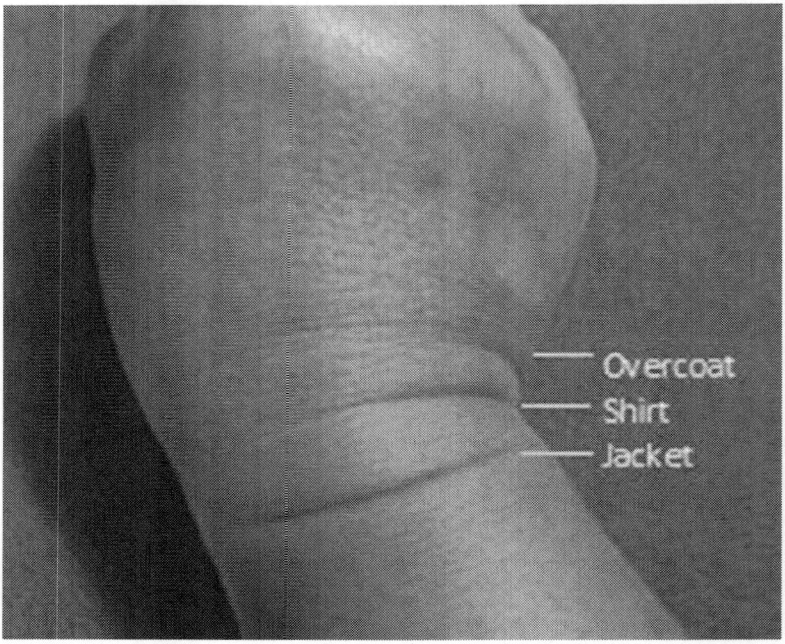

It has never been a shame for a man to show his sleeves.

Shimon Peres properly showed his shirt sleeves whereas President Obama did not.

Shirt sleeves should extend ¼" to ½" beneath the jacket sleeves.

The sleeves of a formal dress shirt should peek out of the formal jacket sleeves ¾" instead of the normal ½". This means that the sleeve length of a formal jacket should be slightly shorter than that of a business suit or sport jacket.

President Kennedy and French Culture Minister André Malraux wore their diner jacket sleeves too long, showing no shirt sleeves.

Gavin Newsom was the Keynote Speaker at the 2009 Black Tie Dinner. He pointed his finger to emphasize something, but his shirt sleeve did not show. It is hard to lecture someone when you cannot get the simple thing right.

President Bush pointed his finger with his shirt sleeve properly shown.

Overcoat sleeves should be long enough to cover both shirt and suit jacket sleeves.

6. *You need only one button on your shirt sleeve.*

World Economic Forum, CC-BY-SA 2.0.

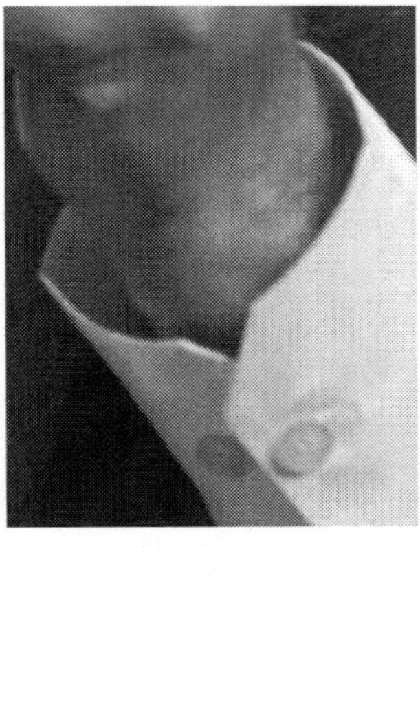

Prince Albert once said, "A gentleman will take care that his clothes are of the best quality, well-made and **suitable to his rank and position**." It is hard to believe that Prime Minister Blair wore a cheap shirt. What is worse is that he fastened the wrong button, leaving a large gap between the hand and the sleeve. President Reagan wore correctly a tight barrel cuff with one button showing.

Better made dress shirts are generally sold in exact sleeve length. Some dress shirts come with a so-called average sleeve length, such as 32-33", 34-35", and 36-37". The term, average sleeve length, is somehow misleading because the sleeve length 32-33" is actually a 33", sleeve length of 34-35" is a 35", and so forth. A 32-33" was designed to fit both a person with a 32" sleeve length and a person with a 33" sleeve length. You may think a 33" is going to be too long for a person who needs only a 32" sleeve. This is how it works. There are two horizontal buttons on the cuff of an average sleeve shirt. If a person needs a 32" sleeve and wears a 32-33" sleeve, he can button the second button. It is possible that some manufacturers may produce a true average sleeve length, to say, a 32 ½" for a 32-33" sleeve. Sport shirts that come with a small, medium, large or extra-large size are usually equipped with two horizontal buttons on the sleeve.

Many customers told me that they need a 35" sleeve length. The 34-35" sleeve is too short. It is a custom in the garment industry to give a brand new shirt ½" to ⅝" allowance in sleeve length to compensate for the shrinkage after the shirt is repeatedly washed or cleaned. Some manufacturers may not provide the allowance for an average sleeve length shirt since the allowance will make the sleeve be too long for persons who need a shorter length. Therefore, it is possible that a 34-35" sleeve is shorter than a 35" sleeve.

Many men prefer fancy dress shirts and have their shirts starched or pressed regularly. It is unconvincing to show how much you care about your shirt with two buttons on the sleeve, which is a mark of convenience and indolence. A man needs only one horizontal button on his shirt sleeve. If you occupy a high position in your workplace or community, or if you simply like to dress up, you may consider removing one of the two buttons. No one will notice that you wear an average sleeve length shirt when there is only one button on the cuff. One justification for having two buttons on the sleeve cuff is wearing a wrist watch.

Unlike women's apparels, men's business clothing lacks variety. Many men are bored with the uniformity of menswear. They are eager in search of ways to dress differently. The turndown sleeve cuff is one of the examples. It is my opinion that dressing differently is unnecessarily the same as dressing better. There are good ways and bad ways to dress differently. The turndown cuff does not appear as clean and elegant as the simple French or barrel cuff.

Screenshot, fair use.

The turndown cuffs look like the turndown collar of the shirt.

Screenshot, fair use.

They even made button-down version of the turndown cuff.

7. *Shirt body and collar Size*

7-1. It is more effective to reduce the body size by choosing a smaller collar.

Frequently, I met customers, who wanted to buy fitted shirts. They said they did not like shirts that are too blousy. I wrote a book, entitled *The Stupid Things Men Do about Their Clothing*. One of the most foolish things men do is to buy an oversized dress shirt and ask for a fitted one. Dress shirts are sold by collar width and sleeve length. The body of a dress shirt is based on the collar size. For every inch increase in the collar, the body size increases about four inches. Many men wear a shirt collar that is much larger than their neck. It is no wonder that some of them wish to wear fitted shirts. If they buy the correct collar size, they may not need slim-cut shirts.

The federal government has established standards of collar size in relation to chest size.

14 ½"	collar	=	36"	chest
15"	collar	=	38"	chest
15 ½"	collar	=	40"	chest
16"	collar	=	42"	chest
16 ½"	collar	=	44"	chest
17"	collar	=	46"	chest
17 ½"	collar	=	48"	chest
18"	collar	=	50"	chest
18 ½"	collar	=	52"	chest

The guideline is somewhat impractical because most men vary quite differently in the neck and chest. There is no consistent relationship between the two measures. When you shop for sport shirts, you should be more concerned about the chest size. If you are shopping for dress shirts, you should focus on the collar width, providing that the chest size is sufficient enough to accommodate your torso.

7-2. Fitted shirts are ideal for men with a relatively large neck, small torso, or both.

Fitted shirts are ideal for men with a relatively large neck, small torso, or both. The body difference between a regular and a fitted shirt of the same collar size is about two inches. Some tailored or slim fit shirts may be four inches smaller than regular or full cut shirts, depending on the manufacturers and the fashion of the time. For a normal man who is used to wear oversized collars, it is more effective and beneficial to reduce the body size by wearing a smaller shirt collar. The man can cut down the body size by two inches if he buys a collar size that is ½" smaller, or reduce the body size by four inches if he selects a collar that is 1" smaller. Fitted shirts are less common than regular shirts. They tend to have smaller shoulders, which are uncomfortable to wear for a built chest. They may also have a shorter tail, which is less likely to stay tucked in.

Some men have a built upper body. They tend to buy shirts with a larger collar just trying to acquire a larger body size. A better strategy is to buy shirts with a snug collar but with a fuller body cut.

No matter if you have a relatively small or large torso, it is always better to buy shirts with a close-fitting collar and use different cuts to accommodate your specific body shape.

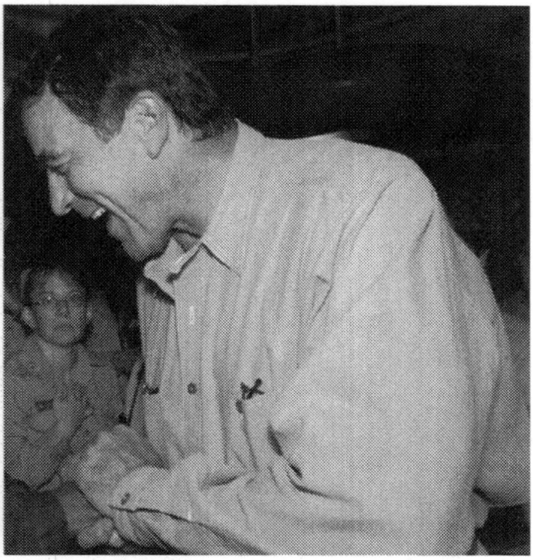

Tom Selleck either wore an oversized shirt or a correct-sized shirt with a full-cut.

Kevin Costner in a slim-fit (left) and a regular-fit shirt.

7-3. The body fit may be affected by the sleeve length.

Many men chose dress shirt sleeves that were too short for their arms. I suggested them to buy shirts with longer sleeves. After trying on the shirts, some of them complained that there was too much fabric hanging under the armpit. Sleeve length is measured from the center back under the collar, along the shoulder, and down thought the arm to the wrist. When manufacturers change from a shorter to longer sleeve, such as from 34" to 36", they tend to widen the shoulder as well as to lengthen the arm. This minor adjustment does not usually affect an average body shape. Nonetheless, if a man has an odd body shape such as a prominent or slim shoulder and chest, he should take this factor into consideration. A man with a built body shape may be better off to err on a longer sleeve length.

8. *Top fused shirts*

I used to get amazed by many journalists, such as David Broder and Charles Krauthammer, who wore wrinkled or bubbled shirt collars on television. As technologies progress rapidly, readymade dress shirts are much better made these days. It has become increasingly difficult to find dress shirt collars that wrinkle and pucker terribly.

William F. Buckley, Jr. wore a wrinkled shirt collar.

8-1. Better made dress shirts are top fused.

The collar of a dressier shirt is made stiff so that the collar will not bend or wrinkle as the neck moves around. To make the collar stiff, firm layers of interfacing are used to add thickness to the collar. Then, the surface of the collar puckers owing to shrinkage difference between the interfacing and shirt fabric. To prevent puckering, layers of interfacing are often glued to the top layer of the shirt fabric, called top fused. In the past, a fused collar may bubble owing to the breakdown of adhesive after repeated laundering and ironing. Dented spots may also occur due to excessive or uneven application of adhesive. Nowadays, the adhesives used in the fusing process are reliable. Collars bonded with quality adhesive seldom come apart and bubble. You should feel comfortable to wear top fused shirts. The best dress shirts in today's market are made with top fused collar. Sleeve cuffs and placket front are usually made the same way the collar is made.

Occasionally, I met few consumers who complained about the collars of their dress shirts. The adhesive leaks out, or layers of fabric become loose, showing bubbles. This has been an unsettled debate between the industries. The garment industry complains that the dry cleaning business ruins garments by using harsh chemicals and high heat. The dry cleaning industry fights back by suggesting that some manufacturers make faulty products because not every fused suit or shirt suffers from the same problem.

If you prefer to send your shirts to the cleaner, avoid dry cleaning your cotton shirts. Prefer hand ironing or soft press to hard press. If the cleaner cannot fulfill your wish, you should look for another cleaner. Or, you can always iron the shirts yourself. I have often spotted that many men wear shirts with unattractive impressions or unwanted creases in the collar and other places. Several of my customers own a dry cleaning business. They complained about how difficult it is to find competent workers.

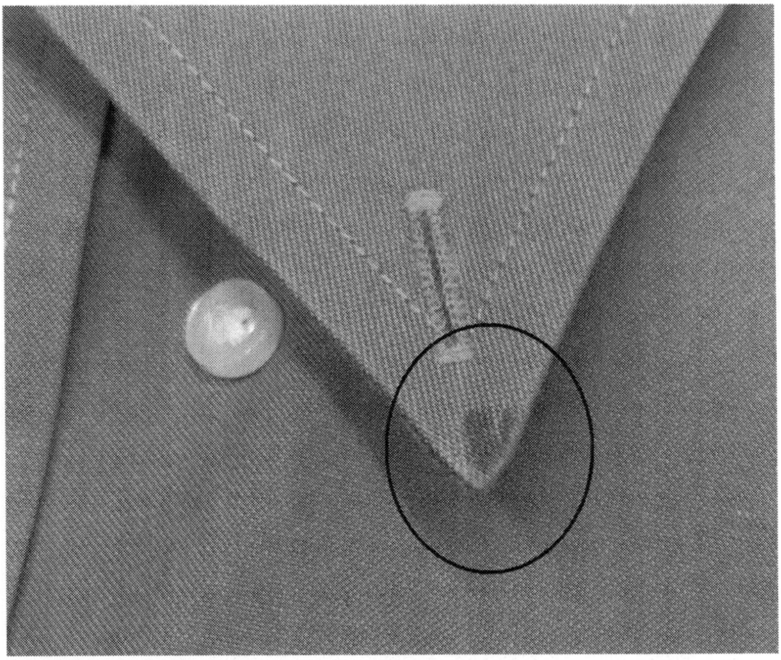

The adhesive in a fused collar leaks out through the tip of the collar wing and turns black under high heat during hard press.

8-2. Wrinkle-free dress shirts should have fused seams.

A great number of men wear ironed and starched dress shirts. Most parts of the shirt appear crisp, but the seams throughout the shirt are wrinkled and puckered. Many sports shirts are intentionally made puckered at the seams to provide a casual look. Some famous sportswear designers often make their dress shirts almost the same way they make their sport shirts. Many men wear a plain sport shirt in the place of a dress shirt perhaps because they cannot tell the difference between a dress shirt and a sport shirt, or because they prefer shirts made by famous sportswear designers. I wonder why people want to buy a dress shirt that is not dressy. If you happen to own a shirt that puckers at the seams, try not to iron or starch your shirt too much. A crisp look shirt with puckered seams appears pretentious and ridiculous.

To reduce the chance of puckering at the seams, you should choose a shirt that is tailored in single-needle stitching. Some areas of a shirt, such as armhole and side seam, require a double-seam construction. Manufacturers can sew two lines of stitching at the same time by using a twin set of needles, call double-needle stitching. They can also sew two lines of stitching one at a time, called single-needle stitching. Most experts prefer single-needle stitching because the double-needle method tends to cause the fabric to pucker between the two lines. The single-needle method may help reduce the puckering caused by sewing machine but may not help reduce the puckering caused by shrinkage after cleaning. Stitching affects the mobility of yarns within the fabric and therefore influences the shrinkage rate of the fabric near the stitching. This is the reason that puckering often occurs at the stitching, especially the double-seam areas. Some puckering can be smoothed out by ironing if the fabric is thin enough. It is difficult to flatten puckered seams by any mean if the fabric is thick or stiff such as an oxford or denim cloth.

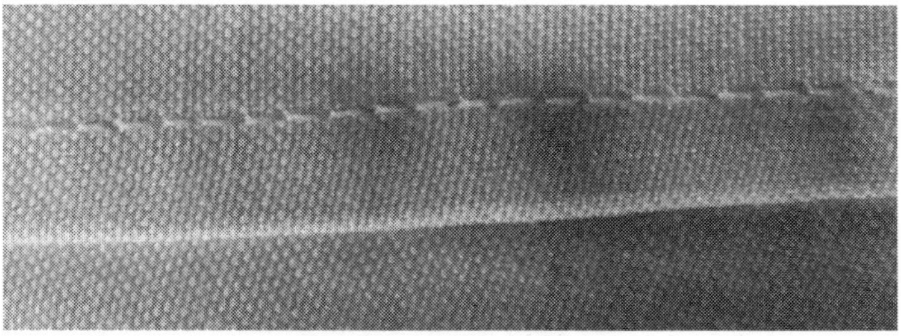

Single-needle stitching

Double-needle stitching

The best way to prevent puckered seams is to fuse the seams with interfacing. Traditionally, a quality dress shirt is top fused at the collar, cuffs and placket front but not at the seams. Fused shirts are not the same as the wrinkle-free shirts. The ordinary shirts have to be ironed to maintain their crisp look.

With increasing demand on wrinkle-resistant shirts, manufacturers are producing more permanent press shirts made of cotton-polyester blend or non-iron shirts made of 100% cotton. Nevertheless, a shirt that is made of wrinkle-free fabric does not mean that it is tailored in a wrinkle-free fashion. Many wrinkle-free shirts do not wrinkle except at the seams. My advice is that a true wrinkle-free shirt should be wrinkle-free throughout the entire shirt. Notice that fused seams are often sewn with a double-needle instead of the single-needle stitching. This may not be considered a deficiency because a fused seam does not pucker and therefore does not require a single-needle stitching, which is more time-consuming.

It is difficult to smooth out puckered seams, especially those on thick fabrics.

A non-fused shirt tends to pucker at the seams.

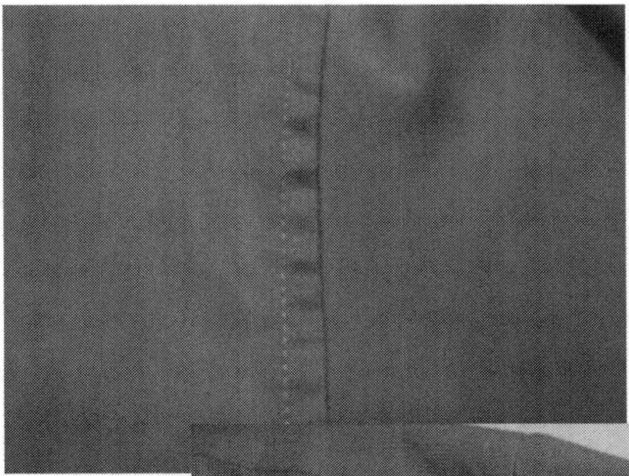

A true wrinkle-free shirt should be wrinkle-free throughout the entire shirt without puckered seams.

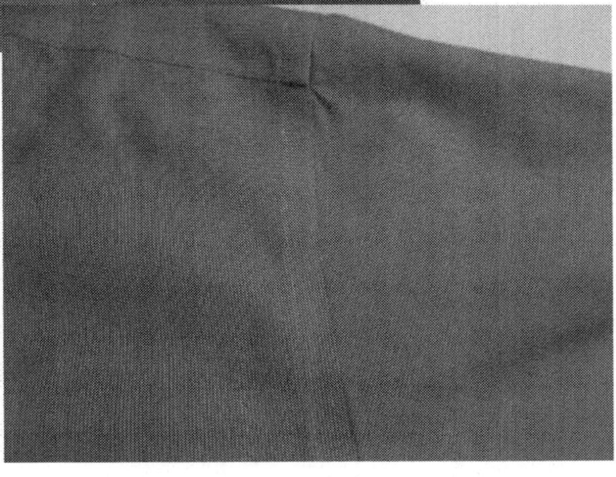

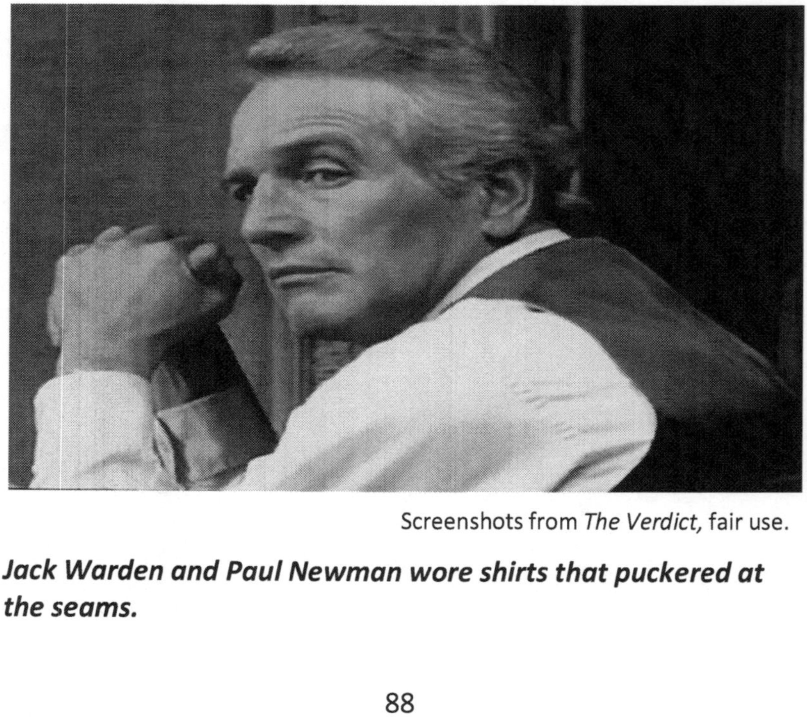

Screenshots from *The Verdict,* fair use.

Jack Warden and Paul Newman wore shirts that puckered at the seams.

9. *One-stage vs. two-stage non-iron shirts*

Since the invention of non-iron technology in the 1990s, non-iron shirts have revolutionized the garment industry. Many men refuse to buy any other types of shirts, but they do not realize that there are two types of non-iron shirts.

Many non-iron shirts do not have sharp creases at the arms, pleats, plackets, or pocket folds. The reason is that manufacturers dipped the shirts in the non-iron chemicals and cure the chemicals with high heat, known as the one-stage process. The cured chemicals make the fabrics resist creases the same way they resist wrinkles. A shirt without creases looks swollen and puffy, especially at the folds. The whole shirt looks like a cheap polyester shirt. Better made non-iron shirts use a two-stage process. The shirts are dipped in the chemicals and cured by heat. Before the chemicals are completely set, the shirts have to be pulled out and creased. After that, the shirts are returned to finish the curing process. Once the chemicals are cured, they secure the creases indefinitely and at the same time prevent the rest part of the shirt from wrinkling.

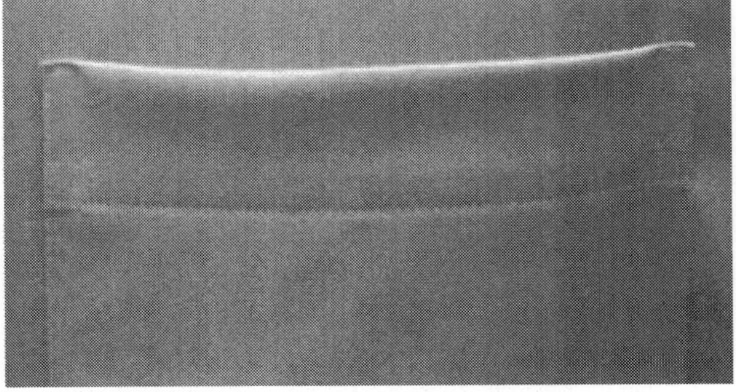

A swollen pocket fold tells you that something is wrong about the shirt.

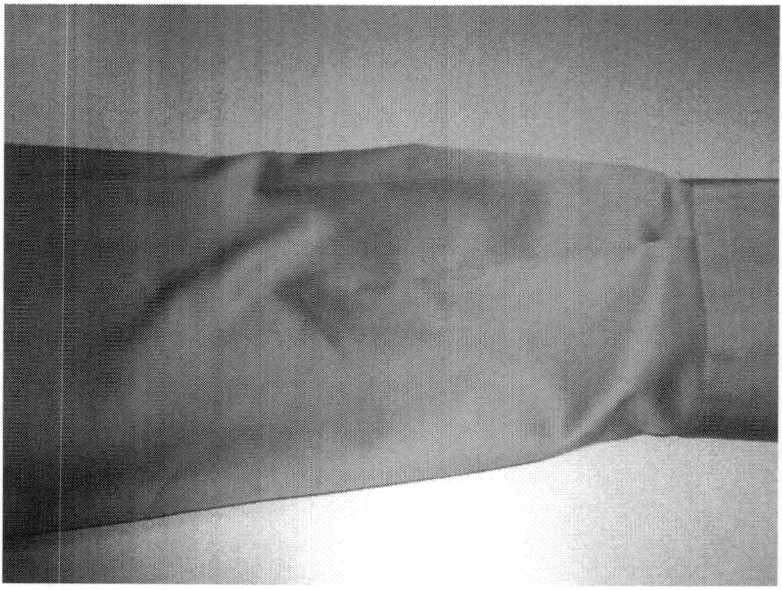

A bad non-iron shirt without creases.

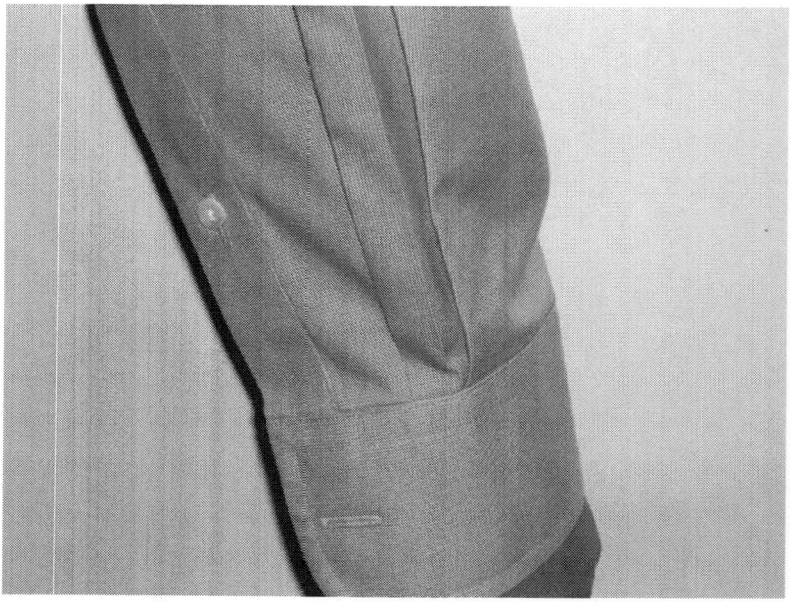

A good non-iron shirt with sharp creases.

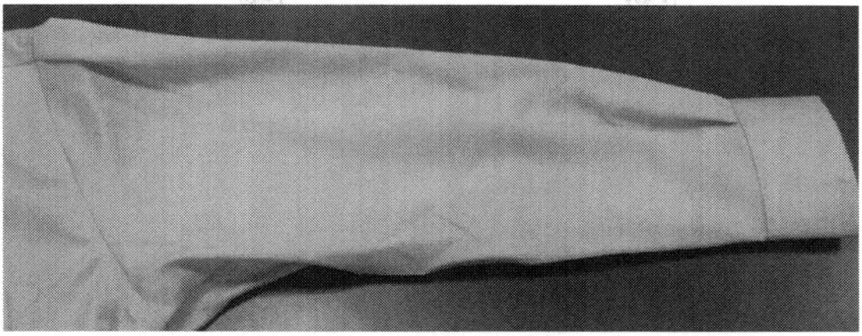

The pleated sleeve was once the trademark of Perry Ellis dress shirts. What makes the sleeve so attractive is actually not the pleat but the sharp crease that comes with the pleat. The one-stage non-iron process erases the sharp crease, making the pleat look redundant and unappealing.

One of the important factors that distinguish between the new non-iron shirts and the traditional poly-blend wrinkle-free shirts is that it is difficult to crease the polyester or poly-blend shirts. If you desire a wrinkle-free shirt, the 100% cotton non-iron shirt seems to be a better choice than the poly-blend permanent press shirt. Bad non-iron shirts cost no less than good non-iron shirts. If you shop for non-iron shirts, be sure that the shirts have sharp creases. It is foolish to spend extra money to buy a shirt that you cannot even crease it when you want to.

Alan Ladd wore pleated sleeves without sharp creases.

Fair use.

10. The hidden button on a double-breasted jacket

10-1. Traditionally, double-breasted jackets are cut shorter than single-breasted jackets.

Double-breasted jackets are those jackets that close by having one half of the jacket front overlapping the other half. To offset the effect of having extra amount of fabric in the jacket front, double-breasted jackets are traditionally cut shorter than single-breasted jackets.

The top photo shows that U.S. bandleader, Ted Lewis, wore a double-breasted jacket in a perfect length. The bottom photo shows that both General Smedley Butler and New York Governor Al Smith wore a double-breasted jacket that was too long.

10-2. A double-breasted jacket should be buttoned at all-time except when the wearer is sitting.

Double-breasted jackets are considered dressier than single-breasted jacket. The Duke of Windsor started the trend in the early 20th century by wearing double-breasted jackets instead of tuxedos to attend formal parties. It is regarded extremely rude to wear a double-breasted jacket unfastened. The overlapping two halves of the jacket front keep flapping around. Yet, many men wear a double-breasted jacket in such a bad manner. The hanging of extra cloth is the mark of someone who is trying to look more important than he actually is. If a man is unwilling to fasten a double-breasted jacket at all-time except when sitting, he has no business to wear one.

by David Shankbone

Sir Thomas Lipton, the creator of Lipton tea brand, and New York Governor Al Smith would not button their double-breasted coat. The extra amount of fabric ripples in the coat front and looks unattractive.

10-3. *The two sides of the double-breasted jacket front should overlap evenly.*

Occasionally, I have seen men wear a double-breasted jacket and the two halves of the jacket front do not overlap horizontally. One side of the jacket front is higher or lower than the other half. The problem can be fixed easily by moving the functional button or buttons to a new location so that both sides of the jacket front can be hung evenly.

Howard Hughes wore a double-breasted jacket. The two sides of the jacket front did not meet evenly.

10-4. Don't forget to fasten the hidden button.

Some men are smart enough to button a double-breasted jacket, but they forget to fasten the hidden button located inside the left half of the jacket front. Consequently, the right half of the jacket front sags and does not line up with the other half evenly. If the hidden button is fastened but the two halves do not meet or the inner half is still sagging, the button is at the wrong place and needs to be relocated.

It is ridiculous to wear a double-breasted jacket front that is sagging, twisted and uneven.

Fred Astaire must have forgotten to close the hidden button.

It is unclear what happened to Boris Becker's dinner jacket. He either fastened the wrong button, or simply did not button the jacket.

10-5. Avoid a double-breasted jacket with all the buttons clustering on one side of the jacket front.

The shape of the jacket front is affected by the way the jacket buttons. The two major styles are the single-breasted and the double-breasted front. A single-breasted jacket front has the two sides meet at the front down a single row of buttons. A double-breasted front allows overlapping at front closing with two vertical rows of buttons and a single row of buttonholes. Double-breasted jackets are considered dressier than single-breasted ones. You should avoid a double-breasted jacket with all the buttons clustering on the left side of the jacket front. In other words, all the front buttons are better to be centered and spaced evenly. It is pointless to wear a double-breasted jacket that does not overlap sufficiently.

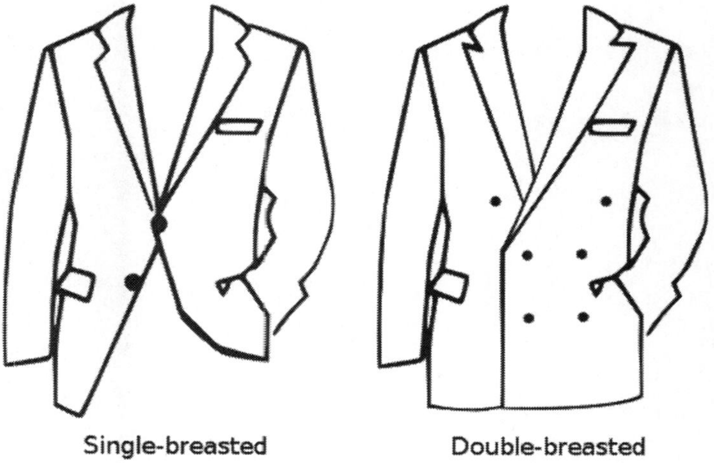

(by Arbapp under GNU)

Al Jolson's jacket does not overlap much, making you wonder if it is a single-breasted or double-breasted jacket.

11. *Watch the collar and back of the jacket.*

11-1. The jacket collar should hug the shirt collar smoothly.

Alan Flusser suggested that 50% of all tailored jackets need some kind of collar alteration to make them hug the neck of the wearer. One common problem is that the jacket collar stands away from the shirt collar. This may be because the jacket is too tight for the shoulders, or simply because the collar is too large for the neck. If the collar is slightly large, it can be shrunk by steaming. If the collar is large enough and leaves a hole, it needs to be shortened. Another common problem is the horizontal ridges of fabric bunching in the back below the base of the neck. The problem can be solved by cutting away the excess fabric under the collar, such as lowering the collar or raising the jacket's back. If tension lines appear across the shoulder blades, the back is too tight and must be let out. If bubbles instead of tension lines appear, the back is too roomy and can be taken in a little.

by א (Aleph), CC-BY 2.5

by Caroline Bonarde Ucci

Hans-Gert Pöttering, President of the European Parliament, Daniel Craig and Kevin Bacon wore a jacket collar that stood away from the shirt collar.

11-2. *The jacket should not be so tight that it shows the arch of the back.*

Many men look in the mirror to check if the jacket front looks all right, but they pay less attention to the back of the jacket perhaps because they cannot see the back well. If you try on a jacket, be sure that you stand in front of a three-way mirror and give a careful look at your back.

The back of the jacket should drape from the shoulders smoothly without showing columns of extra fabric, or showing the curve of the body. Many men wear a tight jacket without noticing that the arch of the back is showing. The jacket's front is often reinforced with extra layers of fabric or interlining to make it stiff; hence, the jacket's front tends to look smooth even if the jacket is too tight. The jacket's back, on the other hand, is not reinforced. It is thinner than the front and tends to show wrinkles and shape of the body.

Screenshots, fair use.

Fifty percent of all tailored jackets need some kind of collar alteration. One common problem is the bump or horizontal ridges below the base of the collar.

Screen shots from the movie, *Blue Dahlia*. Fair use.

A jacket that looks marvelous in the front may not look good at all in the back.

Screenshot, fair use.

Judging from the working buttons on the sleeves, Bill Hemmer wore a fancy suit, but the suit looked horrible because it was far too tight.

The back of the jacket should drape gracefully without any folds or wrinkles.

11-3. *There should be a break behind the armpits.*

When a man tries on a jacket, he needs to be sure that there are no excessive wrinkles in the jacket except in the areas near the back of the two armpits. There should be sufficient fullness over the shoulder blades for a slight break, or fold of fabric, to extend up the back from below the two armholes. Without the extra fabric behind the armpits, the wearer will be unable to move his arms comfortably.

Extra fabric is necessary in the back of the armpit to allow the arm to move freely.

11-4. *The center vent of a jacket should overlap one and a half inches.*

Among the most serious sartorial violations, one is to wear a jacket with its center vent wide-open. Yet, a great number of men wear their center vented jacket this way.

As the work environment and life style is changing, the body shape of an average American man is also changing. Most American men are less involved in vigorous physical activities these days. The lack of physical activities and exercise along with bad diet contributes to the fact that many American men have a relative small chest and a large waist. Yet, suit manufacturers continue to produce suits based on the body shapes of ideal men, making it difficult to fit an ordinary body. The most common problem in fitting is that the center vent keeps opening up or popping out like a cock's tail. Ironically, most American men seem to fall in love with the center vent, judging from the inventory sold in the stores.

The purpose of the vent is to release the stress when the wearer puts his hand in his trouser pocket or when the wearer bends his body. There is no justification that the center vent should open if the wearer stands straight and fastens the waist button. If a man tries on a jacket and the top layer of the center vent does not overlap the bottom layer one and a half inches, the jacket may be too small and the man should try on a larger size jacket. If a jacket seems to fit but the back vent open because the wearer has a large seat, the man should consider a ventless or side-vented jacket. Or, the man can choose a different cut of jacket, such as an American sack suit with a four-inch drop instead of a European athletic suit with an eight-inch drop. A four-inch drop means that the difference between the chest and the waist size is four inches, to say, a 42 size jacket with a trouser waist size of 38 inches. It is desirable to keep the back vent closed. Alan Flusser believes that a center vent "can occasionally be employed to better conceal a prominent hip than either the ready-made ventless or side-vented jacket back." But, isn't the prominent hip the exact reason that a center vent is unable to shut properly?

Clark Gable's back vent was wide open.

by Hans Bernhard, CC-BY-SA 3.0.

The vent in a double side-vented jacket does not overlap as much as the vent in a single center-vented jacket; however, the two side vents should stay closed when the wearer stands straight and fastens the waist button.

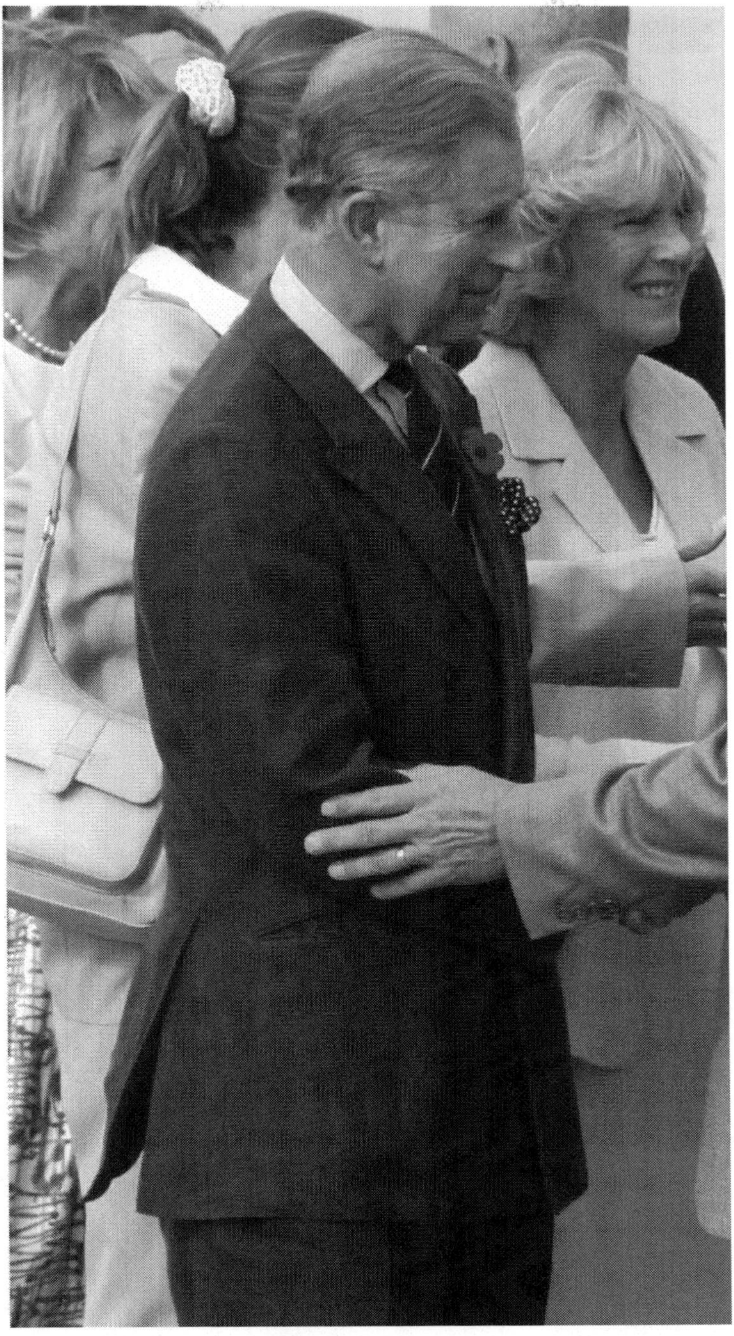

Prince Charles' side vents were wide open.

Many manufacturers sealed the center and side vents with stitches. A sealed vent will not open even if the jacket is too tight. Hence, it is pointless to try on a jacket with the vent or vents being sealed. Nevertheless, I have seen thousands of men try on a brand new jacket with a sealed vent or vents. They should have requested the fitter or salesclerk to open the vent or vents before the trial.

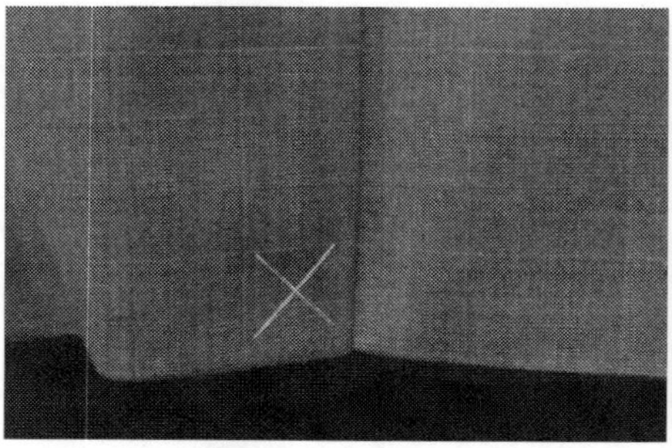

An unfinished functional sleeve (bottom left photo) is sealed to prevent it from being damaged during handling. It is redundant, however, to seal a finished nonfunctional sleeve (bottom right photo). Whether the vent of a sleeve is sealed or not will not affect the fitting of the jacket.

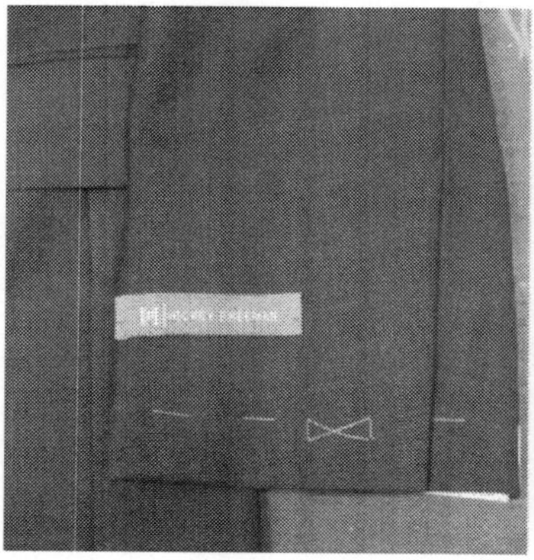

12. Jacket sleeves

12-1. The devil is in the arm.

People often say that the devil is in the detail. If there is a devil in a suit, it must be the arm. The most neglected area in a suit is perhaps the sleeves. There are countless discussions in literature concerning the length of jacket sleeves, but few mentions about the fitting of sleeves. When you turn on a television set or open a magazine, you see men everywhere dress in puckered jacket sleeves.

Because men move their arms constantly, it is understandable that the jacket sleeves tend to wrinkle more than the rest of the jacket. Nevertheless, many men wear a jacket that wrinkles terribly even when the arm does not move or bend. Most men pay much attention to the color, pattern and fit of the jacket, but never realize that the devil is in the arms. The last thing you want to do is wear a nice jacket with wrinkled arms.

12-2. Wear a correct sleeve length.

Many men wear too long their jacket sleeves for fear that the sleeves may retreat and expose too much of the shirt cuffs when the arms bend. They do not realize the consequences of wearing too long the jacket sleeves. One is that the extra length in the sleeve will bunch up and form excessive wrinkles when the arm bends. As mentioned before, Alan Flusser suggested that 90% of all men wear too long their jacket sleeves. These 90% of men must have worn wrinkled sleeves also.

Prime Minister Blair and President Bush welcomed each other with wrinkled arms.

Everyone knows that the sleeve tends to wrinkle when the arm bends, but no one would expect a sleeve to wrinkle so terribly like the one worn by Mikhail Gorbachev.

Steven Spielberg accepting a public service award with a wrinkled arm.

Photo courtesy of www.kremlin.ru.

Russian President Putin and three Russian sport leaders had a contest for wrinkled sleeves. Can't tell which gentleman was the winner.

(Photo Courtesy of Alan Light)

The longer the sleeves, the more they bunch up when the arms bend.

12-3. Fit the curve of the sleeve with the arch of the arm.

When a man drops his arm, the arm is slightly bent. Hence, most jacket sleeves are curved to accommodate this feature. A jacket sleeve tends to wrinkle or pucker if the arch of the sleeve does not fit the curve of the arm. In such case, the sleeve can be rotated at the armhole to attain a better fit.

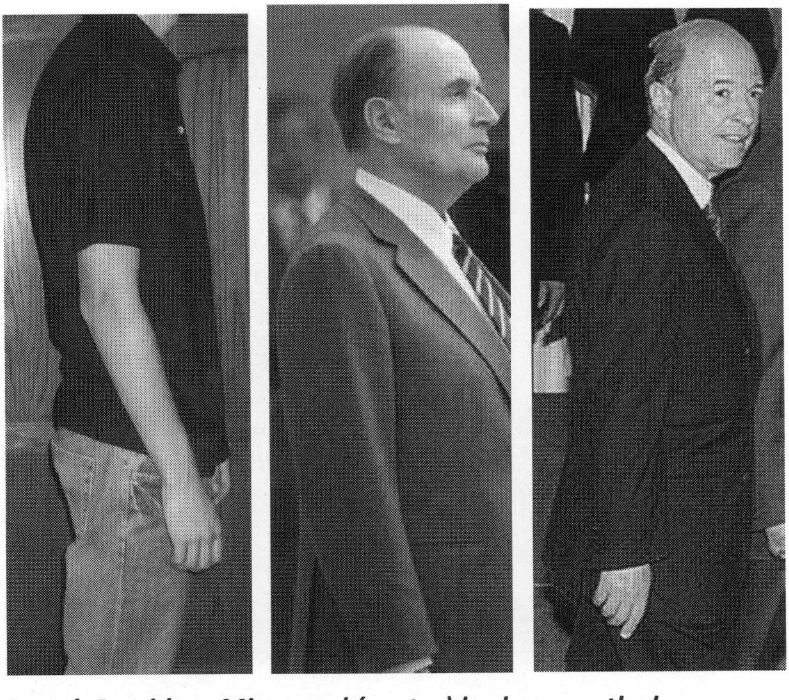

French President Mitterand (center) had a smooth sleeve because he bent his arm slightly. Greek Prime Minister Simitis (right) held his arm back, resulting in a puckered sleeve (source of photo: www.kremlin.ru).

12-4. How to avoid wrinkled arms

To avoid wearing a jacket with excessive wrinkles in the arms, you may want to pay attention to the following factors.

1) Wear correct size jackets.

Jacket size is determined by taking the chest measurement. There are two methods to measure the chest. One is simply placing the measuring tape around the chest under the arms. The other is using the tape to encircle the chest over the arms, and deducting the measurement by 7 inches. This is because most apparel manufacturers construct jackets to meet a 7" difference between the chest size and the over-arm size. The two methods often produce different results. The measured difference is usually greater than 7", which suggests that the larger coat size may fit better. Hence, most professionals prefer the second method. Notice that most manufacturers allow the actual chest measurement of a suit to be typically two inches larger than the size of the suit to allow room for adequate movement.

A tight jacket not only restricts the body movement, but also creates more puckering and wrinkles in the arms. If a man has a pair of prominent arms, he may consider having his suit custom made.

***2) Be aware of tailoring defect*s.**

I watched the movie, *The Man in the Net*, and noticed that Alan Ladd wore a jacket in the movie. The right arm was wrinkled, while the left arm was not. Apparently, the right sleeve was defected since Alan Ladd did not have a pair of uneven arms.

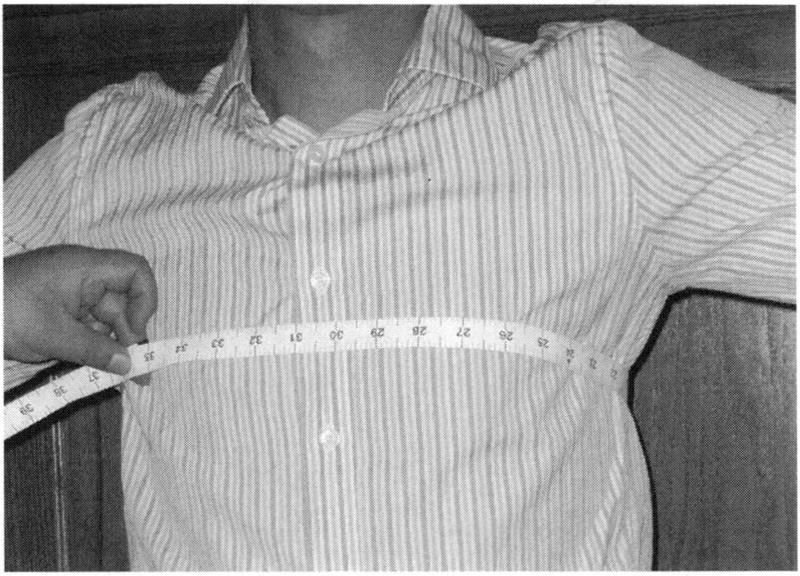

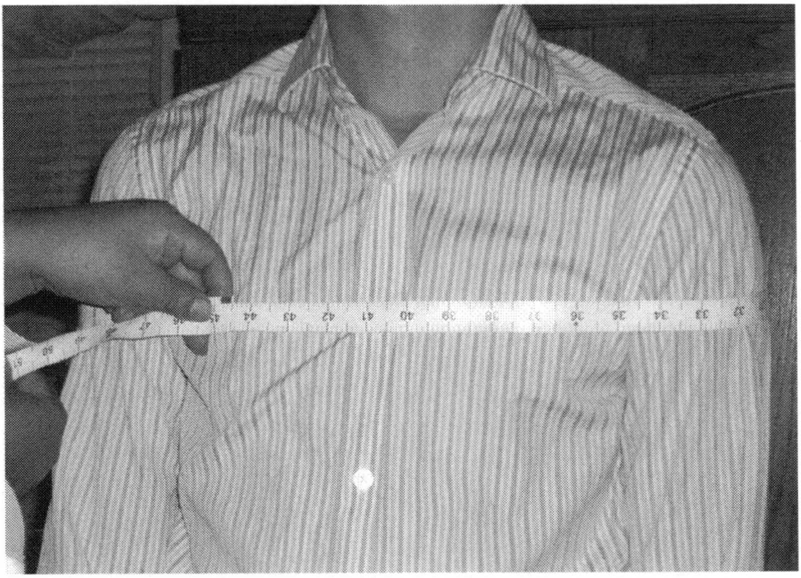

Two methods of measuring the chest: under the arms (top photo) and over the arms (bottom photo).

Screenshot from *The man in the Net*, fair use.

It seemed that the right arm of Alan Ladd's jacket is defected.

3) *Sleeve lining affects the drape of sleeve.*

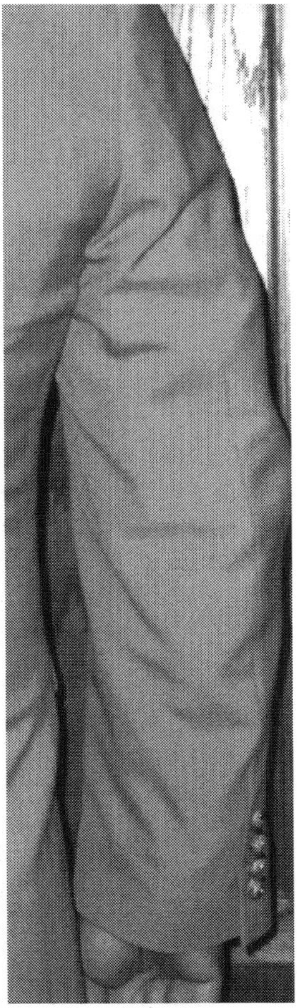

While fashion experts maintain that lining in the jacket and pants help slide in the hands and legs, I have suspected that lining affects the drape of garments. Improperly installed lining causes unnecessary wrinkles in the arm. When you are shopping for a suit or sport coat, be sure that you examine carefully the installation of lining, especially the lining inside the arms.

Lining is not as important as most people think. If the lining affects the drape or causes deformation to your garment, you may be better off to have the lining redone or removed.

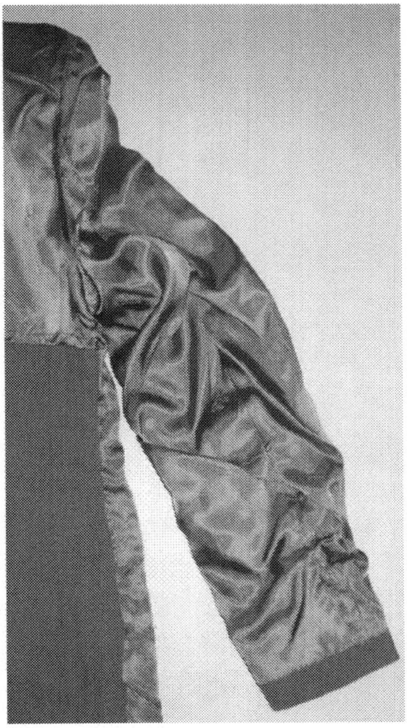

How could you expect a smooth sleeve if the lining of the arm is all messed up?

4) *Reduce the bulk of the shirt sleeves.*

The jacket is often worn over a long sleeve dress or sport shirt. Some shirt sleeves are cut loosely. The extra fabric tends to bunch and wrinkle inside the jacket sleeve. The extra folds and wrinkles may show through the jacket sleeves. If you feel that your jacket sleeves are tight for your arms already, you may want to avoid wearing shirt sleeves that are stiff or bulky.

Avoid wearing bulky shirt sleeves under a jacket for the bulk of the shirt sleeves may wrinkle the jacket sleeves.

5) *Take the weight and softness of the jacket fabric into consideration.*

As technology progresses dramatically, manufacturers are able to produce suits and sport jackets made of ultra-fine wools such as Super 170 or finer. Luxurious fabrics are more delicate and tend to wrinkle more easily. In addition, jacket sleeves made of thinner and softer fabrics are less capable of concealing the wrinkles caused by the shirt sleeves. If you have difficulty in keeping smooth jacket sleeves, you may consider stiffer or thicker suiting materials.

A manufacturer put the humor into its labels, suggesting that super 100's wool is for the king and 140's for the emperor. Uninformed consumers probably can figure it out that 140's is better than 100's since emperors are greater than kings. The higher the S numbers, the finer the fibers and yarns.

The term, Super 100's, is often misunderstood as a measurement of thread count per square inch. Actually, it is a measure of yarn size. The current yarn number system dates back to the 18th century in England, known as the worsted count system. In those days finished yarns were coiled into 560-yard-long loops called hanks. The yarn number indicated how many hanks could be drawn out of a pound of wool.

According to the new laws, the yarn number in fine wool is now a direct measurement of average fiber diameter in microns and fiber distribution in standard deviations. Thus, a wool fabric labeled Super 100's must have an average fiber diameter of 18.75 microns or finer, or the product shall be "misbranded." A micron is one millionth of a meter.

It is common these days that luxurious suits are made of super fine wool such as 170's and finer. Fabrics made of super fine yarns, however, are irritatingly prone to become shiny or to wear through. They also tear and wrinkle more easily.

12-5. Press or steam jacket sleeves regularly.

Because men move their hands and arms constantly, the jacket sleeves are often bent, stretched and twisted.
They look "tired" with a series of wrinkles and require pressing or steaming to smooth the wrinkles out. If you do not have time to press or steam your jacket sleeves, you can simply spray the sleeves with water. Moisture will reset the cross-linked sulfur bonds between wool molecules and restore the sleeves back in shape.

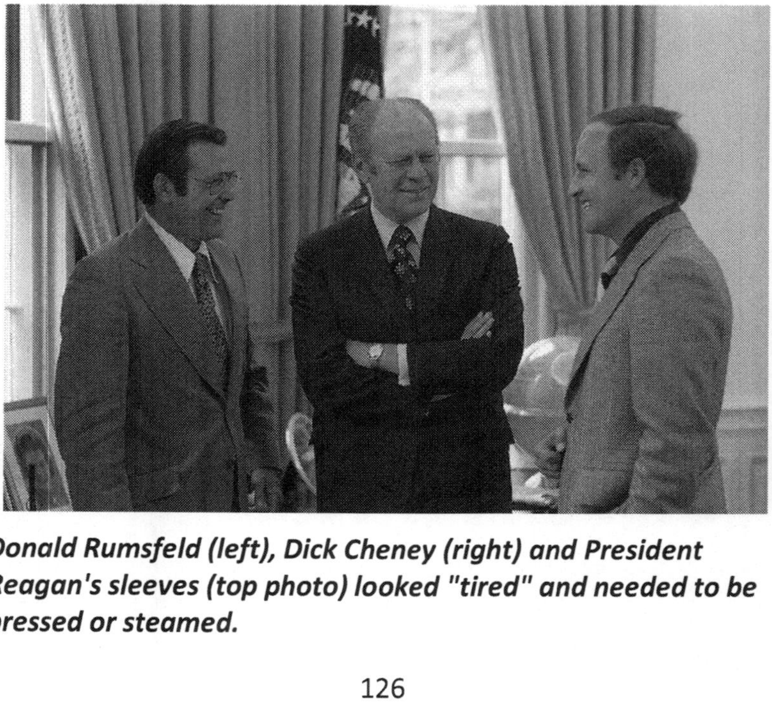

Donald Rumsfeld (left), Dick Cheney (right) and President Reagan's sleeves (top photo) looked "tired" and needed to be pressed or steamed.

13. Jacket sleeve buttons

The sleeve buttons are not an important part of a jacket. They do not affect the fit or the aesthetic aspect of a jacket. In truth, they are usually invisible. Many men do not even notice how many buttons are on their jacket sleeves. If you are a perfectionist and are trying to find faults with a jacket, the sleeve buttons are the best places to start. Experts maintain that buttons on better-made suits or sport coats are made of ox-horn, special nut shell, or other unusual material. As the modern technology goes, manufacturers now produce synthetic buttons that look like horn buttons and yet unbreakable. I have no preference concerning the material of buttons as long as the buttons do not break easily. So many things can go wrong with a few sleeve buttons. I therefore devote this special section to sleeve buttons.

13-1. A single-breasted jacket tends to have more sleeve buttons than the front buttons.

A single-breasted jacket tends to have more sleeve buttons than the front buttons, to say, four sleeve buttons for a three-button jacket and three or four sleeve buttons for a two-button jacket. Some vanguard fashion designers put two, five, or six buttons on the sleeve. One button sleeve is usually found in a diner jacket. Many cheap jackets or women's jackets may have no buttons on the sleeve. For business, you are better off to choose the standard three or four sleeve buttons.

13-2. Each sleeve button should overlap or be overlapped by its adjacent button.

Traditionally, sleeve buttons are arranged in the same way that fish scales lie. Each button lies over or is laid over by the adjacent button. The arrangement is often called the stacked buttons or waterfall. A customer bought a sport jacket that has two buttons spaced apart on each sleeve. After I mentioned that sleeve buttons usually touch one another. The customer went to see a tailor and had the two buttons kiss each other. Some fashion designers put two buttons on the sleeve instead of three or four buttons. The two buttons are usually larger than regular sleeve buttons and are spaced apart to take up more space. It is pointless to lay the two buttons close to each other. Some men do not like that the sleeve buttons kiss one another. Because it is more inconvenient for the sewing machine to stitch a row of stacked buttons, it may be a good sign for better tailoring if the sleeve buttons are sewn close to one another. Personally I prefer that the top button overlaps the lower button, but most manufacturers stack the buttons in the opposite way. No matter what, it is a custom that better-made jacket has stacked sleeve buttons. If you have the sleeves altered, make sure that your tailor stacks the buttons.

13-3. Better-made jackets tend to have functional buttonholes and buttons.

Today's readymade jackets tend not to have buttonholes on the sleeves. The sleeve buttons are mere decorations. There are different stories concerning the origin of the sleeve buttons. Most historians credit the sleeve buttons to either the French or the Prussians, particularly Frederick the Great. One story claims that it was Napoleon himself who ordered the large buttons to be sewn to the top side of the uniform sleeves to keep the soldiers from wiping their noses and mouths. Through the years, the buttons has migrated to the underside of the sleeves.

(a) (b) (c)

Jacket sleeve buttons: (a) not touched, (b) touched but not stacked, and (c) stacked.

In the past, custom jackets have functional buttons. Hence, today's better-made jackets, especially the custom bespoke suits, often have functional buttonholes and buttons. Gentlemen usually leave the lowest one or two buttons undone to show that their jackets are of the best quality. Not every good quality readymade suit comes with functional buttons because it is more difficult to shorten the sleeve when the buttonholes are in the way. On the other hand, many mediocre jackets made by popular designers often have functional buttons. Fashion designers tend to emphasize style over quality, form over substance. If you see a jacket with functional buttons, do not assume that the jacket must be a good quality one.

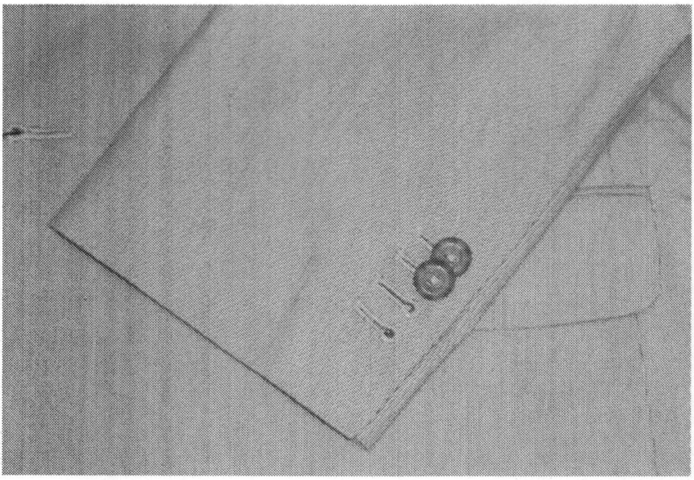

Because buttonholes create difficulty for sleeve alteration, some manufacturers provide unfinished functional sleeves. The buttonholes and buttons can be added to the right locations after the sleeves are shortened or lengthened. The problem is that most retailers do not have the expensive buttonhole machine to finish the job. Some retailers put non-functional buttons on the sleeve instead. Tailors in a small town or city may be unable to afford a buttonhole machine. Nevertheless, the buttonholes can be hand finished.

Customarily, the lowest one or two buttons of a functional sleeve are often undone to indicate that the suit is an expensive one. The <u>Men's Style Manual</u> by <u>Details</u> magazine suggests that "Some flashier types like undoing these buttons in order to show off the superior hand tailoring of their garment." Why is it a show-off simply because you undo one or two sleeve buttons? If you do not unfasten the last button of your vest, sophisticate dressers may think you are ignorant for not knowing the custom. Most business suits have three or four nonfunctional buttons on each sleeve. No one would consider it showy for having a row of buttons that do not fasten anything. The biggest show-off is wearing a suit that does not fit. If you do not want to be accused of showing off, you can forget the whole thing or undo one instead of two buttons.

San Francisco Major, Gavin Newsome (top), unfastened the last two while Russian President, Dmitry Medvedev, unfastened the last one of their functional sleeve buttons.
(Photo of Newsome by GreenJobsNow, CC-BY 2.0. Photo of Medvedev courtesy of www.kremlin.ru)

Many suit makers provide sleeves that have buttonhole stitches without holes. I have seen many men wear a jacket with this type of sleeves. It is ridiculous to wear a sleeve in such

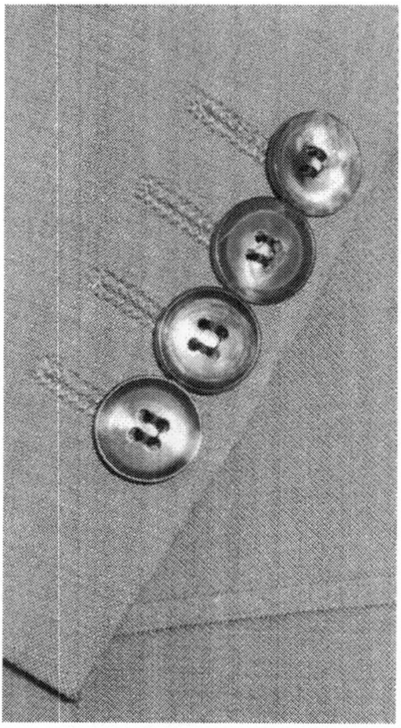

a manner. The buttonholes should be punctured, or the stitches should be removed. Then again, what is the purpose of making holes through fake buttonhole stitches? These sleeves tend to be non-functional. Manufacturers put on the buttonhole stitches simply as a gimmick. If you own a jacket such as this, I suggest that you redo the buttonhole stitches and convert the sleeve into a functional one. A good buttonhole has the shape of a key hole.

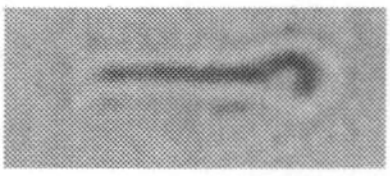

13-4. The lowest button should be close to the edge of the sleeve.

Fashion experts suggest that the lowest sleeve button should not be away from the edge of the sleeve more than three quarters of an inch. In most readymade jacket, however, the lowest button is often one and a quarter inches or more above the edge of the sleeve perhaps because suit makers realize that most jackets will be shortened. If a jacket is shortened about half an inch, you would think that the buttons will be in the correct positions. It is funny that most tailors will move up the buttons after they shorten the sleeves. Hence, you should request your tailor to place the buttons at the location where you desire. If your jacket sleeves are lengthened instead of being shortened, you should ask your tailor to move down the buttons. It looks weird to have the sleeve buttons laid high above the edge of the sleeve.

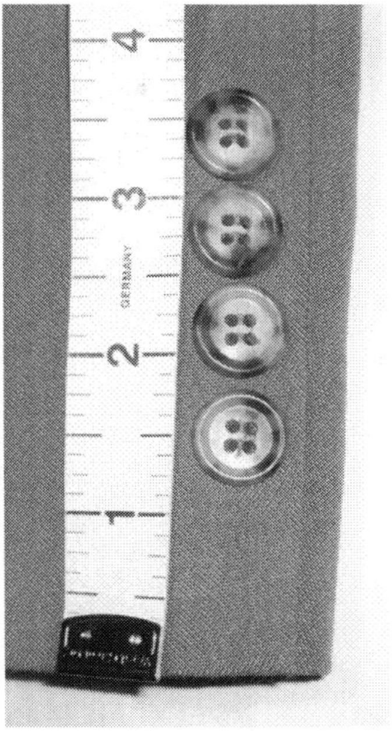

If the sleeve is shortened more than one and a half inches, the sleeve may lose its vent. A jacket sleeve without a vent looks cheap. You may request your tailor to make a new vent or to convert the decorative buttons into functional buttons.

The sleeve buttons on readymade suits tend to be placed high above the edge perhaps because manufacturers realize that most sleeves will be shortened after purchase. What is funny is that ignorant tailors often move up the buttons after the sleeve has been shortened. If the sleeve length is perfect and does not require an alteration, you may want the buttons to be lowered.

Comedian, Ernest Hare's sleeve buttons were placed high at the middle of the fore arms.

Fashion experts suggest that the lowest jacket sleeve button should not be more than ¾" above the edge. Buttons that are placed high on the sleeve suggest that the jacket is not altered and belongs to the shop.

By Alan Light

Screenshot, fair use.

Screenshot, fair use.

13-5. *Buttons on hand- sewn suits tend to be parallel- stitched rather than cross-stitched.*

Most buttons on readymade garments are cross stitched because garment makers believe that cross stitching secures the button better than other methods. Sewing machines in most factories are set for cross stitching. To distinguish hand sewn suits from machine made ones, tailors often intentionally sew the buttons with parallel stitching instead of cross stitching. This is not to suggest that a suit with parallel-stitched buttons must be a hand sewn suit. On the other hand, some hand sewn suits may have cross-stitched buttons. There are no laws or regulations to tell suit makers what to do with the buttons. The advantage of cross-stitched buttons is minute. You need not be shy away from a suit made with parallel-stitched buttons. It can be a good sign.

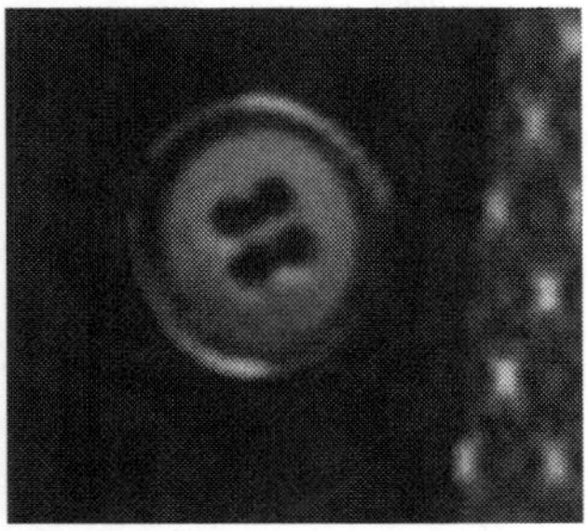

President Obama wore a suit with parallel-stitched buttons.

14. *Jacket lapel size, shirt collar length and tie width*

Fashion experts maintain that the length of the shirt collar and the width of the tie should not exceed the widest part of a notched lapel. Fashion designers and producers change the size of lapels frequently, but they seldom make the announcement. Fashion-unconscious men buy the new style suits, but they do not know to shop new styles of shirts and ties to go with their new suits. Consequently, they wear articles of clothing that do not coordinate properly.

It makes no sense to change the size of lapels simply to render a fashion statement because the width of the jacket lapels should base on a person's head size. Since a man does not change the size of his head, why should he change the size of lapels? Thus, Oscar Wilde commented, "Fashion is a form of ugliness so intolerable that we have to alter it every six months."

I have no problem with the fashion industry changing the size of lapels. The problem is that suit manufacturers tend to produce the same style of lapels throughout the seasons. When narrow lapels are in fashion, it is difficult to find suits with large lapels unless you buy new old stock. If a man buys everything according to his face, he has less to worry about whether the articles of clothing coordinate well with one another. Nevertheless, it is hard to buy the right clothes if they are unavailable.

Nelson Rockefeller wearing narrow lapels with a short shirt collar and narrow tie in 1968. Jimmy Carter wearing wide lapels with a long shirt collar and wide tie in 1977. Elvis wearing a giant shirt collar with giant lapels in 1970.

Robert Duvall either did not know or did not care that the shirt collar and tie width are related to the size of jacket lapels. He wore a large shirt collar and wide tie with narrow lapels.

15. Wear double-sided cufflinks.

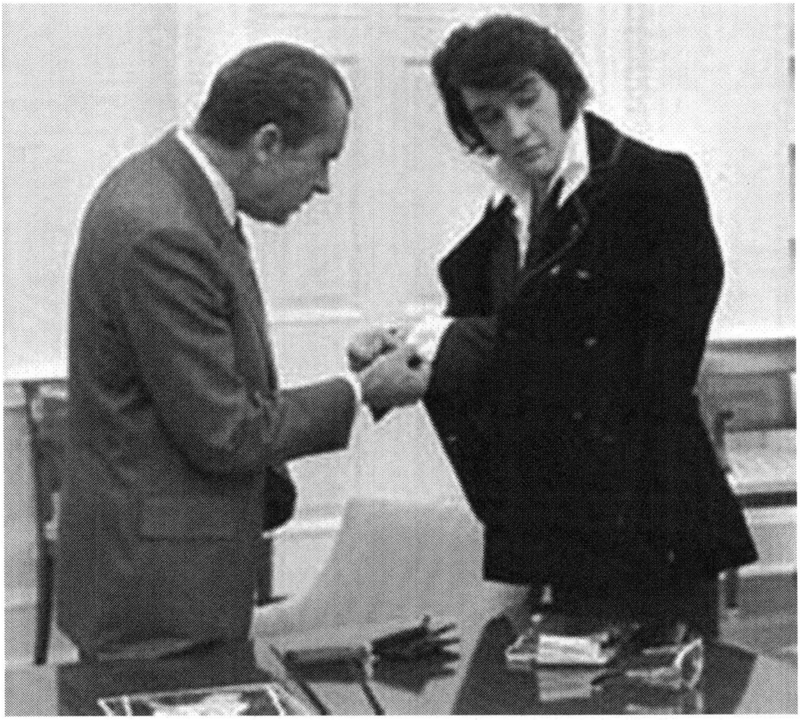

Present Nixon admired Elvis's cufflinks.

French cuff sleeves are fastened with a pair of cufflinks. Wikipedia describes the styles of cufflinks.

> Cufflink designs vary widely. The simplest design consists of a short post or chain connecting two disc-shaped parts. The part positioned on the most visible side is usually larger; a variety of designs can connect the smaller piece: It may be small enough to fit through the button hole like a button would; it may be separated and attached from the other side; or it may have a portion that swivels on the central post, aligning with the post while the link is threaded through the button-hole and swiveling into a position at right angles to the post when worn.

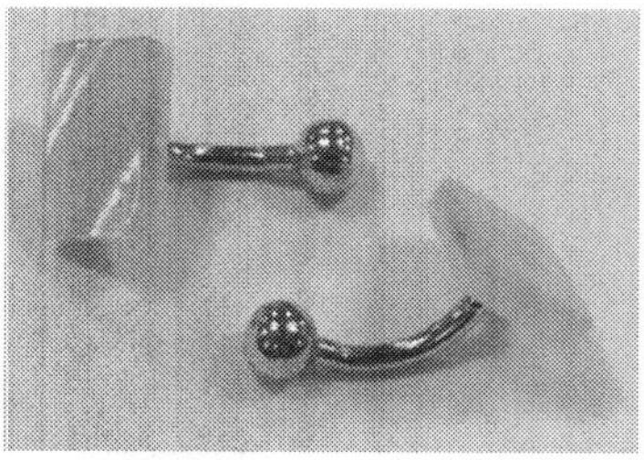

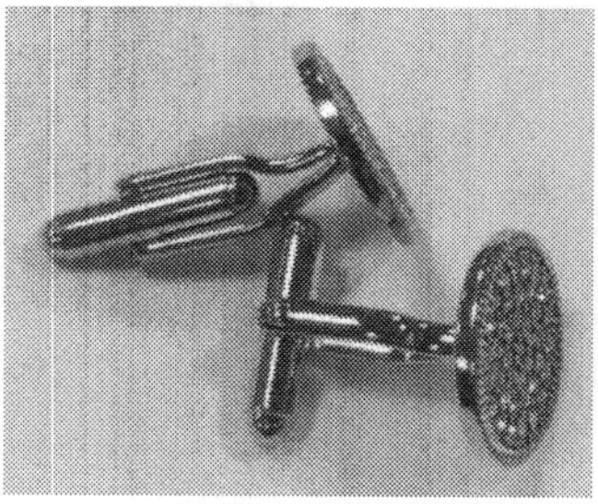

In general, cufflinks can be classified into two groups, the one-sided and the two-sided. If a man cannot afford both sides, suggest some fashion experts, he can forget wearing cufflinks. Nonetheless, most cufflinks sold in the market are one-sided.

One-sided links ***two-sided links***

Two-sided cufflinks are uncommon and costly. If you cannot find a pair at a price you are willing to pay, you can make one by yourself. All you have to do is to find two buttons and connect them with a few strings. So, what is the excuse not to wear a pair of two-faced links?

A prominent designer put the image of a two-faced cufflinks on one of his 7-fold ties perhaps because the double-sided link is a symbol of good taste.

I have worked at a reputed department store chain for more than a decade. I have seen only one style of double-sided cufflinks for one season. A customer returned a pair of this double-sided links, complaining about his being unable to thread the face of the link through the buttonhole. The customer preferred a pair of single-faced links for its being easy to use. I wonder why the customer did not simply enlarge the buttonholes to accommodate a pair of good cufflinks. It is rare to find a pair of double-faced links. Why give up so easily?

The main purpose of the cufflinks is to fasten the shirt cuffs. Hence, they should be simple and elegant, advised fashion experts. If you like gems, buy real ones. Some French cuff shirts come with a pair of cufflinks. They are generally not in good quality. You may want to replace them with a pair of good quality ones.

Screenshot, fair use.

Clark Gable wearing double-sided cufflinks.

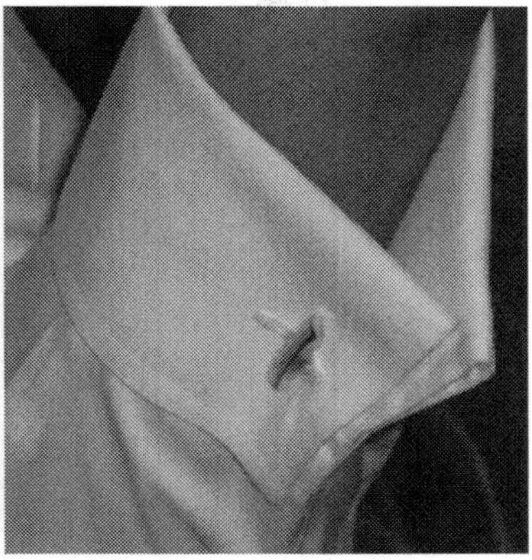

An overwhelming number of cufflinks in the market are single-sided (above photos). Don't you think it is a golden opportunity for you to dress differently and better than other men by wearing a pair of double-sided links (bottom photo)?

Part Two:

Compromise not on proportion

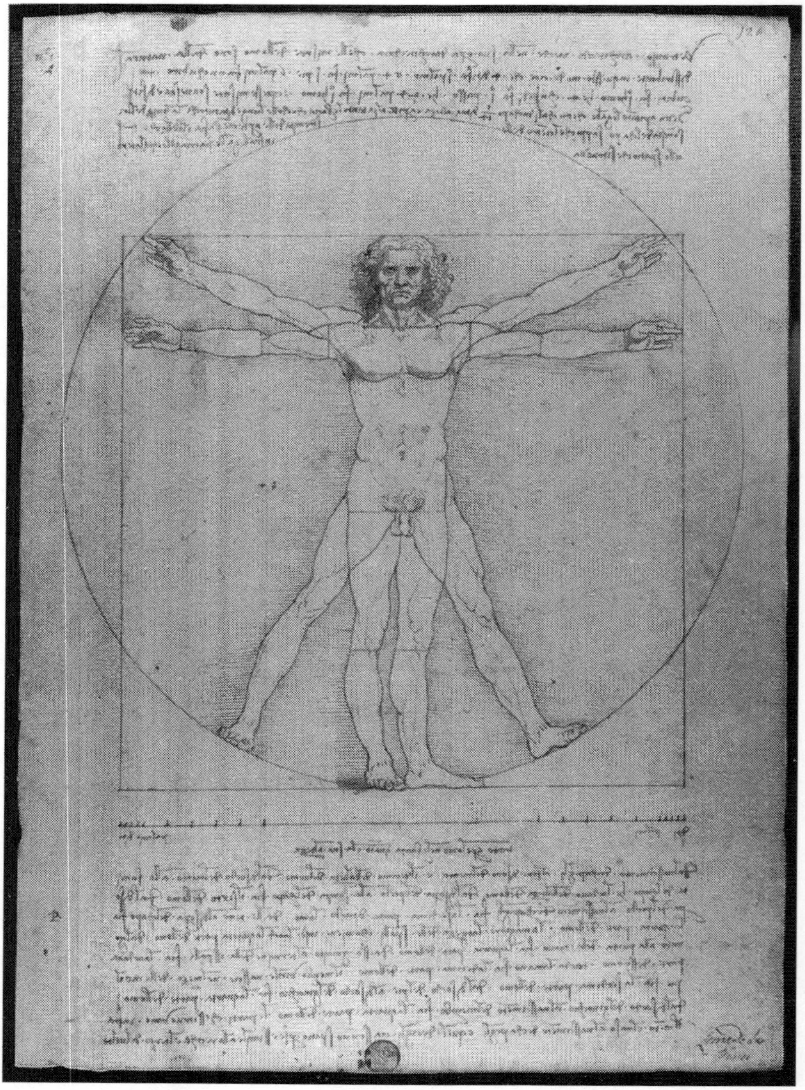

Vitruvian Man by Leonardo da Vinci

Ideal Human Body

The purpose of clothing is to hide the bad parts and showcase the good parts of the body. It is wise to proportion the articles of clothing based on the ideal human figure.

Ludwig van Beethoven

The face is the most expressive part of a human body. It is wise to relate everything a man wears to his face.

16. *Jacket length and the ideal man's figure*

An old tailor's dictum goes, "Compromise on quality if you must, never proportion." A jacket changes the proportion of a man's head and body dramatically. President Reagan's long legs disappeared once he put on a jacket. A well-dressed man should never neglect the effect of his jacket length.

16-1. A man should wear a jacket length according to the inches he needs, not the size manufacturer gives.

Frequently I encountered tall men who were looking for a long size jacket. When I mentioned to them the coat they were trying on is too long, most of them were offended. They yelled at me and said that they had worn long size jackets all their lives. Readymade jackets are usually sold in short, regular, long, and extra-long size. Every designer or manufacturer uses the same system but interprets the size differently. Most consumers understand that a 42-long jacket made by one manufacturer can be longer or shorter than another same size jacket made by a different maker. Consumers seldom realize that the same designer or manufacturer also interprets the size differently each season. During early 2000s, slim fit became fashionable. Most designers or manufacturers made their jackets much longer than those they made a decade or a few decades ago. Most men never noticed the difference and continued to wear the same size jacket they wore many years ago.

Fashion trend changes frequently but a grown man's height does not. For this reason, a man should stick to the inches he needs instead of the size manufacturer gives. If a man needs a 32- inch-long jacket, measuring from the bottom of the collar to the base of the buttocks, why should he care about how the coat makers label the jacket?

16-2. Do not cup the fingers to judge the length of a suit or sport coat.

I often hear customers comment that men look their best in a jacket. A suit or sport jacket has definite shape. It hides the bad parts and showcases the good parts of a man's body. No other men's clothing item requires more precision in fitting than the suit and sport jacket. A man ought to know how a jacket should fit his body. Even so, I have not met any man who really knows how a jacket should fit, especially the coat length. Almost every man cups his fingers to determine the length of a jacket. When I told the customers it had been wrong perhaps for hundreds of years to measure the length of the coat by cupping the fingers, they were stunned and did not know what else they should do.

The length of a jacket has more to do with the length of a man's torso and rise than the length of his arms. Men of the same height and size often have a different arm length. Manufacturers do not make jacket length according to the length of arms. Why should a man buy a jacket based on his arm length?

16-3. Choose the correct jacket length according to the length of torso, not the length of arm.

Most men wear their jacket too long because they have no idea about how long a jacket should be and what the consequences of wearing a wrong size jacket are. Some men have long arms. They would rather buy a longer coat to satisfy the need of their arms even if the long jacket will shorten their leg line and make them look ridiculous. As I have often suggested, manufacturers have a bad habit of making garments that fit most of the target population instead of an average person. Because a longer sleeve can be shortened whereas a shorter sleeve cannot be lengthened beyond a certain length, manufacturers have the tendency of making the jacket sleeves longer than an average man needs. This is the reason that most men need to shorten their new jacket sleeves. Unless a man has extremely long arms, a jacket that fits his body usually has enough sleeve length to cover his arms. Between a jacket that fits the body perfectly but is slightly too short for the arms and a jacket that fits the arms perfectly but is too long for the body, a man should choose the jacket that fits his body. It is just as easy to lengthen as to shorten a sleeve of a brand new jacket. Most jacket sleeves can be lengthened up to 1 ½".

16-4. If a tall man is tall because of his long legs, the man may not need a long size jacket.

Men's clothing stores nationwide are training their salespersons to recommend long size jackets to any man who is six feet or taller. Some stores even give out brochures to promote this erroneous belief. Their recommendation is as follows.

Short:	under 5' 8"
Regular:	5' 8" to 6'
Long:	6' to 6' 4"
Extra Long:	over 6' 4"

A man is tall mostly because his legs are long. But, the jacket does not cover the legs. The legs of an ideal body are about one half to one head length longer than the combination of the torso and pelvis. Unless a man has a long upper body, or his legs exceed this perfect proportion, a man should not ruin his asset by wearing a long coat. John Wayne and James Stewart were tall men. They look marvelous in the movies with a short coat.

Manufacturers proportion the length of a jacket to the chest size of the jacket. A 44-Regular jacket is likely to be longer than a 42-Regular jacket. For this reason a tall man with a small chest may need a long size jacket, whereas a man of the same height with a larger chest may not need a long size jacket.

16-5. Why should a man avoid a long jacket?

Most men these days wear too long their jacket. There are at least five good reasons that a man should not wear a long jacket.

First, a jacket will be sat on if it is too long. Although it seems obvious, few men ever notice the problem.

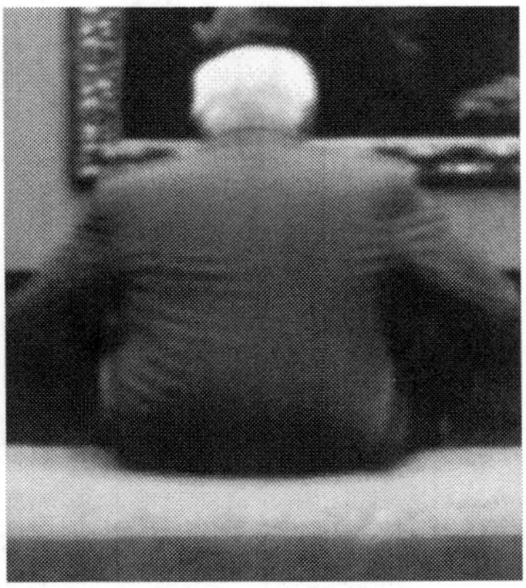

A long jacket not only runs the risk of being sat on, but also creates more lines of wrinkles when the wearer is seated.

(Screenshots, fair use)

Second, a jacket that is too long may distort the proportion of the head and torso. The ideal human body has a torso of two head lengths, a pelvis of one head length, and a pair of lower limbs of three and half to four head lengths. A long jacket diminishes the head and shortens the leg line.

President Bush and Prof. Joachim Sauer, husband of German Chancellor Merkel, appeared having short legs because their jackets were too long.

Third, a jacket that is too long creates excessive lines of wrinkles when the wearer sits or places his hand in the trouser pocket. For some reasons, many men prefer a jacket length and sleeve length that is longer than what they should wear. To show them the consequence of wearing a long jacket length and sleeve length, I often asked the customers to button the jacket and place both hands inside the trouser pockets. The extra length of fabric bunched up at the elbows and above the pockets, which looked very unbecoming.

Many customers changed their mind and wanted a shorter jacket or sleeve length.

Fourth, the long jacket tail tends to flap against the rear of the wearer, especially when the jacket is vented.

Last, a longer jacket may create a larger gap between the jacket and the pants as the legs become smaller toward the ground. The larger the gap, the less attractive the outfit is.

Because pant legs are tapered toward the ground, a longer jacket tends to create a larger gap between the jacket and the trousers.

It looks unbecoming to have a large gap between the jacket and the trousers. A pair of full-cut pants not only provides a better transition from the upper- to the lower-body, but also provides a better balance between the volume of the upper- and the volume of the lower body.

16-6. *The tailor's method*

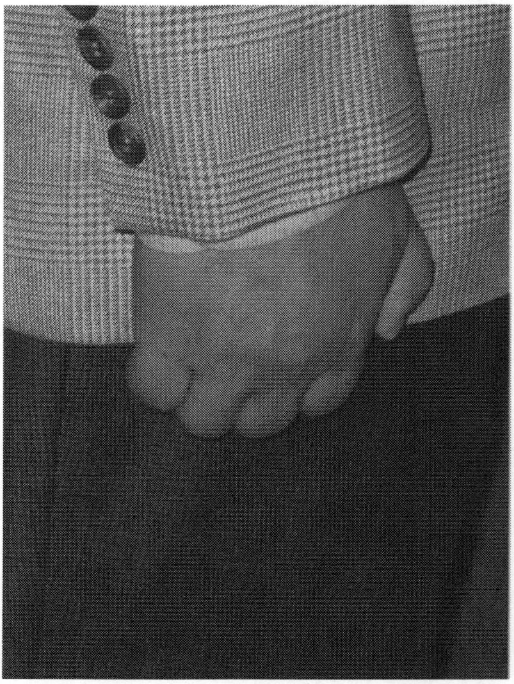

To determine the length of a jacket, most men line up the bottom of the jacket with their thumb knuckle. When a man bends his fingers, the tips of his four fingers are in line with the thumb knuckle. This is why men all over the country cup their fingers when they try on a new jacket. Using this method, a man with a short or average torso but long arms can end up with too long a jacket.

Another method is less known by the general public but is popular with tailors since the method is taught in most formal tailoring schools. The method measures the length from under the jacket's back collar down to the floor and divides by two. This method never works for a short man or tall man. The method also contradicts the perfect proportion of an ideal body.

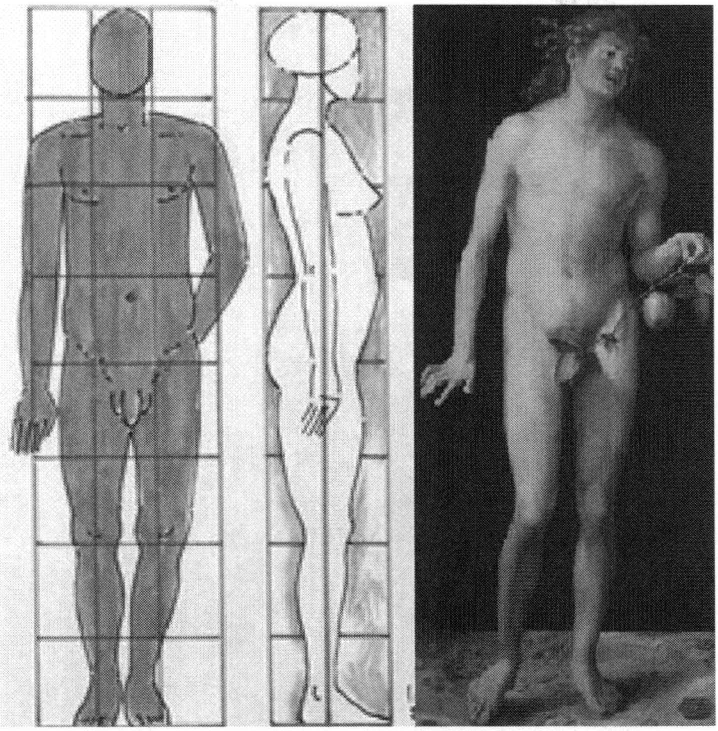

Left illustration by Bernard Ingeborg, CC-BY-SA 3.0.

Ideal human figure

16-7. What is the proper length of a jacket?

I am amazed by the fact that our current knowledge allows us to send men out of space and to alter our gene but does not enable us to find a simple method that can determine the proper length of a jacket. Isn't it so obvious to find the correct length just by considering the following two factors? One factor is that the coat has to cover the curvature of a man's buttocks. The other factor involves the components of an ideal human body. As mentioned previously, the ideal human body has a torso of two head lengths, a pelvis of one head length, and a pair of lower limbs of three and half to four head lengths. A suit or sport coat should be short enough just to cover a man's torso and pelvis. This will help elongate the leg line and achieve the esthetic proportion of an ideal human body. Putting these two factors together, the only conclusion is that the jacket should end at the joint where a man's buttocks and legs meet. If a jacket extends too much beyond the buttocks, the jacket length will shorten the leg line when the man is standing and the jacket tail may be sat on when the man is seated.

Over the years, I have devised a few guidelines to determine the proper length of a jacket. Customers call my guidelines scientific. I would consider these guidelines simply "common sense."

1) The jacket must cover a man's seat. Hence, the bottom of the jacket should line up with the base of the buttocks.

2) If a man has a built lower body in relation to his upper body, the man should exaggerate his upper body by wearing a slightly larger or longer coat. If he chooses a longer one, the man can wear a jacket length up to one inch longer.

3) A tall man can wear slightly longer jacket and still looks all right. But in no time, should the jacket length exceed the length from the bottom of the coat to the ground.

4) A short man should wear a short jacket length but not shorter than one inch above the base of the buttocks. According to my experience, a short size jacket is still too long for most short men. A short man can have his jacket shortened but the jacket should cover most of his buttocks. Women's suit jackets are often made so short that the bottom of the jacket cuts across middle of the pelvis, inviting eyes to focus on the center of the buttocks and genital area, which is extremely unbecoming. A jacket should either cover the seat or end at the waist such as in the case of a waistcoat.

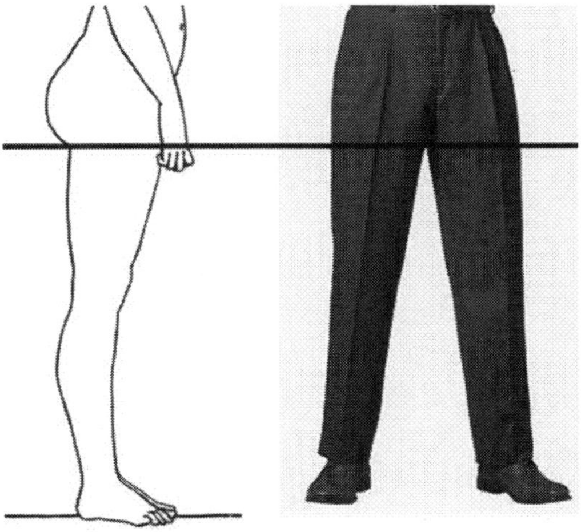

While the best jacket length depends on individual's height and body proportion, the proper jacket length for an average man should end at the base of the buttocks, or where the pant legs part, providing that the man wears his pants correctly.

Women's suit jackets are often made so short that the bottom of the jacket cuts across middle of the pelvis, inviting eyes to focus on the center of the buttocks and genital area

16-8. Better to be short than to be long

Fashion experts suggest that a jacket should be ½ the length from under the back collar to the ground. This may be undesirable because it contradicts the figure of an ideal man. For a tall man, I am inclined to recommend a jacket length that is slightly shorter than ½ of the total length unless the man has a relative large lower body, which may make a short jacket appear insignificant.

Bob Hope wore a jacket that is less than ½ of the total length.

One of the biggest fashion mistakes that today's men commit is wearing too long their jackets. Among the leaders in the G-7 Economic Summit of 1983, President Reagan wore the shortest jacket in proportion to body height. He looked marvelous.

Between a long coat, short legs and a short coat, long legs, which is more attractive?

Hugh Jackman looks marvelous in a short jacket, which keeps eyes looking up toward the chest and the face. In contrast, John Travolta's long coat forces viewers to look downward.

17. Balance the Mass.

Following my recommendations on choosing the proper jacket length, some men found that they are between sizes. They had difficulty to choose between two sizes, such as the short and the regular, the regular and the long, or the long and the extra-long. I suggested them to take the concept of mass into consideration.

17-1. The illusion of Mass

If you place two boxes of the equal size, one white one black, next to each other. The white box looks larger but lighter, whereas the black box appears smaller but heavier. It looks unstable if you put the black box on top of the white box. Hence, it is wise to reduce the volume of the jacket to make the whole outfit appear more stable and balanced.

17-2. The difference between a suit jacket and a sport jacket

One key difference between a suit jacket and a sport coat is that a suit jacket is worn with a pair of matching trousers whereas a sport coat is usually worn with non-matching pants. To highlight the concept of non-matching, it is more effective to wear contrast colors. Thus, a navy blazer worn with whit dock pants, or with grey flannel or khaki pants becomes a classic model. If a man wears a matching suit, the effect of mass illusion becomes less noticeable since the jacket and the trousers are viewed as a unit. If a man wears a sport coat with contrast slacks, the effect of mass becomes apparent.

For those men who are between two jacket lengths, it may be wise for them to choose a shorter jacket if the jacket is dark and the pants are light, and vice versa.

Mass Balance

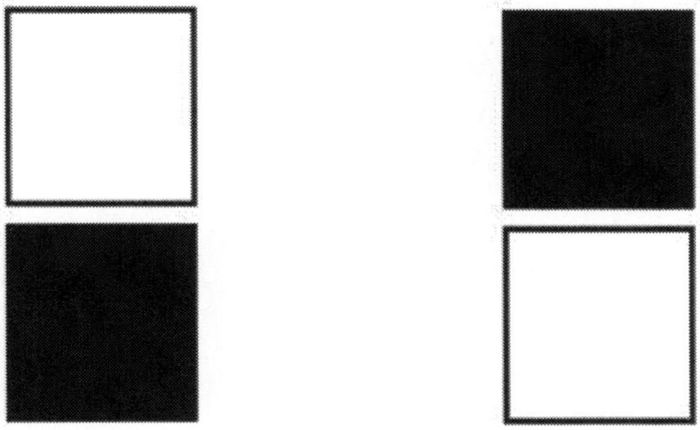

1. ***The white box looks larger and lighter than the black box even though both boxes are the same size.***

2. ***The figure on the top right appears less stable than the figure on the top left because the black box is on the top.***

3. ***The figure becomes more stable if the volume of the black box is reduced (bottom left) or broken into sections (bottom right).***

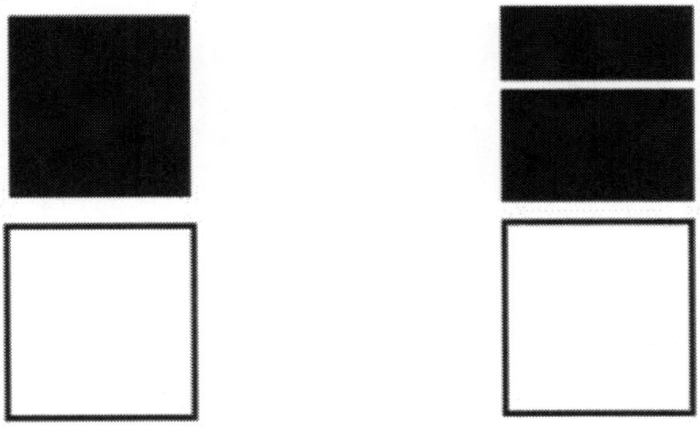

18. Proportion the volume of shirt and pants

18-1. Proportion the volume of shirt according to the ideal body figure.

No matter how good quality, how stylish, or how well-fit a shirt is, the shirt is not going to look marvelous if the volume of the shirt is not proportional to the wearer's overall body length. Many men wear a pair of pants a few inches below the waistline, showing too much the upper body and the shirt. A large volume of shirt diminishes the significance of the face. A large volume of shirt also upsets the balance between the upper and the lower portion of the body, especially when a dark shirt is worn with a light color pair of pants. To make the body appear sturdy, you either reduce the volume of the top or increase the size of the bottom.

As I have explained previously, an ideal human figure has a torso of two head lengths, a rise of one head length, and a pair of legs of three and a half to four head lengths. Because a dress shirt is supposed to cover only two out of eight sections or one quarter of the body length, it is imperative not to oversize the volume of the shirt. Fashion designers use patterns such as stripes and checks to break the shirt into smaller sections so that the volume of the shirt does not appear as large as its actual size. The best way to reduce the volume of the shirt is to wear a pair of high-waisted pants, especially when a man is short.

18-2. Wear pants on the waist.

The great majority of men wear their pants in the wrong place mostly because they do not know the proper place to hang their pants. Most men wear their pants a few inches below the waist because they feel more comfortable this way. Indeed, most of the readymade pants these days tend to have a low rise. It is uncomfortable to wear a pair of low-rise pants high on or above the waist.

The waist is supposedly the smallest part of the torso. Logically, the waist is the ideal place to hang the pants. Many American middle age men are overweight and have a large belly. Their waist happens to be the largest part of their torso. It is very difficult to keep the pants up if a man has a large stomach. This is the reason that many men cannot wear their pants on the waist even if they want to.

Most readymade pants in the current market are available in even-numbered waist sizes, like 30", 32", 34" and so forth. Odd-numbered waist sizes are available but only in smaller waist sizes. Size 29" and 31" are common whereas size 33" and 35" are uncommon. Size 37" and beyond are rare. If a man needs a waist size of 35", he often has to choose between the 34"and the 36". Most men prefer a slightly larger waist to a slightly smaller waist. Some men continue to wear a larger size waist because they have lost weight. Whatever the reason is, it is difficult to keep a larger pair of pants on the waist unless the wearer hangs the pants with a pair of suspenders instead of a belt.

Most men and women are conscious about whether a particular color or pattern looks good on them or whether the color or pattern of a garment coordinates well with the rest of their outfit; few men and women ever pay attention to the proportion of each garment. A good quality garment that does not suit the wearer is less attractive than a bad quality garment that fits. Proportion is one of the key elements that determine the fit of a garment. Many fashion designers consider proportion the foundation of style.

To achieve the aesthetic balance of an ideal human figure, most men should wear their pants high on the waist. For those men with short legs or long torsos, they should by-pass their natural waist and should wear their pants above their waistline to shorten the torso and to lengthen the leg line. Men with a high rise can wear long rise pants. For those men who cannot find their waist because of their being overweight, they ought to know that the waistline is about the same position of the navel.

Many young people these days intentionally hang their pants from the hip instead of waist because they think the style is appealing. John T. Molloy said that lower-middle-class men tend to let their pants droop and hang from the hips. Nonetheless, I have seen many upper-middle-class men wear their pants the same way. Most men do not think it is a big deal whether or not the pair of pants sits on the waist. They never realize the importance of proportions. The best location for an average man to wear his pants is slightly above the navel.

18-3. A pair of low-waisted pants makes the jacket appear shorter than its actual size.

I have been stunned by the fact that a great many men wear their jackets too long. Each day I have to persuade customers to switch their jacket size to a shorter one. Some men tried on a shorter jacket and complained about the jacket's being too short. I asked them to pull up their pants. All of a sudden, the same jacket looked marvelous. This helps explain why so many men wear their jackets too long. If a man wears his pants several inches below his waist, a jacket of proper length may appear too short because the coat may be unable to cover the entire seat of the pants. It is awful to wear a pair of droopy pants with a suit or sport jacket.

Fair use.

The top body overwhelms the lower body.

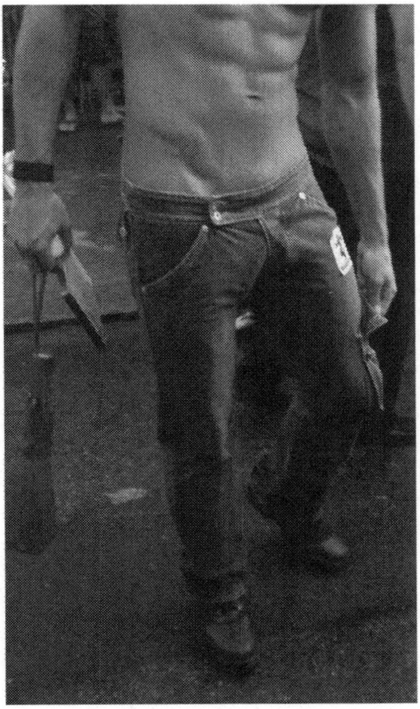

Many men believe that it is their body and they can wear whatever they like on their body. Some wear offensive clothing in public, such as a pair of low-rise jean and a pair of sagging pants. Clothing is like silent language. Just as we should be careful about what we say, we should be vigilant about what we wear.

Top photo by istolethetv, CC-BY 2.0.

by Clq

A pair of low-waisted pants makes the torso appear longer.

The man looks sharp with a pair of high-waisted pants and a well-proportioned shirt.

19. Jacket front opening and balance points

19-1. Most men have two balance Points.

Scholars studied the portraits of great artists and found that the head in the portraits often appears in balance with the upper body. They discovered an important concept of balance and proportion, called balance points. Most people have two balance points. The first balance point on the upper body can be determined by measuring the length of a man's face from hairline to chin with a tape or string and by letting the tape or string fall from the chin down the man's chest. Where the tape or string ends is the man's first balance point. The second balance point can be decided in the same manner except that the length is taken from the widest part of the face to the chin.

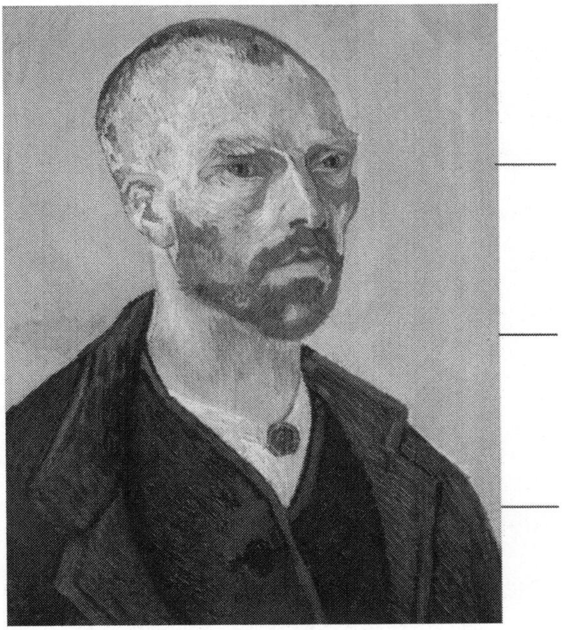

Van Gogh's self-portrait shows that the vest opening corresponds to the second balance point.

Frans Hals's Gipsy Girl

Eva Gozal's Portrait of
a Woman in White

Portrait of John Ruskin (author unknown)

Charles Bird King's Portrait of David Vann

Portraits showing that the chest front opening corresponds to the first balance point.

When a jacket or vest is buttoned, the jacket or vest front forms a V opening and becomes the focus of attention beneath the face. It is wise to have the V opening correspond to the face according to the balance points.

One of the advantages of the three-button jacket is that the V opening of the jacket corresponds to a man's face because both the V opening and the face are about the same length. In other words, the sharp angle of the V opening is at or near the first balance point of the upper body. This makes the jacket very attractive when the head and the upper body are the focus of attention.

Suit designers lower the positions of gorge, chest pocket, and waist, to balance the body line of a tall man. The gorge is the seam that joins the jacket's collar to its lapel. None of these details, however, are as effective as the V opening of a buttoned jacket in playing down the height of a tall man. A short V opening escorts the viewer's eyes upward, whereas a long V opening invites the eyes downward. A small V opening will appear disproportionate to a long or large jacket. For this reason, I would recommend a three-button jacket to a man, who is short or sits a lot. For those men, who are tall or stand up frequently, a two-button jacket may be a better choice.

19-2. Golden Section

The best length of the V opening on a two-button jacket is about 1.6 times the length of the head based on the golden section. The great masters of art have found that the relation of one part to another is very pleasing to the human eye if the ratio is about 5 to 3, or 1.6 to 1. This visual proportion is known as the Golden Section, Golden Mean, or Golden Ratio. Any V opening that approximates or exceeds two times the length of the face will diminish the proper balance of the head.

Golden Ratio

In mathematics and the arts, two quantities are in the golden ratio if the ration of the sum of the quantities to the larger quantity is equal to the ratio of the larger quantity to the smaller one.

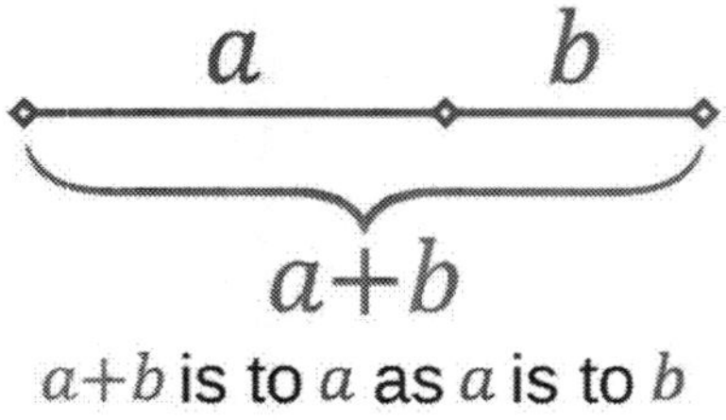

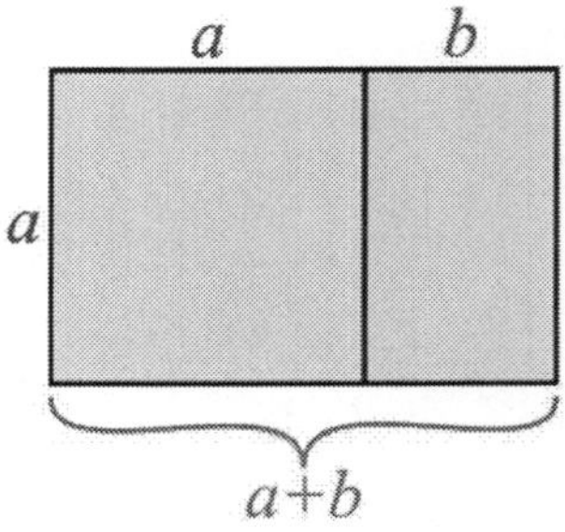

Jacket and Vest V Opening in Relation to the Face

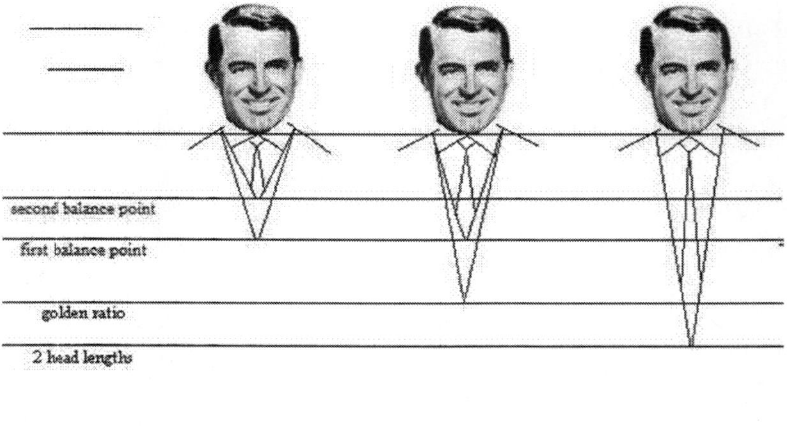

Michael J. Fox is a short man; he would look better with a high-cut jacket that has a higher gorge on the lapel.

By Alan Light.

Young Harry Truman and Gandhi's jacket front opening landed at second balance point.

General Petraeus's jacket V opening, Gary Cooper and Lincoln's vest V opening correspond perfectly to their first balance point.

Douglas Fairbanks, Jr. and President Bush's jacket opening are in the golden ratio whereas President Kennedy's equals two head lengths.

JFK, Jr.'s coat opening exceeds two head lengths, diminishing the head.

20. Cardigan sweater

Sweaters are designed to keep the body warm. Hence, most sweaters have a high-cut neckline. The problem with a high-cut sweater is that it covers a large portion of the shirt collar and the tie. Furthermore, a high-cut neckline does not respond to any balance point.

Many men enjoy wearing a sweater or sweater vest under a jacket. It is my recommendation to wear a low-cut cardigan or V-neck instead of a high-cut V or crew neck sweater because a cardigan sweater tends to have a larger chest opening that balances the head or face of the wearer.

by Martin Kraft, CC-BY-SA 2.5

(a)

(b)

The chest opening of a low-cut cardigan (c) or V-neck (b) allows the shirt collar and the tie to be shown and tends to correspond to the balance point while the chest opening of a high-cut crew or V neck (a) sweater does not.

by Cuidro, CC-BY-SA 3.0

(c)

21. Where to place a tie tack, clip or chain

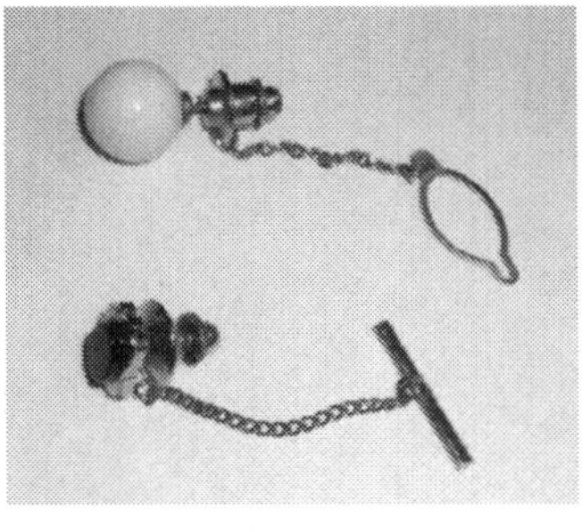

When a man bends his upper body, his tie tends to swing around. A tie bar, clip, tack or chain is used to secure the tie. Nevertheless, few men know the proper location to put on these accessories.

Like President Reagan, most men put on their tie tack, clip or chain at random without thinking there may be a better location for the jewelry. Consequently, the tie tack or bar often lands at a different place each time the man wears the accessory.

Some time ago, men wore high-cut vests and jackets. There was no need to hold down the tie with a tie tack or clip. Most men wore tie accessories for decoration purpose. Tie tacks, clips or chains were placed high near the tie knot for visibility.

Today, most men wear low-cut jackets without the vests. Consequently, men are moving down their tie accessories.

It is mind blowing that President Johnson placed his tie tack right on the triangle point of the jacket V opening. The top button has the same effect of securing the tie as the tie tack does. President Johnson should raise the position of his tie tack, making it more visible. Or, he could just forget wearing one.

To prevent the tie from swinging around, it is more effective to place the tie tack or clip near the bottom of the tie. Nonetheless, the placement lures eyes downward and looks unattractive.

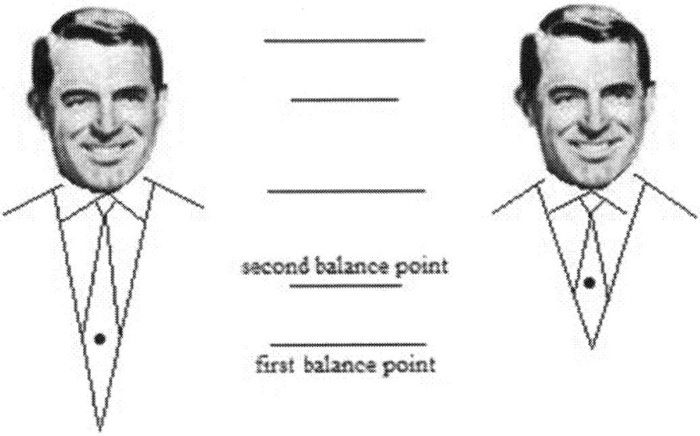

The best place for a tie accessory is the first balance point. The next place is the second balance point if the first point has been taken. The concepts of balance points will be discussed later in this book.

Because a flat tie that falls straight from under the collar is lifeless, it is wise to use the tie tack or clip to help suspend the tie for a lively arch.

Screenshot, fair use

Edward and Robert Kennedy placed their tie clips too low and did not tip the clips. Edward contradicted the effect of his diagonally striped tie by wearing the tie clip horizontally.

It is a custom that a well-attired man should not match his pocket square with his tie. Fashion experts believe that the matching set invites eyes to look sideways instead of looking vertically. For the same reason, the tie bar should tilt a little. A tilted bar is in harmony with the long narrow tie.

One exception is to have the tie bar go across the tie horizontally when wearing it with a square-ended tie.

Screenshot, fair use.

Isn't it redundant to wear a tie clip to hold down a tie when the tie is already tucked inside the pants?

22. Balance the jacket shoulders with the head.

While the jacket front opening should correspond to the head vertically, the jacket shoulder width should also relate to the head horizontally. Some fashion experts consider the relationship between the shoulder width of the jacket and the head size the most important factor in judging the size of a jacket. The jacket's shoulders frame the head. If the shoulders are too narrow, the head will appear larger than actual size. Conversely, if the shoulders are cut too wide, the head will come out disproportionately small.

Narrow shoulders make the head appear larger than it is.

Broad shoulders diminish the head.

fair use.

George Stephanopoulos should widen his jacket shoulders.

The theory sounds great. In reality, it is difficult to maneuver between the head size and the shoulder width. If a man has a large head and a slim body, he may be able to counterbalance the large head by wearing a slightly larger shoulder width. But, it is unworkable to wear a smaller shoulder to accommodate a small head. A man with an undersized head has no option of reducing his shoulder but has the option of enlarging his head by wearing long hair or a hat. Another approach is to use the slope of the shoulder line to balance the head. Most men choose readymade jackets that fit their body shape. But if the body shape is flawed, what is the point to highlight the imperfection? The purpose of clothing is to conceal the weakness and showcase the strength of the body. Few men ever think about adjusting the slope of the shoulders to balance with the head and the body.

When I gave customers the right size jacket, many of them, especially their spouses, often complained that the shoulders were too big. Most people do not know the proper width of the jacket shoulders. The ideal width, in my humble opinion, should follow the golden ratio, which is 3-5-8. The ratio of total shoulder width to head should be 8 to 3, or 2.67 to 1.

A mother was shopping for a blazer for her son. I gave her son a jacket of the correct size. Both complained about the shoulders' being too large. I asked them why they thought so. Like everybody else, they could not give me the answer. Most people think the jacket's shoulders are too wide as long as the edges of the shoulder blade stick out a little. I measured the widest part of her son's face, which is 8". The shoulder width is 21". I told them the shoulders matched the golden section perfectly, 8 ÷ 3 x 8 = 21.3. Both were excited and shouted in the store, "It is science."

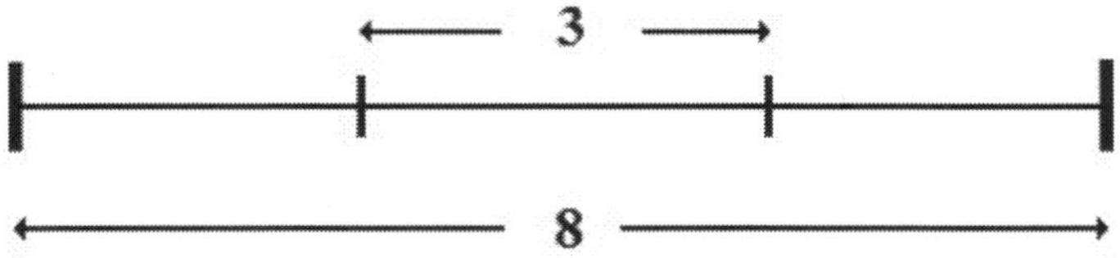

The ideal shoulder width is 8 to 3 (or 2.67 to 1) in relation to the widest part of the face.

The photos below show that ancient Japanese samurais and modern football players extend their shoulders to promote the image of physical power and strength. A man should not be afraid of wearing a jacket width that is slightly larger than his natural shoulders if the width helps achieve aesthetic balance to the head.

It is possible to enlarge the shoulder of a jacket to counterbalance a large head, but is unworkable to narrow down the shoulder width to match up a small head. It is easier to make a head appear larger by wearing a hat or long hair.

Sloped shoulders harmonize with a narrow face and thin frame while built shoulders support a wide head and large body.

A long neck isolates the head from the body. Tom Hanks, and the former President (bottom left) and Vice President of South Vietnam needed a tall shirt collar and raised jacket shoulders to offset their tall neck.

by Alan Light

Squared shoulders can make the short neck disappeared and bury the head.

Sloped shoulders help lift the head.

Part Three:

The great myths

There are a few myths about menswear. One pervasive misbelief is that a knotted tie should reach the waistband of the trousers. Another misconception is that plain front pants are slimmer than pleated pants. And, all pants should have a little break. In this section, different views are presented to challenge these erroneous ideas and thoughts.

23. *Hang the tie according to the length of head and torso.*

23-1. Should the tie reach the waistband of the trousers?

The vast majority of men and women believe that a knotted tie should reach the waistband of the pants. There is no clear justification for such belief.

Experts suggest that the tip of the tie blade should cover the belt buckle or reach the waistband of the trousers. By doing so, the tie divides the wearer's upper body into two sections, known as gores in fashion design. This seems to be a good idea. The problem is that the majority of men wear their pants a few inches below the waistline. Contemporary trousers have a lower rise than those in the past. Many men feel it is more comfortable to wear pants on the hip than on the waist. As a result, their torso appears to be out of proportion. It makes no sense to wear a tie length that reaches the hip. Experts claim: if a tie does not hang to the waistband, it will expose a patch of the shirtfront and lure eyes to the midriff. I do not understand how these experts think. To lure eyes to your midriff is much better than to lure eyes to your private part. An ideal man has a torso about two lengths of his head. The torso starts at the bottom of the neck and ends at the waist. The waist is the part of the abdomen between the rib cage and hips. On proportionate people, the waist is the narrowest part of the torso. Many people do not have a clear waistline because they are overweight. For most men, the waist is near the navel.

In my humble opinion, a tie should hang to the waistline or to the navel. If a man wears his pants correctly at the waistline, the tie should touch the pants. If a man wears his pants several inches below the waist, there is no reason to lengthen the tie a few inches just trying to cover his mistake. A tie that drapes below the waist and points at the genital area not only looks unbalanced but also looks inappropriate.

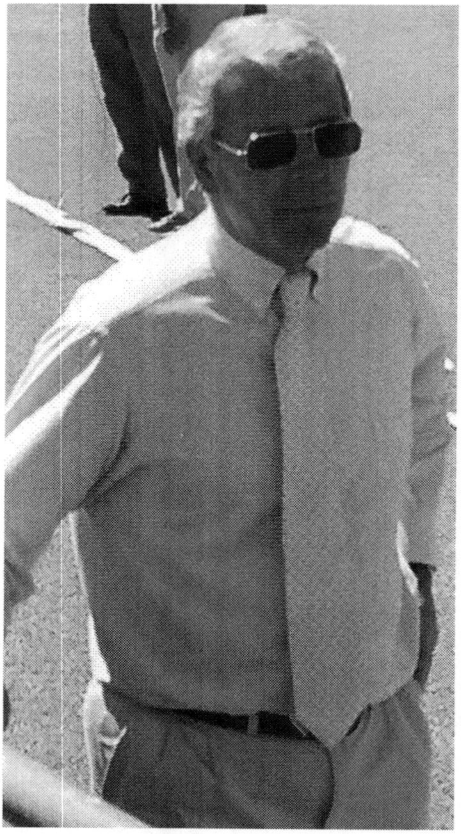

Some people have a long torso. They wear high-waisted pants to reduce the volume of the upper body. Some people do not have a long torso but wish to create the image of having longer legs by wearing high-waisted pants. When the waistband of pants is higher than the actual waist of the body, the tie is better worn short enough just to touch the waistband. Or, the extra tie length will contradict the effect created by the high-waisted trousers.

Most short men are short because of their short legs. Since short men cannot make their legs longer, they should reduce the volume of their upper body by wearing high-waisted pants and short ties. If a short man is unwilling to wear high-waisted slacks, he will still look better with a short tie.

When a man sits down, his upper body bends and his torso gets shorter. Thus, every man tends to have his tie length wrong when he sits. For those men who sit most of the time, they should wear their ties one or two inches shorter than they normally wear when they stand up.

I have met a number of tall men who insist on wearing an extra-long tie. In most cases, they really do not need one. Some of them wear a shirt collar that is too big for their neck, most of them use the Windsor knot, and, worst of all, they do not know the proper length of a knotted tie. Most tall men are tall because they have long legs, not because they have long torso. Unless a man has a very large neck or very long torso, a regular size tie should be long enough for the man if he uses a simple tie knot. Sometimes customers ask for extra-long ties because they want to tie the Windsor knot. I wonder why a man would choose the Windsor. It is not a good knot. Some men want extra-long tie to go around their big belly because they mistakenly think the tie must touch the belt or waistband. Extra-long ties cost more than regular size ties. In addition, the selection of extra-long ties tends to be limited.

23-2. Why do so many men wear their tie too long?

You may think men will wear a tie length that is proportional to the length of their torsos. They do not. Most men wear a tie according to the length of the tie fabric, ranging from 53" to 60". Although the average tie length varies according to the fashion trend of the time, most ties are made about the same length during the same season. Consequently, it seems like every man is wearing the same length of tie. This is wrong. Each man should wear the right length of tie based on the height of his top body; he should not wear a certain length of tie only because tie manufacturers make him to do so. But, what is the correct length of a knotted tie? I find it disturbing that most men wear their ties too long. Manufacturers have the tendency to produce clothing items that fit most of the consumers instead of an average consumer. What do you expect a man to do if all the ties he can buy are about the same long length?

The conventional wisdom is to wear a tie length that is long enough to reach the waistband of the pants.

It is better to wear a short tie with a pair of high-waisted pants.

By Vmadeira, GNU

It is extremely unattractive to have the tie point at the sensitive part of the body.

by Robert Scoble

23-3. Adjust tie length to head length.

Fashion experts maintain that the width of the tie should not exceed the widest part of a notched jacket lapel, and the width of the jacket lapel should be proportional to the head size of the wearer. No expert ever suggests that length of a knotted tie should relate to the length of head. The ideal human body has a torso about two times the length of the head. It is my recommendation that any man should not wear his tie longer than twice the length of his head, especially if the man has a relatively small head.

23-4. Neckties belong to the neck; it is better to wear them short than long.

It is a shame for a man to choose wearing a tie but wearing it at the wrong length. I hope that I have argued forcefully about the correct way of wearing a tie. If a man is incapable of wearing a tie at the right length, he ought to consider that the full name of a tie is "necktie." This means neckties belong to the neck. A man would rather wear a tie too short than wear it too long if he cannot hang it right. A long tie lures eyes downward and ruins the proportion between a man's face and his torso.

Any man who has a small head, who wears high-waisted pants, or who sits down a lot should wear his tie short. Short men should also wear short ties.

By Antonio Zugaldia

A man with a small head should wear a short tie.

Tie Length and Head Length

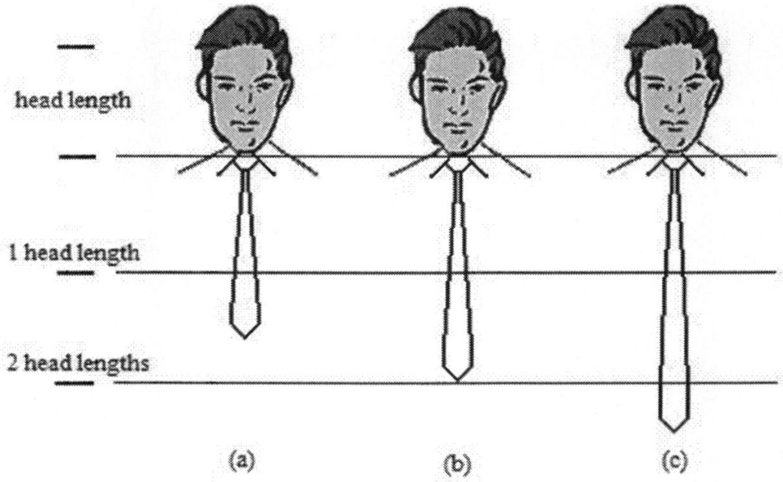

The great masters of art have found that the relation of one part to another is very pleasing to the human eye if the ratio is about 5 to 3, or 1.6 to 1. This visual proportion is known as the Golden Section, Golden Mean, or Golden Ratio.

(a) ***The best tie length is about 1.6 times the length of the face based on the Golden Ratio.***

(b) ***Nevertheless, an ideal man has a torso of two head lengths. It is wise not to wear a tie length that exceeds two head lengths.***

(c) ***A tie length that exceeds two head lengths will diminish the face.***

It looks silly for American author and radio show host, Garrison Keillor, to wear such a long tie.

There has never been any golden rule, suggesting that the tie must cover the belt buckle.

At one time, men including the big and tall ones wore a short tie.

I showed customers photos of men wearing short ties. Many of them rejected the idea and complained that the photos were old. It is true that necktie were made shorter in the past, making it more difficult to wear the tie long. But why should a man wear his tie long only because the tie cloth is long? Does it make more sense to wear a tie based on the length of the wearer's head and torso?

The body shape of mankind has not changed for millions of years. The following photos show that some men prefer a short tie even if they had a chance to wear it long.

James Stewart and Spencer Tracy could wear their tie long but they chose not to.

The Duke of Windsor, trendsetter of the early 20th century, wore a short tie. What is significant is that the back piece extended beyond the front blade and was tucked inside the trousers. This indicates that it was intentional to wear the tie in such a manner.

The Spanish painter, Salvador Dali, wore a short tie in the same manner that the Duke of Windsor wore his.

by Carl Van Vechten

Screenshot, fair use.

If short ties look cute on girls, they may look good on men too.

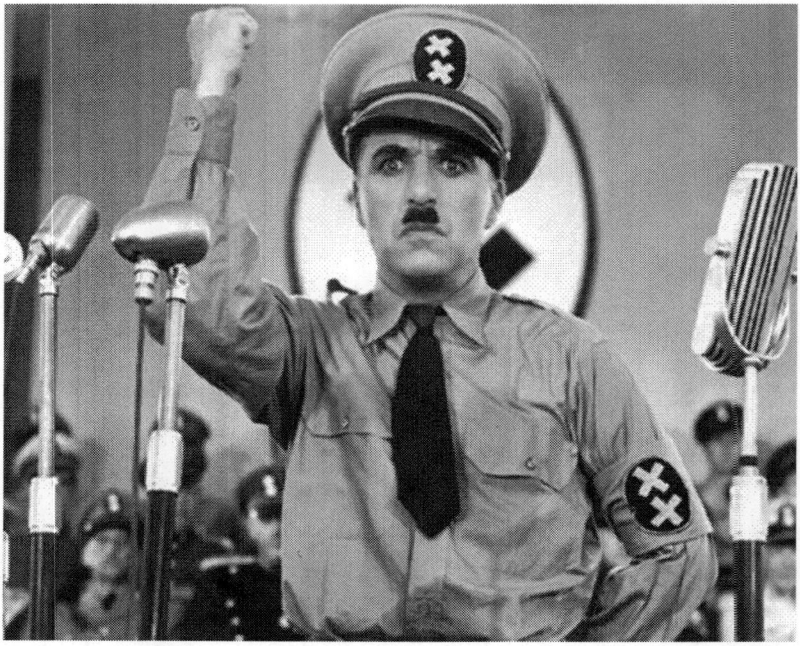

23-5. A long tie prevents the knot from arching out.

To help arch out a tie, the tie should not be knotted longer than necessary. A shorter tie carries less weight and reduces the burden of the tie knot. A shorter tie also means that the tie is knotted at a lower location of the tie blade. The lower the location, the larger the tie width is. A wider piece of fabric passing through a narrow knot opening will create a larger dimple and add strength to the tie knot. A strong tie knot provides the forward thrust for an arched tie.

24. Are plain-front pants trimmer than pleated pants?

Many men prefer non-pleated to pleated pants because they think the flat front makes them look trimmer. Connoisseurs mock this idea and consider the effect of the flat front opposite to what those men have expected. When people look at a pair of flat-front pants, the eyes see the edges or sides of the pants. As for a pair of pleated-front pants, the eyes will focus on the two vertical lines of the pleats. According to the experts, pleated-front actually promotes the illusion of a slimmer look.

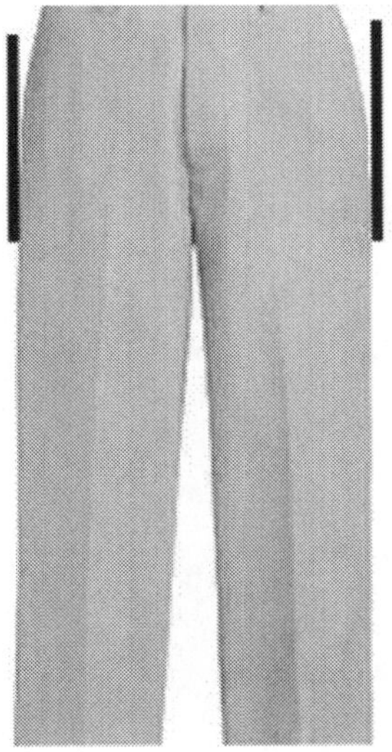

Eyes tend to focus on the edges of a pair of plain-front pants and concentrate on the two sharp creases of a pair of pleated pants. Hence, the pleats have a trimming effect.

Those men, who think flat front pants make them look trimmer, confuse pleats with the cuts of pants. Manufacturers make the same size of pants in different cuts. Some pants are cut fuller in the rise, thighs and derriere. Manufacturers often produce a more relaxed or looser cut for pleated than for non-pleated pants. Hence, pleated pants tend to be baggier than non-pleated pants because of the cut and not because of the pleats. You can have a pair of pleated pants in tailored fit or slim cut. You can also have a pair of plain-front paints in relaxed fit or baggy cut. A pair of pleated pants and a pair of non-pleated pants should have the same fit if both pants are the same size and the same cut, and the wearer is standing. The advantage of the pleated pants is that the pleats will open and give the pants more room when the wearer sits or bends.

Alan Ladd wore a pair of plain-front pants in loose cut.

Fair use.

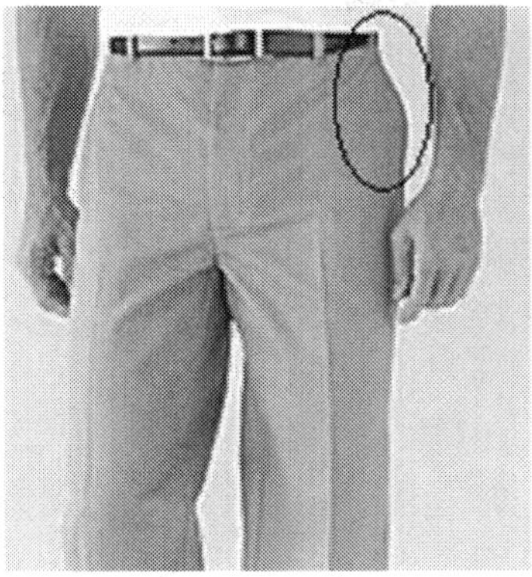

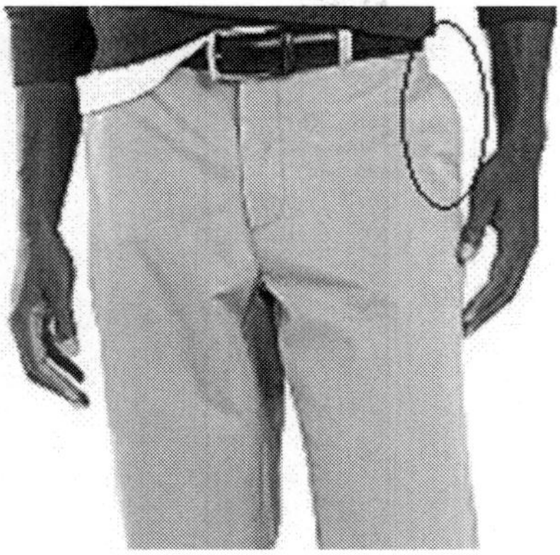

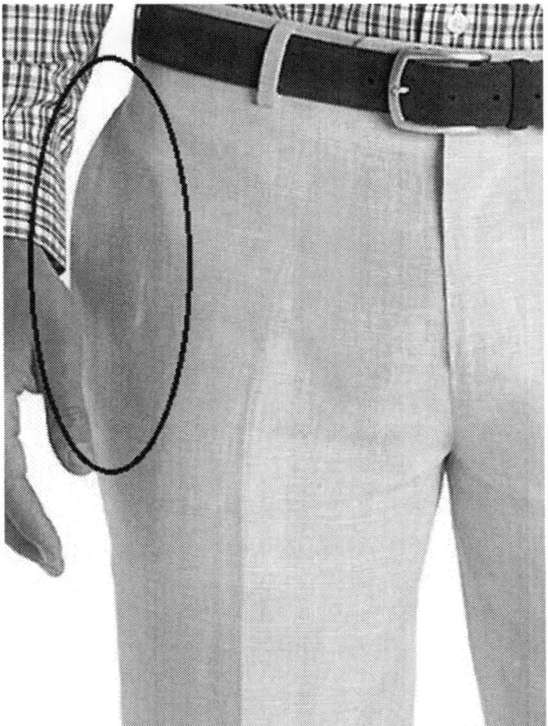

Because there are no pleats to conceal the extra fabric in the hip area, the side pockets of the plain-front pants tend to be pulled open a little. Many men like tight-fitting flat-front pants but do not like the way the pocket pop-opens. It is bizarre.

One remedy to reduce the tendency to pull open the side pockets is to wear diagonal or besom pockets. The front pockets come in four basic styles in men's dress pants based on the positions of the pockets. They are on-seam, diagonal, horizontal, and besom. The most common style is the one that aligns with the side seam of the pants. This design looks neat when the wearer is standing, but it opens up wide when the pants are tight or when wearer sits. Hence, many designers slant the pocket seams toward the middle of the pant front.

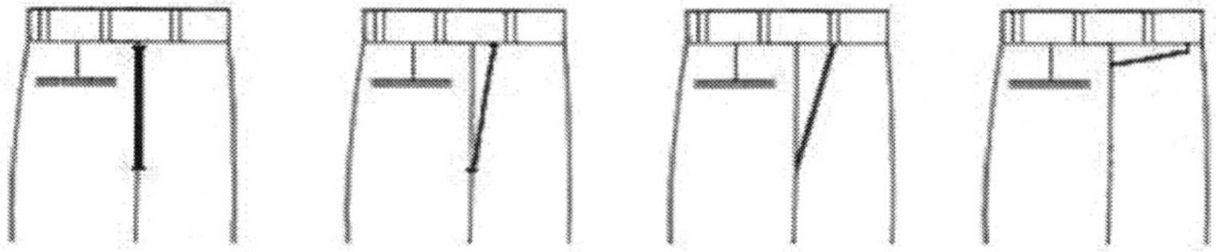

On-seam ***Eighth top*** ***Quart top*** ***Full top***

A slanted pocket reduces the amount of fabric that pops up when the wearer sits. The diagonal pocket seam adds an interesting line to the appearance of the pant front. When the top of a slanted pocket seam ends at about a quarter portion of the pant leg, the pocket is called a quarter top pocket. Whether a slanted pocket should be a half top, a quarter top or an eighth top depends on the number of pleats and the waist size of the pants. A half top pocket does not coexist with a pleated front because the pocket seam will interfere with the main pleat, which divides the pant leg into two halves. For the same reason, a quarter top does not work with a double pleat.

When the pocket opening is horizontal to the waistband, the pocket style is called a full top. The full top pockets are extremely popular in jeans and western wear but they are out of favor in dress slacks these days perhaps because the full top pockets only exist in plain front pants.

The besom pockets are considered the most elegant style of the four designs. The opening of a besom pocket is bound by strips of fabric, called welts. A double-welt besom pocket resembles a beautifully finished buttonhole. Nevertheless, I found it troublesome that the two sides of a double-welt besom pocket tend to stay apart after the pocket is used many times, leaving a gap that is very unbecoming. If you prefer a welt pocket but do not like the pocket to stay open, consider a single-welt instead of a double-welt pocket.

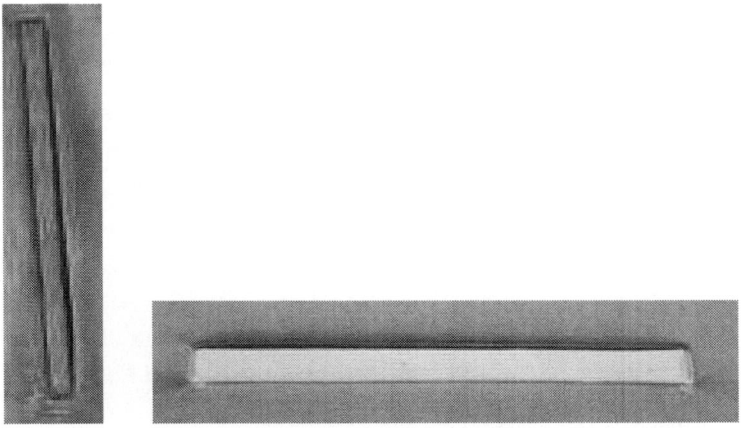

Single-welt pocket

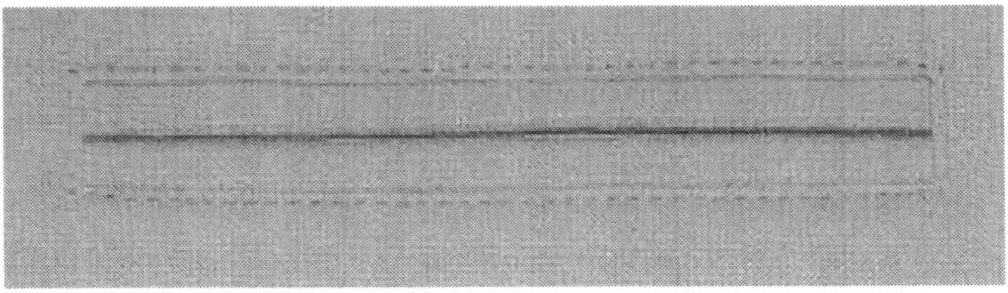

Double-welt pocket

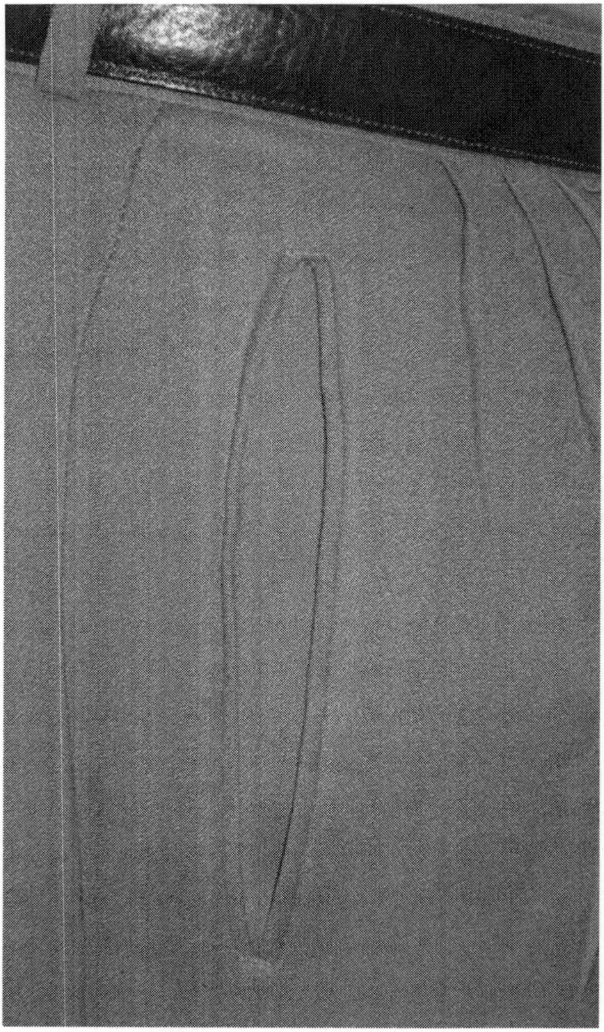

The two sides of a besom pocket tend to stay apart after the pocket has been used over time.

25. Should you give your trousers a break?

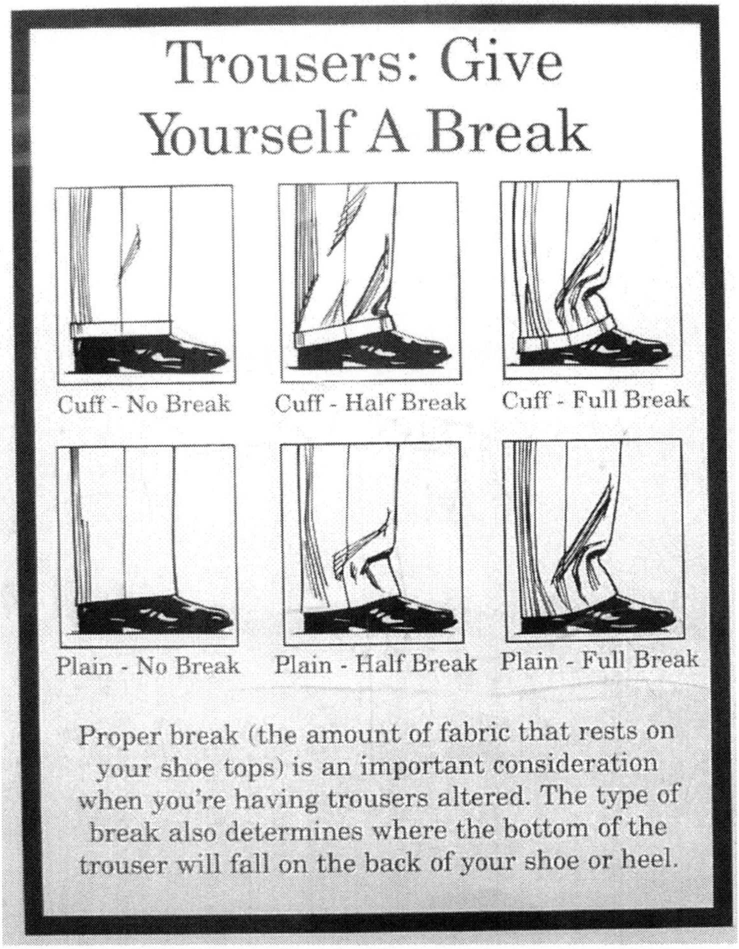

Alteration and tailor shops use the "break" to determine the length of pants. The concept is somehow flawed. Many men look at the poster and tell their fitter or tailor what type of break they prefer without considering various factors that cause a break.

Many clothing stores and tailor shops use the concept of break to help consumers determine the length of their pants. The concept is misleading. All the salesperson or tailor does is to cut the pants shorter if the customer wants "no break" and to cut the pants longer if the customer wants "full break." The break is the result of the pants' being too long. Why would any man want to wear a pair of pants that is too long? If a man prefers a pair of long pants, why can he just say so? It is silly that many men use the term to justify their wearing a pair of sloppy long pants. They think they wear their pants appropriately because the pair of pants has a half or full break. They do not realize there is no criterion to determine how long the pants is considered having a full or half break. Many men wear their pants so long that the pants have multiple breaks in the back, which is inexcusable. They also do not realize that they can have a pair of long pants with little or no break if they finish the bottom of the pants properly.

Pants with excessive break look ridiculous no matter how you call it, a half or full break.

By Fredrik Tersmeden,

Pants that fall straight down from the waist without any break look marvelous.

Breaks interrupt the crease and leg line. They should be avoided. Dress pants are better off to be finished with a slanted bottom, which helps eliminate or reduce the amount of fabric resting on the shoe tops. Cuffed bottom cannot be slanted using conventional hemming methods. Hence, break may be unavoidable with cuffed bottom unless you cut your pants short or use other methods. There are confounding factors that influence the amount of break. You should consider these factors before you tell your fitter or tailor what type of break you prefer. To reduce the amount of unnecessary break, you should keep your waistband horizontal to the ground all the way around. You may also choose pants with a wider leg opening and avoid bulky shoes.

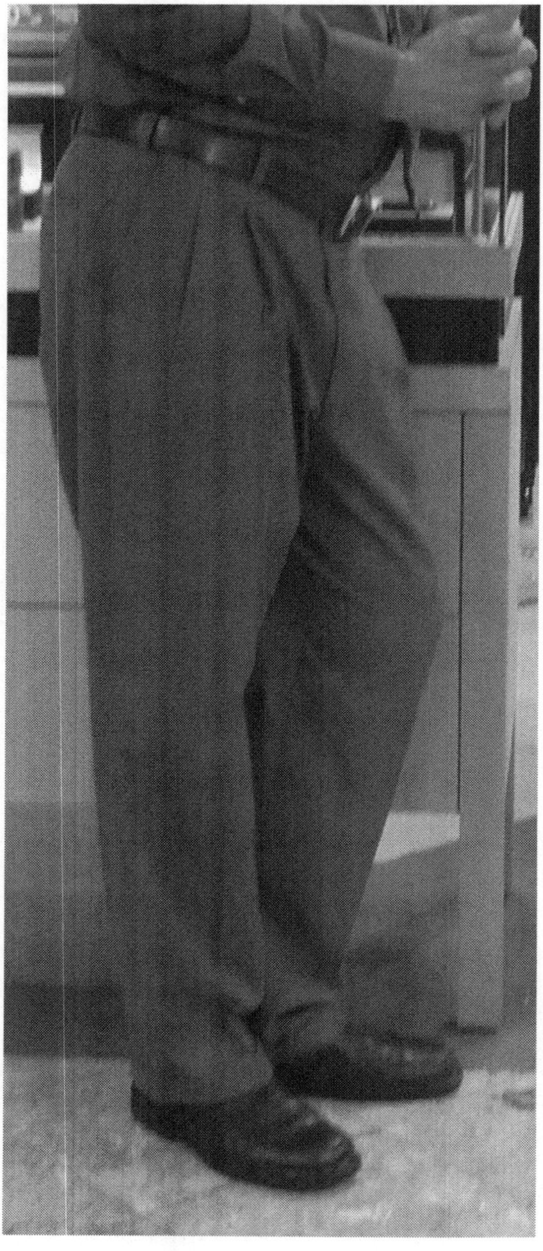

The way you wear your pants will affect the break on top of your shoe.

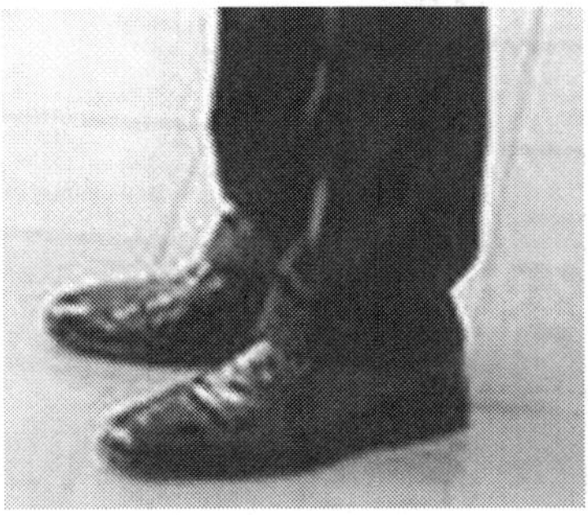

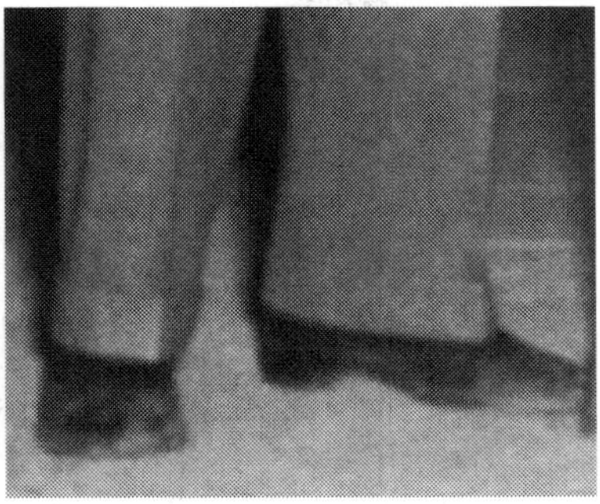

The bottom width of the pant legs and the type of shoes also affect the amount of break.

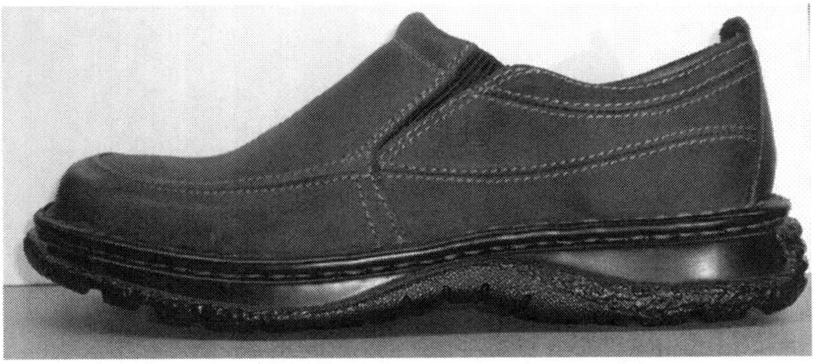

26. Lined and unlined trousers

26-1. The lining of the pant front and pant legs is unnecessary.

Many luxurious dress pants are lined from the waist to the knees inside the front of the pants. Experts tend to advise consumers to look for lining as an indication of quality. They believe that lining serves several purposes. First, the lining conceals the inner construction by providing a neat and clean finish. Second, the lining acts as a buffer between the fabric and the skin; therefore, it helps the pants fit better. Third, the lining reduces wear from the inside out. Last, the lining makes it easier to put the pants on and to take the pants off because the lining is usually made from smooth and shiny materials. The most popular lining material is Bemberg, which refers to a silky soft type of rayon fabric known as cuprammonium. The Bemberg lining is named for the German man who created it.

Fashion experts exaggerate the importance of the lining. If the lining is so important, why are most lined pants only lined in the front and only to the knees? The lining of the pants is not only unnecessary, but also has negative impacts on the appearance and the fit of the pants.

First, there is no inner construction in the pant legs that needs to be concealed. Experts maintain that a jacket without lining is usually better in quality and is more expensive than a similar jacket with lining because manufacturers are unlikely to expose poor tailoring details. Shouldn't the same logic apply to the lining of the pants?

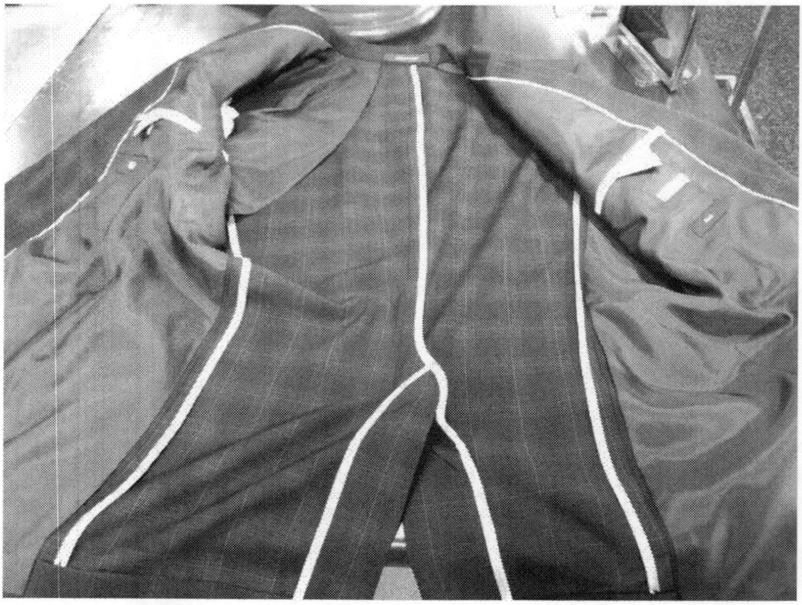

An unlined jacket tends to cost more than a lined one if everything else is equal.

Second, no matter how good the quality of the lining is, the lining is a much inferior material to the shell fabric. The lining is not as comfortable to the skin as the shell fabric. It is ludicrous to promote the lining because it reduces wear. When you have a pair of nice pants, you wear them often. The more you wear the pair of pants, the sooner they wear out. When those pants wear out, you move on to another pair of good pants. Many men buy fancy dress pants because of the soft touch of the fabrics. Do you not think it is silly to prevent the soft fabrics from touching your skin by placing a layer of inferior lining material between your skin and your pants?

Third, the original intention of creating the lining is to make it easier to slide the foot and the leg into the pant leg. I doubt that the lining helps much. A loosely cut pant leg actually makes it easier to put on the pants. I have never heard anyone complain about the lack of lining on shirt sleeves.

Fourth, in order for the lining to function properly, the lining must be cut more loosely than the shell fabric. When the lining is cut loosely, it tends to sag and to pull the pant leg downward, preventing the crease from jutting out. It is brainless for the experts to suggest that the lining helps the pants fit better because the lining serves as a buffer.

Fifth, while the shell fabrics of good dress slacks tend to resist static, the artificial or synthetic lining materials frequently attract static electricity when the air is dry. The lining clings to the skin and sparks.

Finally, the lining adds thickness to the pant leg, making it more difficult to crease the pant leg.

I have heard customers comment that a pair of lined pants is better than a pair of unlined pants. Some customers screamed in the store, accusing the store of deceiving consumers by selling expensive pants without lining. Consumers tend to think lined dress pants are better in quality. Otherwise, the manufacturer would not take extra efforts to put the lining in. It is my opinion that the lining is not as important as the experts have suggested. As the profit and the production efficiency becomes the focus of commerce, more manufacturers are producing quality dress pants without lining. It is foolish for consumers to search for a pair of lined dress pants only because they mistakenly believe a pair of lined pants is better quality than a pair of unlined pants. The lining often interferes with the drape of the pant legs. If you happen to own such a pair of pants, I suggest that you have the lining removed.

27. Collar style and tie knot

27-1. It is unnecessary to wear a large tie knot with a spread collar.

Some men want to buy spread collar shirts because they wish to wear a large Windsor knot, while more men reject the spread collar for the opposite reason. Fashion experts recommend that the size of the tie knot should correspond to the spread of the collar opening. The larger the collar inverted V opening, the larger the tie knot is preferred. Many men mistake this suggestion as a requirement and hold it against the spread collar.

In truth, there are no clear criteria to determine what size of a knot is considered large or small. It is obvious that large tie knots do not fit a narrow pointed collar. On the other hand, there is no reason that a man cannot wear a small knot with a spread collar. Both extreme small and large knots do not appear attractive on any collar style.

The length of the shirt collar and the width of the tie are supposed to correspond to the width of a notched jacket's lapels. Fashion industry keeps changing the width of jacket lapels every so often. This practice makes little sense. The width of the jacket lapels should base on the head size of the wearer. Because a man does not change the size of his head, he has no need to change the size of his lapels periodically. In my humble opinion, a man should balance the size of the tie knot with his head.

Fashion experts recommend that a small tie knot should accompany a narrow point collar while a large knot should go with a wide spread collar.

by Maggie, CC-BY 2.0.

A small or slim knot looks alright with a large collar (top photos), but a large or thick knot looks unattractive with a small collar (bottom photos).

by Tubukas

Sloppy tie knots look unattractive regardless of the size of the knot or the style of the collar.

28. Should socks match shoes, slacks or neither?

28-1. The two theories

There are two pervasive theories concerning the color of socks. One theory says that the color of socks should match the color of shoes. The other suggests that the color of socks should go with the color of pants. Both theories are unfounded. Socks are supposed to be covered until the wearer moves around or bends his leg. Why should something that is mostly hidden match anything else?

An ideal human body has a pair of legs that is one and half to twice the length of the torso. Men with long legs look more attractive. To lengthen the leg line, it is smart to include the foot as part of the leg. If the color of socks contrasts sharply with the color of pants, the socks cut off the leg line. Hence, it is wise to wear light color socks with light color pants, and dark socks with dark pants. But, it is unnecessary to wear the same color socks and pants.

Shoes are important items in an ensemble but they are too remote from the face and the center of body. It is silly to worry about how socks should relate to the shoes. Men wear only two or three different colors of shoes. It is no fun to wear few colors of socks all your life.

28-2. Coordinate socks with something worn above the waist.

Fashion experts recommend that the socks should coordinate with something that is worn above the waist. When a man dresses up from head to toe, he may gradually lose the connection between his upper and lower body. The socks give an opportunity to connect both parts of the body.

J. Edgar Hoover and his assistant Clyde Tolson

Socks are supposed to be covered under the pants until the wearer moves around or bends his leg.

I once saw Fred Astaire wear a tie that matches his socks in a photo. Rich people have the financial means to do whatever they wish. Ordinary people should not lose sleep over the colors of their socks. Some designers do produce few matching tie and socks but you may be unable to find them. If this is the case, do not worry. You can always use socks that coordinate with your shirt, jacket or pocket square, and so forth. Each season our company carries a variety of wild socks in red, yellow, orange and other bright colors by famous designers. Those socks do not usually sell until the end of the season when they are closed out and sold at 90% of the suggested retail price. I do not know why the buyers of the company never learn. Most consumers mistakenly think socks must match either the pants or shoes. Because few men wear red or orange pants or shoes, it is no wonder that few consumers will buy wild socks at $20.00 a pair, when a good quality non-iron shirt or a pair of non-iron pants is about $50.00.

Ralph Lauren produced ties and socks that are matched in color and pattern.

Department stores carry men's socks in a wide variety of patterns, weaves and materials, but in a limited number of colors because consumers mistakenly think socks must match either their shoes or pants.

Part Four:

Personal choice?

When scientists discover a new plant or animal that has never been recorded, they compare the sample with existing species that share similar characteristics. If the features of the sample fall between the traits of two closest species, A and B, and if the difference between the sample and Specie A equals to the difference between the sample and Specie B, scientists may declare the sample a new specie. If the characteristics of sample are overwhelmingly close to Specie A but not Specie B, scientists would rather classify the sample the same specie as A instead of creating a new specie.

Fashion writers list all varieties of styles in major categories of menswear, but they are unable to tell readers which styles are preferable. Most experts believe that whether a pair of pants should be pleated or non-pleated, should be cuffed or non-cuffed is a personal choice. They suggest there are four basic styles of dress shirt collars, and consider collar style a personal preference. Consequently, consumers are confused with the varieties of styles. Does the style matter if it is a personal choice? They often wear the wrong styles of clothing and dress for failure.

If there are two or more different styles and each style has about the same number of advantages or same amount of quality, you may consider each alternative a personal choice since you cannot determine which style is superior. But if one style overwhelmingly has more advantages or better quality than the other styles, would you consider each selection a personal preference?

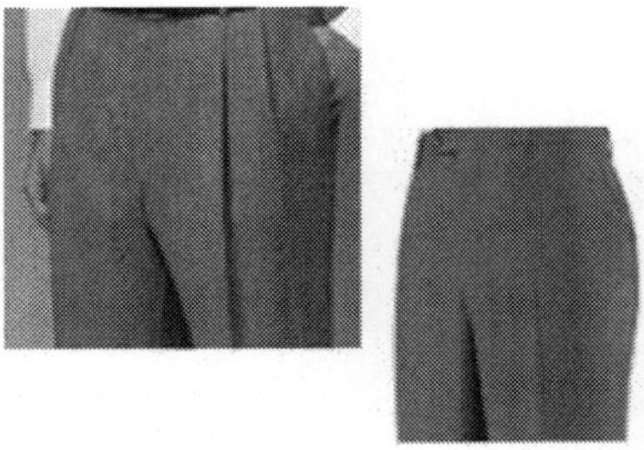

29. The advantages of the spread collar

29-1. The collar is the most important part of a dress shirt.

Fashion experts believe that the collar front is the single most important part of a dress shirt. This makes sense for several reasons. 1) It is directly under your chin and it frames your face when the top shirt button is fastened. 2) It is the place where a necktie is worn. 3) It is the busiest intersection, where the shirt, jacket, vest, and tie meet. 4) It is usually highlighted by color contrast between the jacket and shirt, the jacket and tie, and the tie and dress shirt. In short, no other part of a man's outfit offers more color, pattern and textural activities than the collar front.

Most men look for the right colors or patterns of the shirts when shopping for dress shirts. Few men will pay attention to the style of shirt collars.

29-2. There are four basic collar styles.

The contemporary shirt collar is called a turned-down collar, in which the collar first stands up from the bottom edge of the neck and then falls down to rest on the garment. Although it is possible to have many variations, modern turned-down collars are generally classified into four basic collar styles, which give a shirt its name. They are point, button-down, spread, and pin (or tab) collar. Whereas the great majority of men in the U.S. wear point or button-down collars, fashion experts maintain that spread collars are dressier. Nevertheless, few authors can explain why. I seem to be the only author who can explain the advantages of a spread collar in great details.

Collar Styles

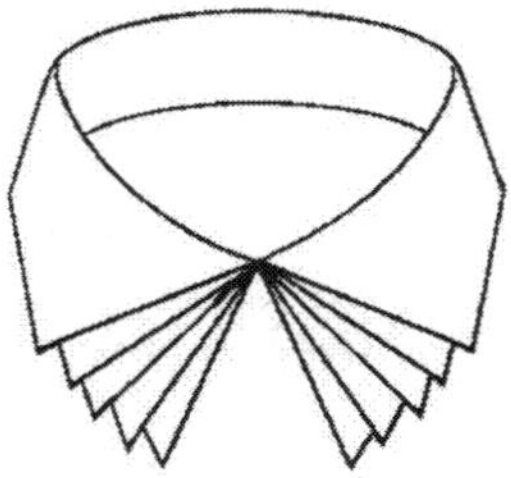

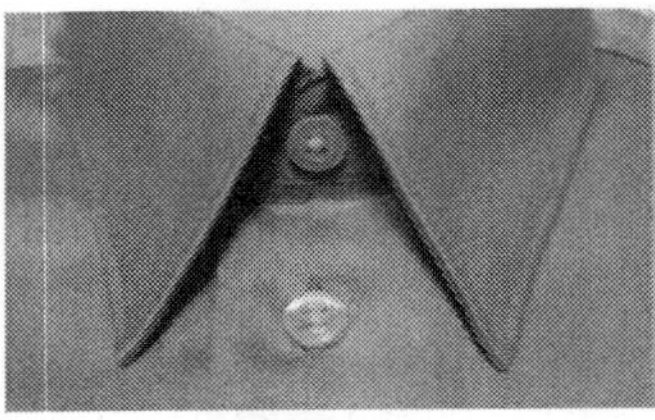

Point ***Spread***

Button-down

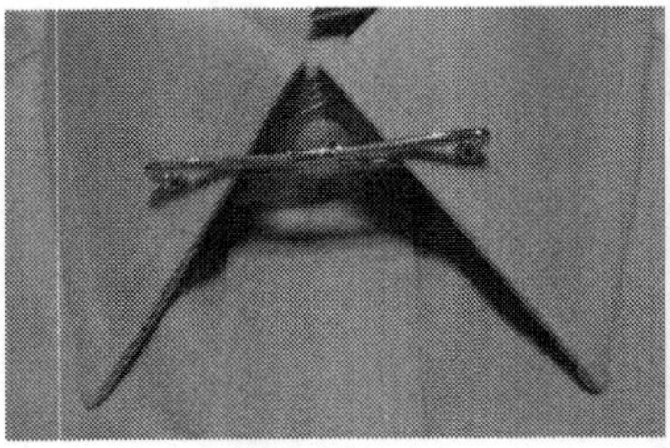

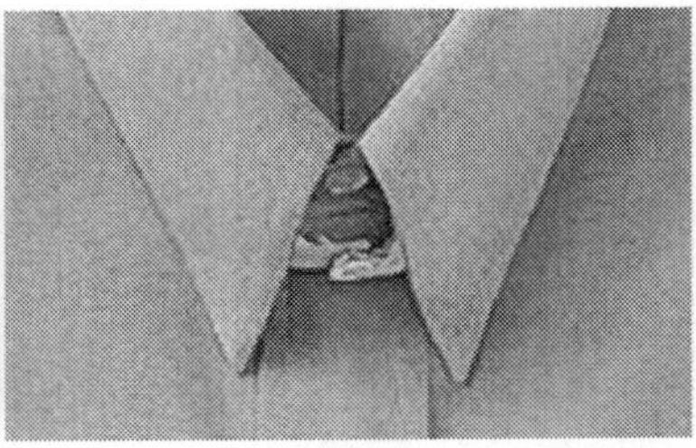

Pin ***Tab***

Although there are infinite possibilities regarding the spread and the length of the collar wings, contemporary dress shirts are generally categorized into four styles: point, spread, button-down, and pin (or tab) collar.

29-3. The advantages of spread collars

A. ***<u>The spread collar fits most face shapes</u>.***

Experts agree that the size of a shirt collar as well as the length and the spread of its points should complement the wearer's face shape and size.

a. Wear a collar size that is proportional to your head size.

1) Common sense tells you a small head will be lost in a big collar with large wings or long points. Conversely, a large head will overshadow a tiny collar with small wings or short points.

2) Just as a large tabletop requires a big pedestal to support its weight, a broad face needs a large inverted V to measure up its breadth.

b. Wear a collar style that is opposite to your face shape.

1) Long straight point collars will extend and narrow the image of a wide face, whereas wide spread short collars will offset the line of a long or narrow face.

2) A round face can be compensated by a sharp straight point collar, just as an angular face can be softened by a rounded or broad-space spread collar.

The above guidelines suggested by image consultants and fashion authorities may not be as useful as they may sound. Experts use adjectives, such as "wide," "narrow," "long," "short," "large," and "small," to describe the size or shape of head and collar. It is unclear what length is considered long or short, and what size is considered large or small. Guideline a-(2) seems to contradict b-(1). A straight point collar may offset a round face slightly better than a spread collar, but the advantage is insignificant. A short and wide face does not exist and does not need a point collar to compensate the breadth of a wide face. What is the benefit of wearing a point collar? Point collars are useless these days. The only benefit of a point collar is that it looks good with a bowtie.

A customer told me he needed a point collar to go with his long face. I suggested a spread collar to counterbalance his long face. Women wear oval or rectangular earrings to match a narrow face and wear round or square earrings to complement a wide face. Nonetheless, earrings are worn beside the face. Shirt collars are directly under the face. A long point collar will extend a narrow face and make the face appear even longer.

The decision to harmonize by choosing a similar shape or to counterbalance by choosing an opposite shape is more an art than a science. If you are as confused as this customer was, you may set aside these guidelines and wear a spread collar, which has more advantages over any other collar style and looks appropriate for most men. Some men including fashion writers believe that straight point collars can offset facial rotundity. It is unclear that a straight collar is more pointed or sharply angled than a spread collar. Even if it is true, the difference is often insignificant.

Most dress shirts sold in the U.S. are either point or button-down. I am puzzled by the popularity of these collars, considering the many shortcomings of these two styles. The dress shirt is designed to be worn with a jacket and some sort of neckwear such as a tie. It is inappropriate to discuss the fit of a collar without taking the jacket and the tie into considerations.

Women use the same forms of earrings to complement the shapes of their face. Men are better off to use the opposite forms of shirt collar to counterbalance their face shapes. This is because earrings are worn beside the face while shirt collars are directly under the face.

By Lan Bui, CC-BY-SA 2.0.

A long straight point collar narrows the image of a face and makes a long face look even longer. A spread collar cuts short the extension of the face line and offsets the shape of a long and narrow face.

B. ***<u>The points of a spread collar tend to reach the jacket front</u>.***

Men look best in a suit or sport jacket. When a jacket is worn and buttoned, a triangle is formed by the V opening of the jacket front. The triangle is topped by another triangle formed by the inverted V opening of the collar front. **Ideal design: the more spread out the two wings of the collar, the shorter the length of the wings.**

The idea behind this design is to ensure the two points of the collar will touch the jacket front. Thus, to wear a point or button-down collar with a jacket is a serious mistake. The length of the collar is seldom long enough to reach the jacket front. Just as a small roof does not cover a big house, a small collar does not fit a large jacket opening.

Ideal Collar Design

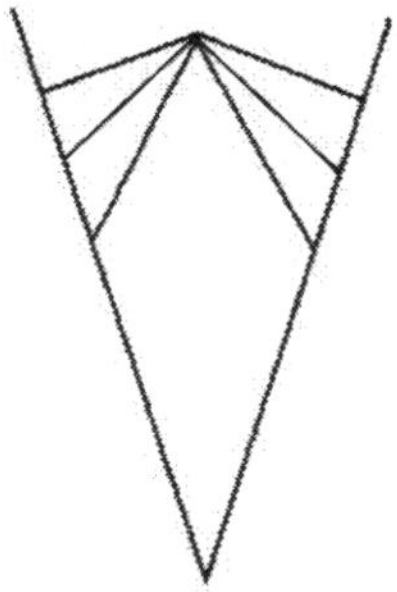

The ideal collar design is to have the two points of the collar touch both sides of the jacket lapels.

The point collar is also known as the classic collar perhaps because it was worn from the beginning of the modern turned-down collar shirts. In the old days, jacket fronts were cut high with a small V opening. Jackets were usually worn with a vest, which has an even smaller V. A short length point collar was long enough to reach the front of the vest or jacket. In addition, men wear string tie, which does not require a large opening of the collar front. Nowadays, jacket fronts are cut low to have a large V opening, vests are no longer popular, and the four-in-hand tie knot requires more room than that provided by a point collar. A wide spread collar is needed for this new trend.

Sometimes the edge of the point collar can be covered by the jacket front if a vest is worn or the V opening of the jacket is high. Still, a spread collar will look more attractive than a point collar.

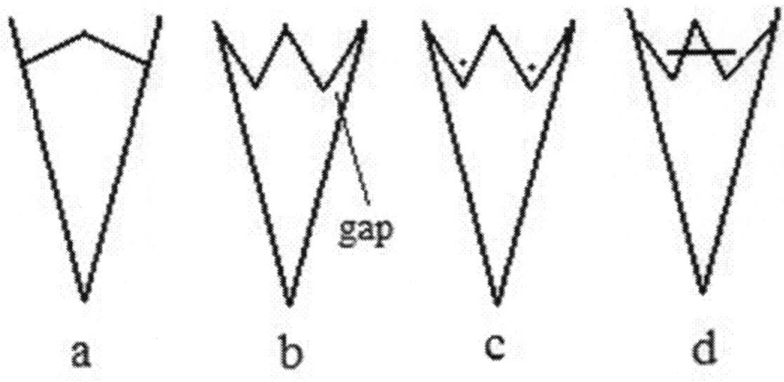

Among the different collar styles, only the spread collar (a) is suitable for contemporary jackets with a large V opening. The button-down (c) and the pin (or tab) collar (d) are actually a point collar (b).

Everyone can see what is wrong when the two collar points extend beyond the edge of jacket lapels. Few men notice the problem when the collar wings are too short to reach the jacket front

A spread collar tends to touch the shirt front and reach the jacket lapels if the jacket is a correct size.

C. *A spread collar provides the aesthetic balance to the head.*

When the top button of the shirt is fastened, the collar frames a person's face. The collar achieves the aesthetic balance between the head and the upper body if the collar opening equals the widest part of the face. Among various collar styles, only a spread collar can attain this artistic balance. If a bowtie is worn, the width of the tie should also match the widest part of the face. If a collarless shirt such as a T-shirt or sweater is worn, the neckline opening should be identical to the widest section of the face.

Some image consultants claim that a spread collar looks unbecoming for a person with a very narrow head. Actually, none of the collar styles, especially a long point collar, looks good on a person with a long head. Consultants often confuse the collar length and the collar opening. The word, spread, refers to the angle of the collar opening and has nothing to do with the length or size of the collar. A wider collar should have a shorter collar length. Nevertheless, many designers make their spread collar long just to render a fashion statement. As the distance between the two points of the collar exceeds the widest part of a person's face, the balance between a person's head and the upper body is disturbed. No one will look good wearing a collar opening that is larger than the widest part of the face.

As long as the aesthetic balance is achieved, a person can wear a spread collar that is as wide open as a 180 degree in angle.

Aesthetic Balance

The two points of the spread collar (right) line up with the largest part of the face, providing an aesthetic balance to the head.

The chest opening of the shirt does not correspond to the size of the head.

Whereas the length of any chest opening should correspond to the length of the face, the width of any treatment under the chin should also relate to the widest part of the face.

by Hs4g at en.wikipedia

The top photo shows that Bill Nye's bowtie corresponded to his face but the shirt collar was too wide for his narrow face. The bottom photo shows the opposite. The shirt collar matched Clive Anderson's face but the bowtie was too narrow for his wide face.

by WikiWebbie at en.wikipedia

It is obvious that a small pointed collar opening will not offset a large head and neck.

A spread collar with a large inverted V opening supports a large head.

D. ***<u>The points of a spread collar tend to touch the shirtfront</u>.***

All shirts sold in the stores are made with the points of collar touching the shirtfront. Yet, it is funny that many men wear point collars that do not stay in touch with the shirtfront. Obviously, these men are wearing a collar that does not fit correctly with the neck. When the top button of the shirt is fastened and the collar stays are in place, the point collar will touch the shirtfront if it is fitted properly; a spread collar will usually touch the shirtfront even if the collar does not fit the neck perfectly.

Fashion experts maintain that the two points of the shirt collar should touch the shirt front. It is very common, however, to see a man wear a point collar that does not reach the shirt front. Many men use this as an excuse to wear button-down collars.

Photo courtesy of Paparazzo.

E. ***The spread collar moves the center of focus up.***

Examine the two diamond shapes in the following illustration. You will notice that the center of attention moves up with a spread collar.

Focus Point

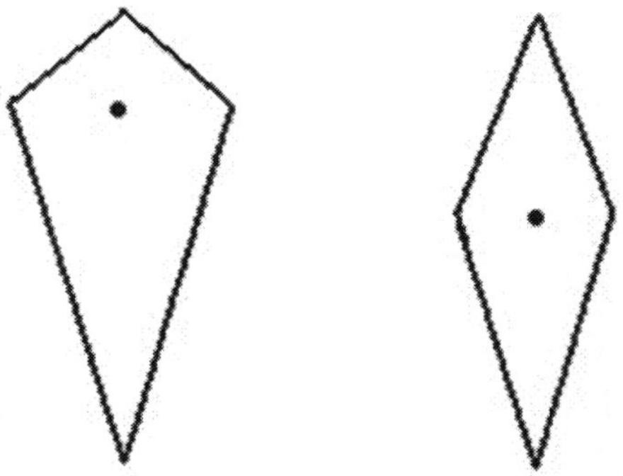

The center of focus moves up when a spread collar is worn.

F. ***The spread collar corresponds to the chin line.***

The wide inverted V of the spread collar corresponds to the chin line of most face shapes by forming a crisscross, which is very becoming.

The wide spread collar (right) crisscrosses with the chin line, providing another aesthetic balance to the face.

The wide spread collar crisscrosses Regis Philbin's Chin line.

G. <u>The wide opening of a spread collar allows even a bulky tie knot to show</u>.

A dress shirt looks fabulous when it is worn with a necktie. The narrow opening of the point collar does not leave enough space to accommodate the modern tie. The beauty of the tie knot cannot be fully revealed if the collar covers part of the knot. Very often, the tie knot lifts the collar up, preventing the points from touching the shirtfront--which is a no-no in menswear. At the same time, the two wings of the collar push the tie downward, preventing the tie from arching out. To accommodate the tie, many point and button-down shirts are intentionally made with a gap between the two sides of the collar. The gap, called tie space, is generally from ¼" to ¾". A collar with tie space looks like a defect, created by a careless or unskillful shirt maker. It is unflattering at least. You should avoid wearing a collar with tie space.

The tie knot is the head of the tie. Let it be shown. It is pointless to hide the knot behind the collar.

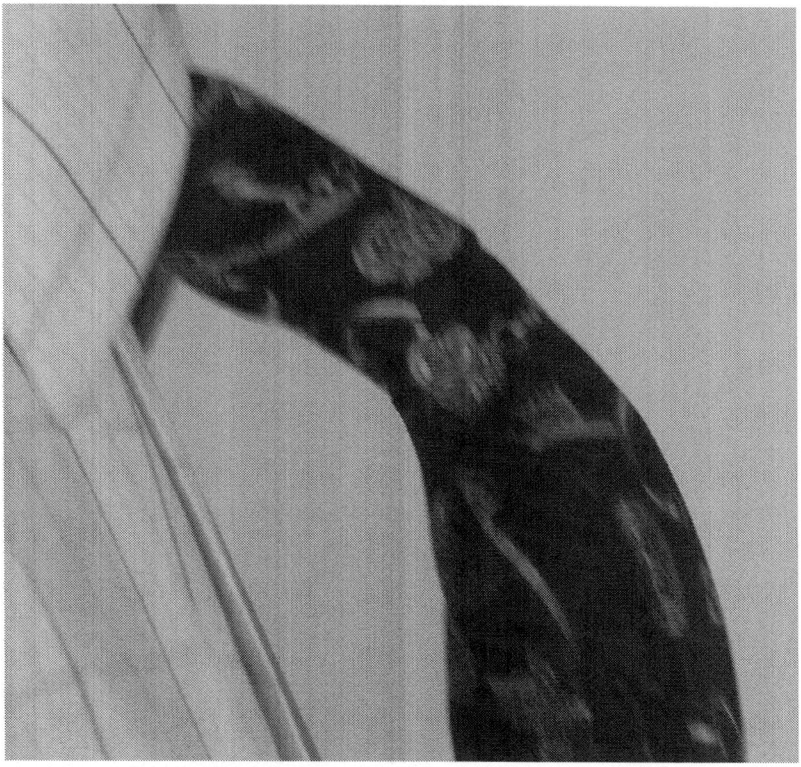

A spread collar allows the tie knot to show and to arch out if the correct knotting method is used.

Gentlemen prefer spread collars.

Because of its overwhelming advantages, gentlemen all over the world prefer spread collars, including the presidents of the United States, Japanese emperor, King of Great Britain, diplomats, celebrities, the influential, and other well-dressed men.

What happens when people become more influential and mature?

They change their shirts from point or button-down collars to spread collars.

1994

1999

2007 (World Resources Institute, CC-BY2.0)

2010 (Tom Raftery, CC-BY-SA2.0)

1975

1977

Unknown date

1993

1993

2007

2010

2004

2006 (Jonathan Blundell, CC-BY-SA 2.0)

2010 (Ed Schipul, CC-BY-SA 2.0)

2011 (Gage Skidmore, CC-BY-SA 3.0)

Congressman Gingrich met with the Great Communicator in 1985, wearing a point or button-down collar.

2010

2011

Gingrich runs for the President of the United States, wearing spread collars. (Both photos by Gage Skidmore, CC-BY-SA 3.0)

29-4. What if the jacket's lapels do not touch the two points of a standard spread collar when the top shirt button is fastened?

The jacket may be too small for the chest or the jacket collar may be too large.

By Alan Light

Pee-Wee Herman's jacket was obviously too small.

It looks weird that the right side of Secretary Paulson's jacket lapels did not touch the point of his spread collar.

30. The advantages of crease and pleat

The contrast between a pair of pants with and without sharp creases

30-1. *The crease helps keep the pant leg in the right shape.*

The crease not only has an aesthetic function by adding a vertical line to the pant leg, but also has a practical function by keeping the pant leg in the right shape. Thus, sophisticated dressers keep their creases sharp and keep their creases uninterrupted by eliminating the break.

Top and Front Views of Two Different Pant Legs

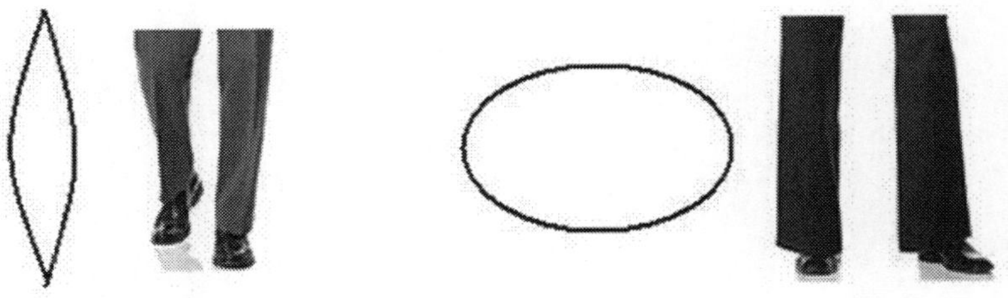

(a) *(b)*

The crease helps keep the pant leg in the right direction (a). A pant leg with sharp crease tends to go forward whereas a pant leg without crease tends to go sideways (b), owing to the stiff seams on both sides of the pant leg.

30-2. *Pleats are designed to absorb the stress and to reduce or eliminate unattractive horizontal lines in the front of pants.*

When a man sits, his waist expands, creating additional stress to the waist and the front of pants. Consequently, unattractive horizontal lines often appear on the top front of pants if the wearer sits a lot and if the pair of pants is not made of wrinkle-resistant materials.

When modern pants were first created, they did not have creases. The dressmakers soon recognized the need for adding extra amount of fabric to the front of pants. The pleated-front became the norm. During World War II, the U.S. government restricted the production of pleated and cuffed pants to save materials for the war.

Pants made of thick or stiff fabrics such as denim or canvas seldom have pleats because thick fabrics cannot be folded or creased effectively.

Dress pants are usually made of fine or soft fabrics and are better off having pleats.

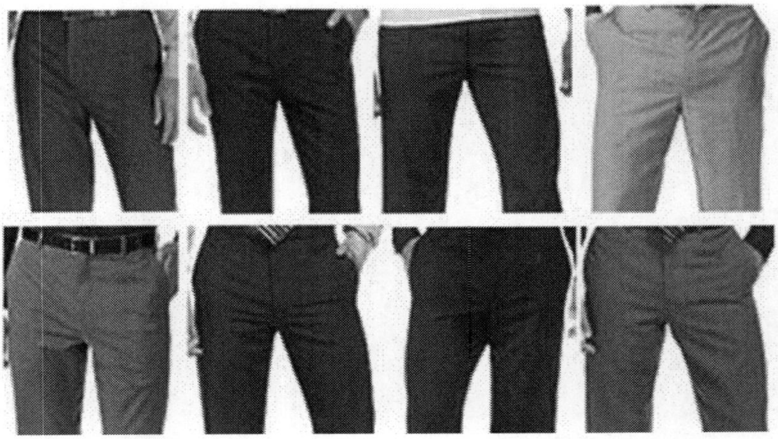

The front of pants tends to wrinkle when it is stressed.

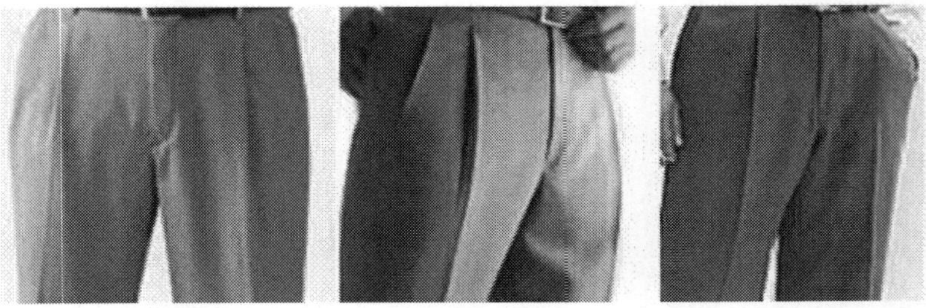

The pleats are created to absorb the stress and reduce wrinkles.

30-3. Pleats guide and maintain the crease lines, and add aesthetic interest to the pants.

Pleated pants have another aesthetic and functional advantage. The creases are the extensions of the pleats. The pleats help guide and maintain the crease lines. In the movie,

Mother, Debbie Reynolds kept telling her son that she had spotted a man whose sideburns were uneven. Without the pleat, the crease seems to disappear at the top front of pants. If you wear a pair of plain-front pants, you need to make sure that the tops of the two front creases are even. Uneven crease lines look as silly as a pair of uneven sideburns. People will notice them.

Flat front or plain-front pants look plain and flat just as their names imply. Pleats in the front of a pair of pants add aesthetic interest to the pants. Darts, which are widely used in suit jackets and women's slacks or skirts, also provide a slimming illusion, but do not have the effect of releasing the stress.

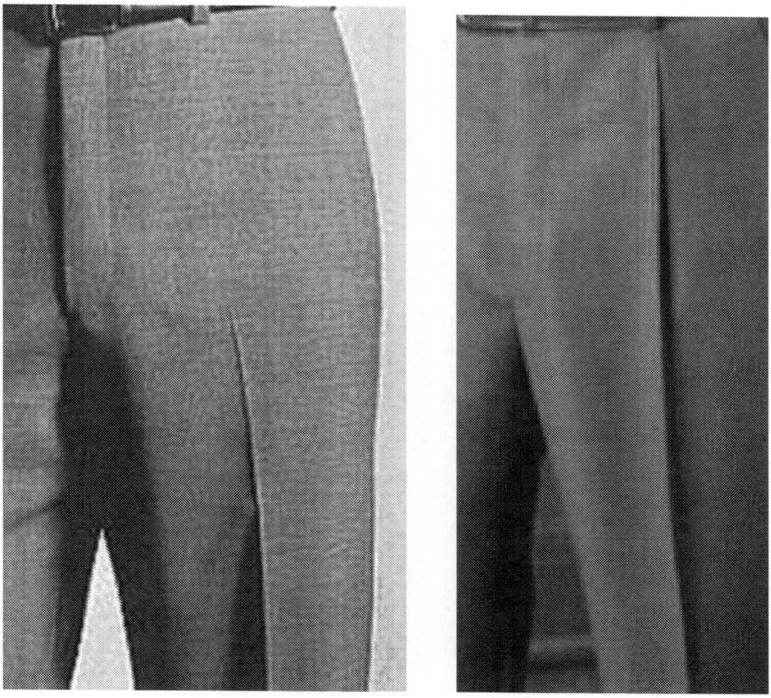

A crease that disappears somewhere in front of the pants (left) look less attractive than a crease that runs through the entire pant leg.

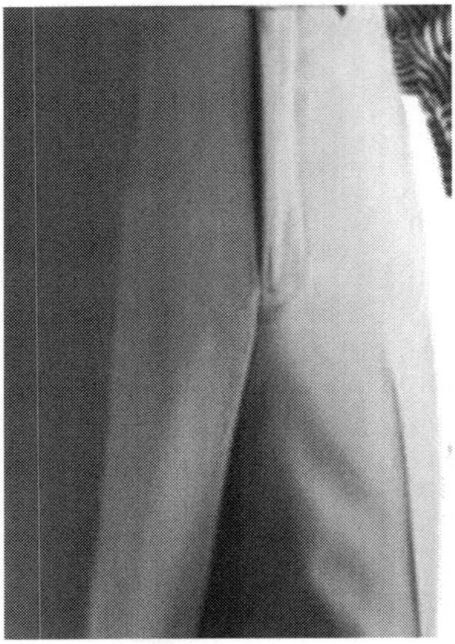

A pair of uneven creases is inexcusable.

Pleats come in several styles in men's dress pants.

1) single-, double-, or triple-forward pleats (which open toward the fly),

2) single-, double-, or triple-reverse pleats (which open toward the pocket),

3) box pleats, (which is a type of knife pleats, look like rectangular folds of fabric with one side opening toward the fly and the other side toward the pocket).

4) inverted box pleats (which are the inside out version of the box pleats).

I recommend the regular triple- or double-pleats over the box pleats because the pleat lines run in the same direction, giving an orderly appearance. Experts are indecisive about which style is better between the forward and the reverse pleats. I prefer the reverse pleats for one simple reason. When a man puts his hand in the pant pocket, the creases of the forward pleats will be pulled toward the pockets before the pleat folds are pulled open. On the other hand, the creases of the reverse pleats will not be disturbed while the pleat folds are opening.

Theoretically, each pair of pants only needs one deep pleat on each side of the pants. Nevertheless, a single pleat is less interesting to the eyes. Most pleated pants have two or three pleats on each side of the pant front. The additional pleats are put on mainly for an aesthetic purpose. They tend not to be folded as deeply as the main pleat. The pleats are designed to accommodate the expansion of the belly when the wearer sits or bends. Hence, the pleats should remain closed when the wearer is standing.

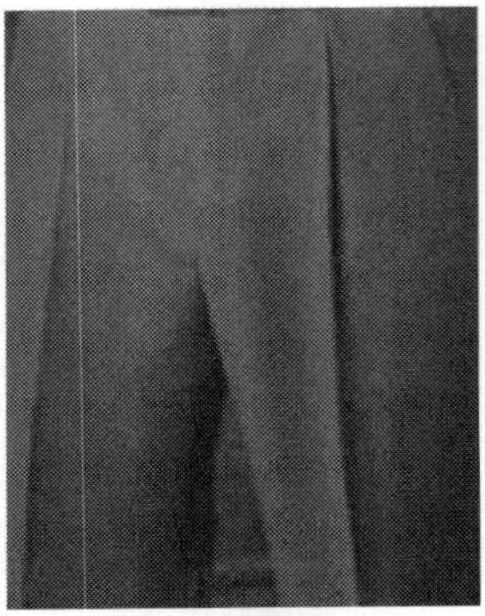
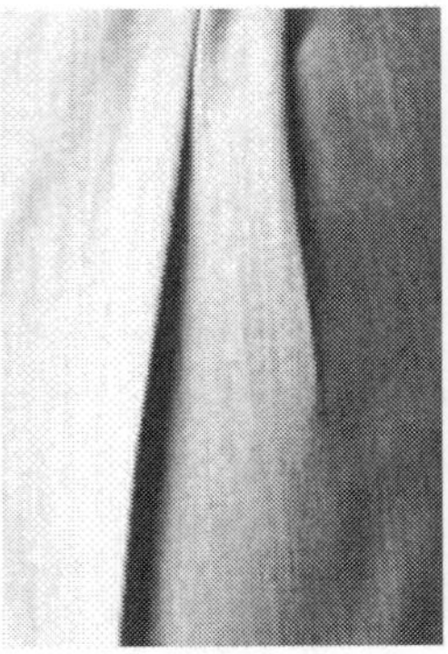
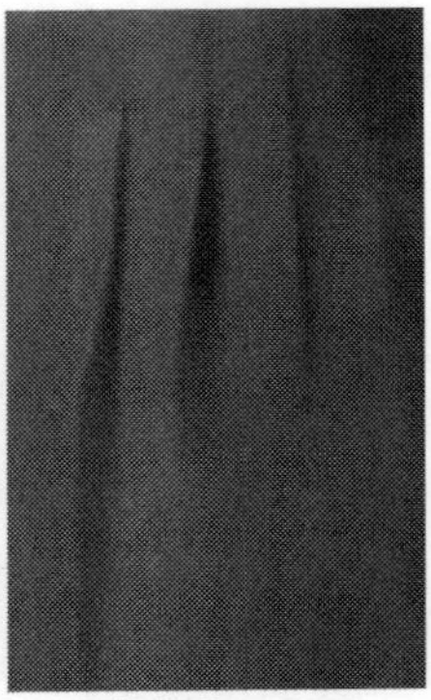

Single Reverse ***Double Reverse*** ***Triple Reverse***

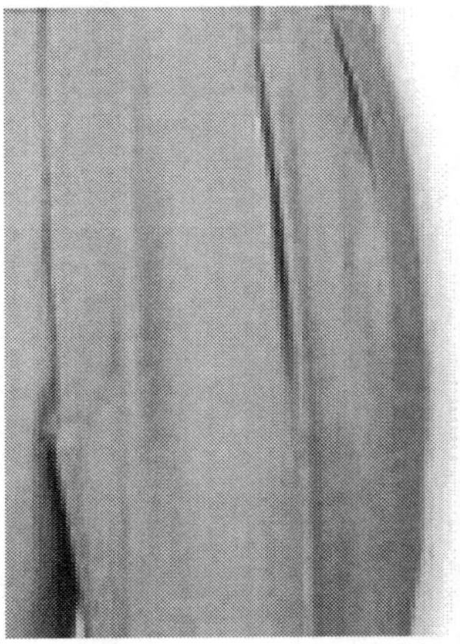
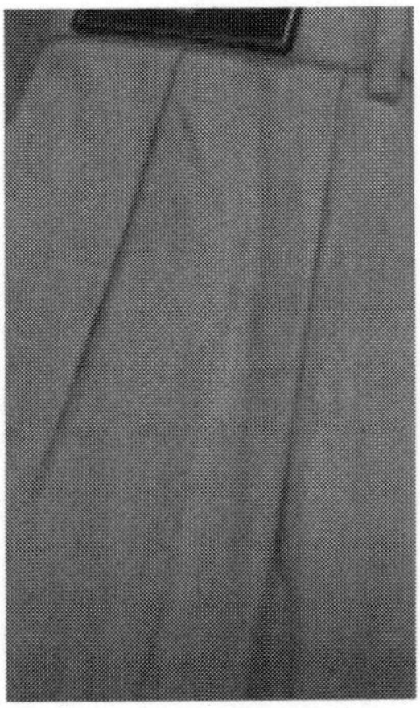

Double Forward

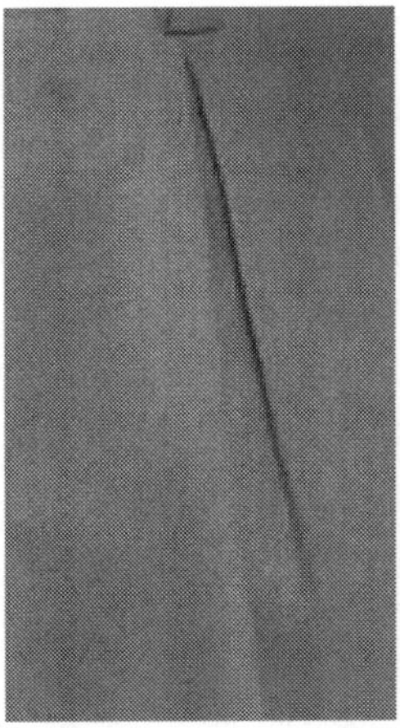
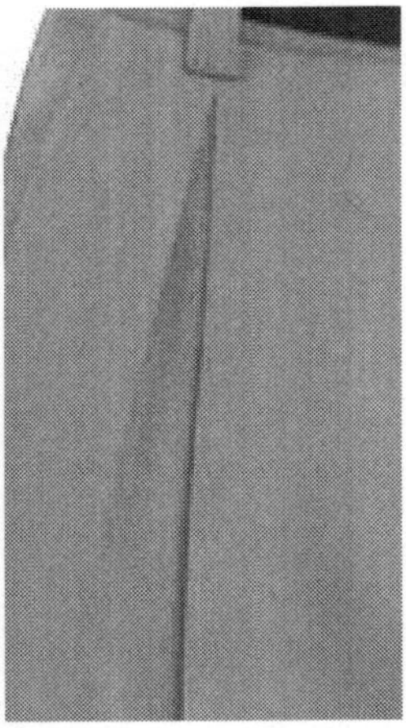

Inverted pleat

30-4. Permanent crease on dress pants

I wrote a book, entitled *The 12 Simple Ways to Dress Differently and Better than Other Men*, in which I stressed that one of the best ways to show a man caring about his clothes is to keep the creases sharp. Creases running vertically down the center of pant legs can help create a smart and sophisticated style. Some fabrics, such as wool, and some weaves, such as plain weave, hold creases more effectively and permanently than others. Still, you may find yourself pressing creases frequently to keep them crisp and sharp. A few methods have been developed to eliminate the need for pressing. One method is to sew a permanent crease by stitching about 1/16 inch away from the folded edge of the crease. The shortcomings of this procedure are 1) the stitching may not match the threads in the pants perfectly, 2) the stitching marks show, and 3) the stitching may come loose after repeated wearing and cleaning.

The recent method is to apply a thin line of silicone beads underneath the crease. The silicone glues the fabric on both sides of the crease together and is able to hold the crease in place indefinitely. Silicone is a very stable and safe adhesive. It can withstand washing, dry-cleaning and routing wears. Because silicone bonds the crease physically rather than chemically, the treatment will not affect the chemical characteristics of the fiber. Nevertheless, silicone may affect the light passing through the fabric. A piece of blue cloth absorbs all color lights except the blue one. Some unabsorbed blue lights reflect back from the surface of the fabric and reach our eyes; thus, we see the cloth blue. Some blue lights pass the fabric through the gap or space between yarns. White cloth does not absorb any color light; it permits all color lights passing through. Loose woven cloth has larger gap between yarns and allows more light to pass through. Hence, a white and thin shirt, especially when it is wet, is more revealing than any colored or dense shirt. Depending on the color, weave and texture of the fabric, silicone gel sometimes leaks through the fabric and interferes with the lighting. An associate of mine had a pair of black suit pants put on the silicone. He showed my coworkers and me that there was a white line running down the crease of his pant legs. He complained that tailor mistakenly applied clear silicone instead of black silicone to his black pants. He felt embarrassed and we never saw him wear the same pair of slacks again.

A permanent crease (above) is created by applying silicone beads underneath the crease (below).

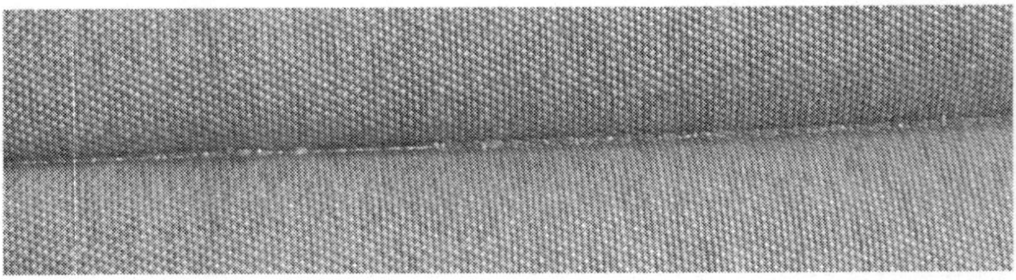

The silicone procedure is gaining popularity among professionals, who wear dress pants. National clothiers, such as Jos. A. Bank and Men's Wearhouse, offer this service at an affordable price.

In order for the silicone to work properly, the right amount of silicone gel must be applied to the underside of the crease. Silicone gel does not create the crease; it simply holds the existing crease in place. Hence, the crease must be pressed before and after the application of silicone gel. The crease should remain closed until the gel is hardened. The cured silicone will be able to bring fabric from both sides of the crease together and keep the crease sharp indefinitely. I doubt that every worker knows this. Some workers may apply inadequate amount of silicone and do not press the crease immediately after the application. The result is a dull instead of a sharp crease. The hardened silicone will make the crease become stiff and will affect the drape of the pant legs. It makes no sense for many men to have their dress pants hemmed with full break and have silicone applied to the crease. The pants will not drape gracefully at the bottom of the pant legs.

Many men are indecisive about whether they should have their trousers put on the permanent creases. The best dress pants are made of 100% wool, which is called miracle fiber for reasons. Wool fabrics hold creases better than other fabrics. If you wear wool slacks, and have problems in maintain the creases. You probably either bought the wrong types of wool fabrics, or did not wear and take care of your slacks correctly. There is little need to put silicone on a good pair of wool pants. Ironically, most clothiers only offer permanent creases on good dress pants.

In the 1990s, the garment industry began to provide non-iron treatment on cotton pants and shirts. Garments treated with the non-iron process are wrinkle-free. Some garments even have permanent creases. Today many wool garments are treated for wrinkle-resistance; some have built-in permanent creases. These wool products are often called "washable wool." The term is misleading, of course. I have washed all my wool slacks, including suit pants, in the laundry machine. One of the newest developments in dry cleaning industry is "wet cleaning," which is washing "dry clean only" goods in water.

You should give special care to any garment that has permanent creases on it. Avoid ironing or pressing on the creases regularly, or tears may occur on the creases. To learn more about creases on pants, please read my books, *A Perfect Pair of Dress pants* and *The Etiquette of Suits and Sport Coats.*

31. To cuff or not to cuff

31-1. Whether a pair of pants should be cuffed or not depends on one single most important factor.

To cuff or not to cuff is an important decision for most men when they buy a suit or a pair of dress pants. The majority of men in the U.S. prefer cuffed pants, whereas a smaller number of men like non-cuffed pants. Some men have no preference. Whatever the choices are, few men know the significant difference between the two options. Even the experts are unsure about which finishing is preferred. Most experts claim that it is a personal choice. Some authors suggest that cuffed pants are dressier than the non-cuffed pants up to a point. This is a silly suggestion. How can one style of pants be dressier up to a point and then become less dressy? Those authors have to say so because their recommendation contradicts the fact that the dressiest slacks in formalwear never have cuffs.

Whether a pair of pants should be cuffed or not, in my humble opinion, should be based on one single important consideration that is how the bottom of the pant legs is cut. In the past, non-cuffed pants are finished with a slanted bottom. Cuffed pants can only be cut horizontally straight across the pant legs using conventional tailoring method. As the workmanship declines along with the rise of the mass production methods, the readymade non-cuffed dress pants are seldom slanted these days. Therefore, it makes little difference now whether a pair of readymade pants is cuffed or not.

None of the five living U.S. presidents in 2009 wore a proper length of trousers.

It is disturbing that all ten leaders from the G-8 nations in 2001 wore too long their trousers. Compare the sloppiness of their trousers with the neatness of those worn by the Queen's Guard at Buckingham Palace.

31-2. What is the proper length of a pair of pants?

The answer is more complex than what an average man thinks. To make it simple, a pair of pants is too short if the bottom front of the pant leg does not touch the top of the shoe. Similarly, a pair of pants is too long if the bottom back of the pant leg touches the ground or has any wrinkle or break.

Experts cannot agree on the proper length of a pair of pants. Some authors suggest that a pair of pants should barely touch the top of the shoes. When a pair of pants is cut this short, several problems emerge.

First, much of the socks will be seen when the wearer moves around.

Second, the bottom of the pants keeps falling inside the shoes, especially when the man wears a pair of loafers instead of oxford shoes.

Third, a pair of shorter pants makes the legs look shorter. Some image consultants suggest that a short man should wear a shorter length of pants to make the legs appear relatively longer. This is dreaming. To help lengthen the leg line, it is more effective to include the foot as part of the leg. To achieve this, the pair of pants should be long enough to stay in contact with the top of shoes without excessive break. The proper length of pants will extend the leg line, whereas a pair of pants that is too short will cut off the leg line above the foot.

Last, uneven pant legs will show through a pair of shorter pants. Some men have an uneven waist or a pair of uneven legs. Other men may have a normal body but they pull their pants up unevenly at the waist. It is also possible that both pant legs are cut unevenly. Regardless of the reasons, the uneven pant legs will be exposed when they are suspended in the air.

The pant leg keeps falling inside the shoe if it is cut too short.

31-3. Why is it better to have the bottom of the pant legs slanted?

Theoretically a pair of pants can reach anywhere on the back of the shoes; however, the ideal position for a pair of pants to end is where the back and the heel of the shoe meet. When a pair of pants is cut this long, the pants will have a break a few inches long in the front. To eliminate the unnecessary break, a man either tilts his feet by wearing high heel shoes or by wearing a pair of pants with a slanted bottom. Because men do not usually wear high heel shoes, the only remedy is to slant the bottom of the pant legs.

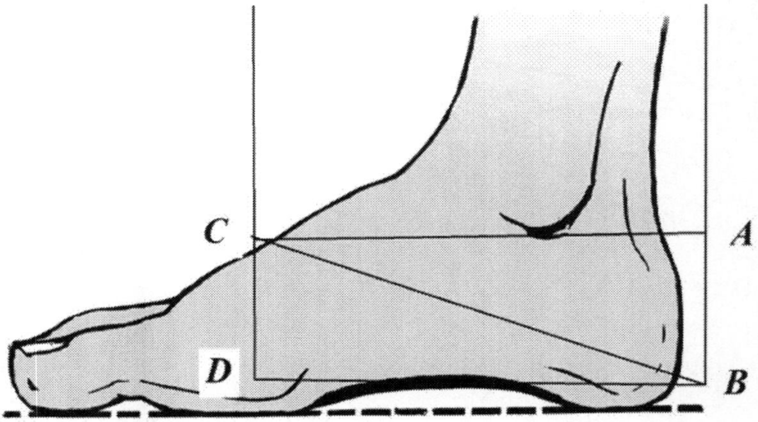

Because of the human foot shape, a man can avoid a break if he wears his pants short (AC). If he wears a pair of long pants (BD), the excess length (CD) will fold on top of the foot or shoe, known as the "break." To avoid a break with a pair of long pants, the man can tilt his foot by wearing high heel shoes. Since men do not usually wear high heel shoes, the only way to avoid a break is to slant his pants (BC).

The amount of break determines how sharp the slant should be. A few factors influence the amount of break.

1) If everything else is held the same, the length of the pants is the most important factor that determines the amount of break.

2) If a man wears his pant waist lower in the front or if a man has bad posture and leans the body forward, additional break will occur.

3) High heel shoes reduce the amount of break. Many women look marvelous wearing a pair of pants with high heel shoes. The pair of pants drapes gracefully without any break, producing two sharp crease lines.

4) The larger the opening of the pant legs, the less the amount of break.

5) The bulkier the top of the shoes, the more the amount of break.

Some experts suggest that a man should wear a pant length that is ¾ inch shorter in the front. Because each individual is affected by a combination of different factors as mentioned above, I urge each man to weigh the factors that apply to him. A man can slant the bottom of his pants up to 1 ¼ inches. A pant bottom that is slanted more than 1 ¼ inches may draw unwanted attention. Keep in mind that the sole purpose of slanting the pant bottom is to eliminate the unnecessary break. If a man prefers to wear his pants short without a break, he needs not to have his pant bottom slanted.

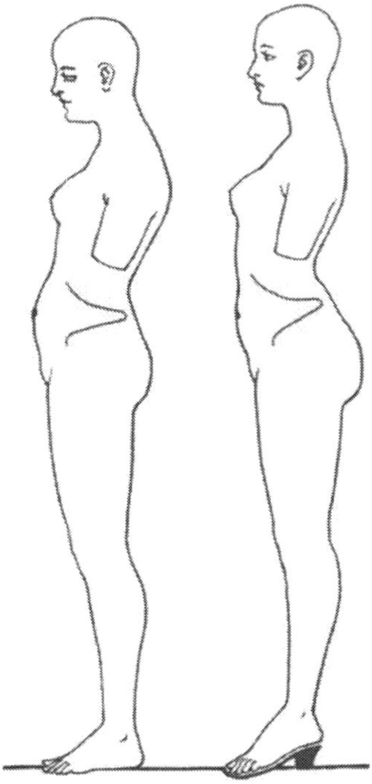

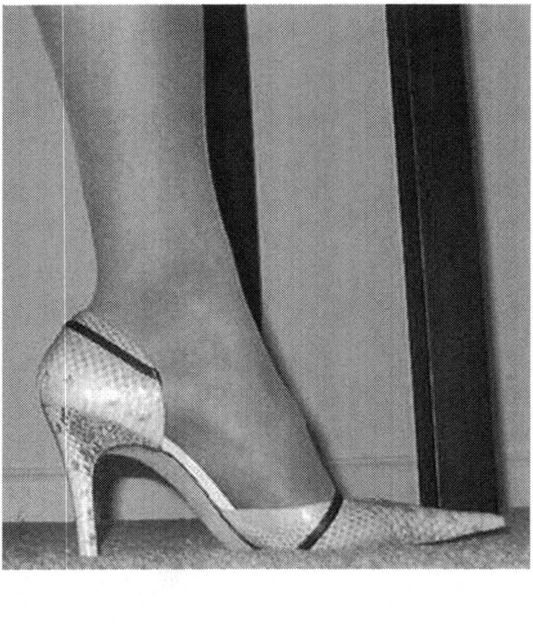

The heels of shoes help keep the body standing erect. A high heel helps eliminate unnecessary break and drape the pants freely.

(a)

(b)

A pair of short length pants, photo (a), shortens the leg line, exposes much of the socks, and may get caught inside the shoes. A pair of long length pants (b), on the other hand, creates too much break in the front. The break disrupts the sharp crease and leg line. The only way to have a long length without unnecessary break is to finish the pair of pants with a slanted bottom.

<u>The perfect pant length</u>

The back of the pants:	***reaches the joint where the back and the heel of the shoe meet.***
The front of the pants:	***barely touches the top of the shoe with very little or no break.***

A pair of properly slanted pants has little or no break even if the pant legs are cut long.

Readymade pants these days are seldom slanted. If you prefer a slanted pant bottom, you may have the pants altered in a tailor shop. Be cautious that many tailors cut the bottom of the pants slightly shorter in the front, but they hem the pants using the wrong method, which produces a straight instead of a slanted bottom finish. To test whether your pant bottom is slanted, flatten your pant leg with the front crease in the center. If you notice that the front crease is shorter than the back crease and the opening of the pant leg looks like a lip or flat diamond shape, then you know your pant bottom is slanted.

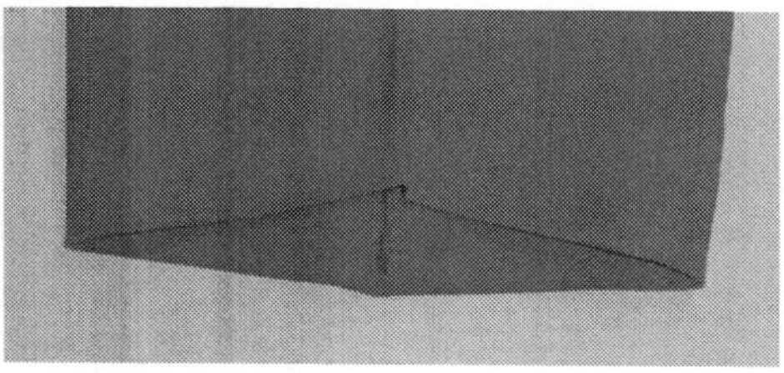

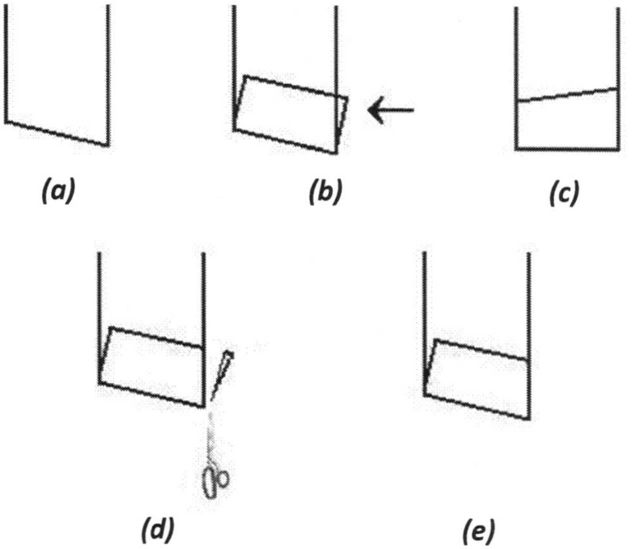

(a) *(b)* *(c)* *(d)* *(e)*

When a pant leg is cut slanted (a), the hem will stick out (b). Most tailors use an easy way to finish the pant leg by pushing the hem inward. The result is a flat (c) instead of a slanted bottom. A better way to finish the pant leg with a slanted bottom (e) is to trim off the excessive fabric that sticks out (d) before hemming.

John T. Molloy recommends cuffed pants simply because most business executives in the country wear them. Cuffed pants offer none or few advantages but many problems. Why should a man wear cuffed pants because other men wear them?

Egon Von Fürstenberg, a fashion designer, suggested that cuffed pants originated some time ago from men rolling up their pant legs while crossing a muddy street. Hence, any serious business suit pants should not have cuffs. When he was a child, Fürstenberg had the opportunities to observe many of the world's most influential people who came to visit his father, the Prince of Austria. Fürstenberg noticed that the most important men wore non-cuffed pants.

It is my opinion that all dressy pants should be finished with a slanted bottom. If you insist on cuffed pants, make sure that the cuffs are done right. It is extremely rude to wear a pair of pants with sloppy cuffs.

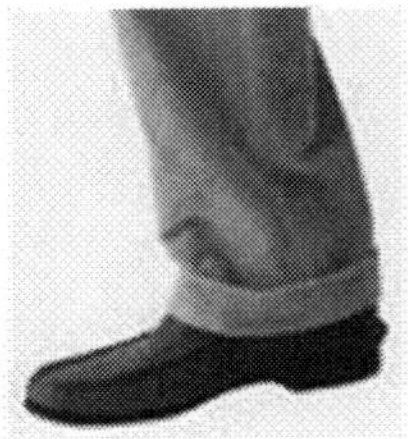

31-4. The common problems with cuffs

The great majority of American men prefer cuffed pants to non-cuffed pants. If you ask those men what the advantages of cuffed pants are, no one will be able to name even one benefit. Some fashion experts claim that the cuff adds weight to the bottom of the pants and pulls to anchor the pants. In truth, a cuff can help anchor the pants only when the pair of pants is worn short without a break. When the pair of pants is long enough to produce a break, the weight of the cuffs rests on the top of the shoes, canceling the effect of adding weight to pull the pant bottom. Non-cuffed pants have a much wider hem than cuffed pants. The wide hem can do the same trick without the many problems of the cuffs, as explained below.

First, a cuffed bottom cannot be slanted and therefore can create more unwanted break that ruins the long vertical crease line in the front of pants.

Second, cuffs add bulkiness to the bottom of the pants. Hence, pants that are made of thick fabrics should not be finished with cuffs. Bulky cuffs draw unwelcome attention and cease the continuation of the leg lines.

Third, creases on both the top and the bottom of the cuffs should be sharp and stay sharp all the time. Pants made of synthetic or thick fabrics are difficult to be creased. They also tend to lose the creases after being cleaned.

Fourth, cuffs produce uneven surfaces, where unsightly shining and impressions often occur when the pair of pants is ironed or pressed. Uneven surfaces also lead to crocking, which is the color of fabric being rubbed off.

Fifth, cuffs add stiffness to the bottom of the pants because of the multi-folds. They often affect the drape of the pant bottoms.

Sixth, cuffs are the best places to collect dust, dirt and other objects. A real estate agent once told me that he could never wear cuffed slacks because the cuffs collected grass every time he showed clients around the house he was selling.

Last, cuffs on modern pants are seldom made correctly. In the past, pant legs were tapered to the knees and then straight down to the bottom. Today, pant legs are tapered all the way to the bottom, making it more challenging to construct hems or cuffs. The dressmakers or tailors have to stitch a smaller circumference of fabric to a larger one. It takes 3 ½" length of fabric to make a 1 ½" cuff. This means that the difference between the two circumferences can be close to half an inch or more. Ordinary dressmakers and tailors will not take time to open the side seams to compensate for such a big difference. Hence, cuffs on modern pants are usually imperfect and tend to have one or more of the following signs.

1) The cuff has a pucker, dent or fold inside the cuff near the crease.

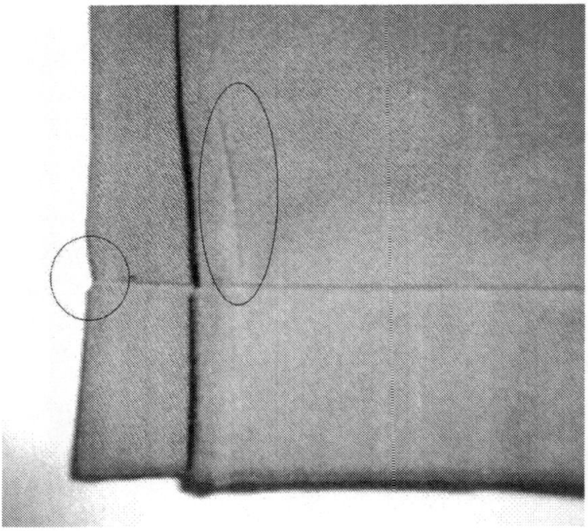

2) The cuff has a tendency to stay open.

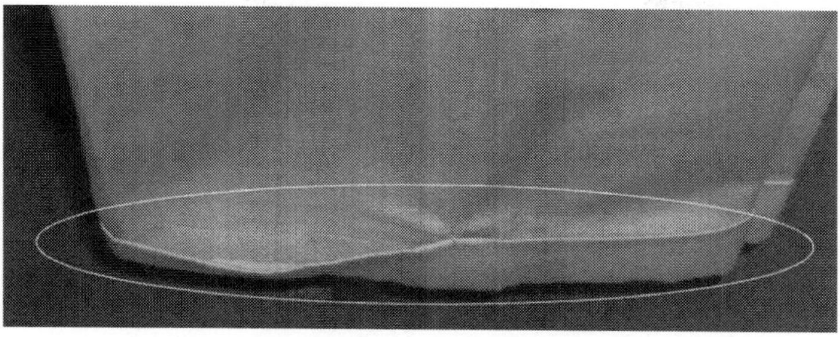

3) The top of the cuff looks like the roof of a house, having two slopes.

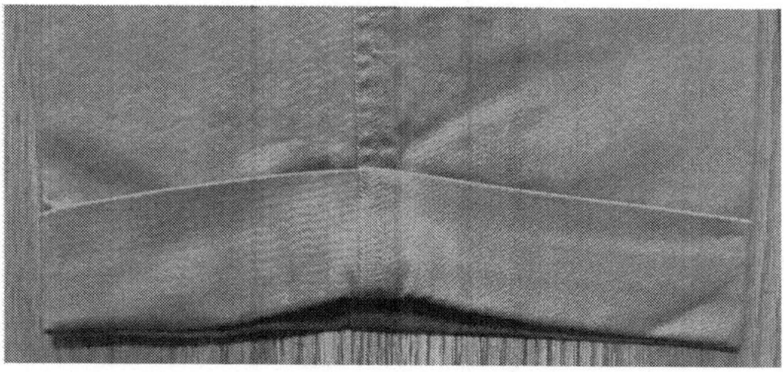

4) Most manufacturers and tailors take the easy way out by making short cuffs.

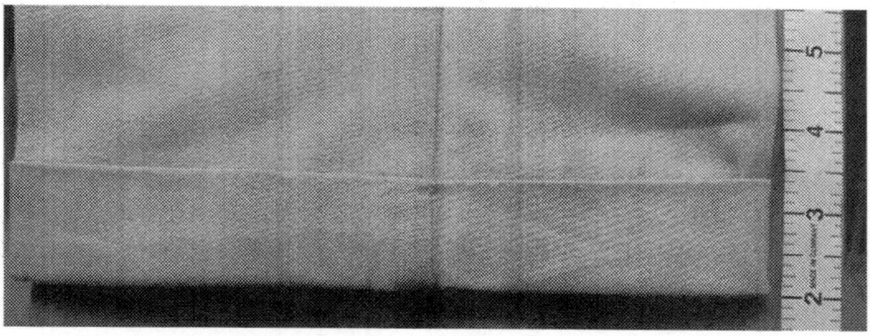

American singer and songwriter, Arthur Fields, wore a pair of puckered and dented cuffs.

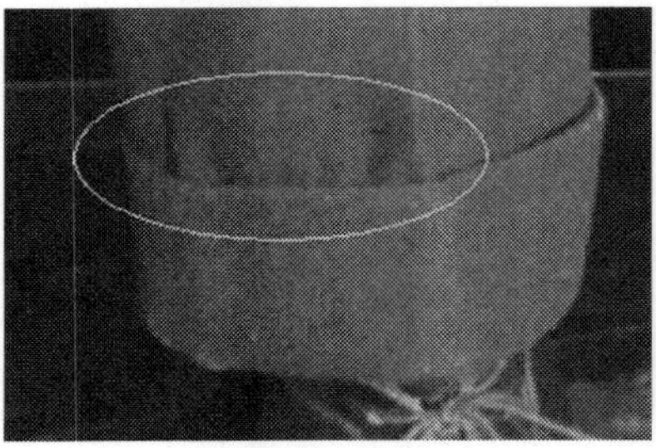

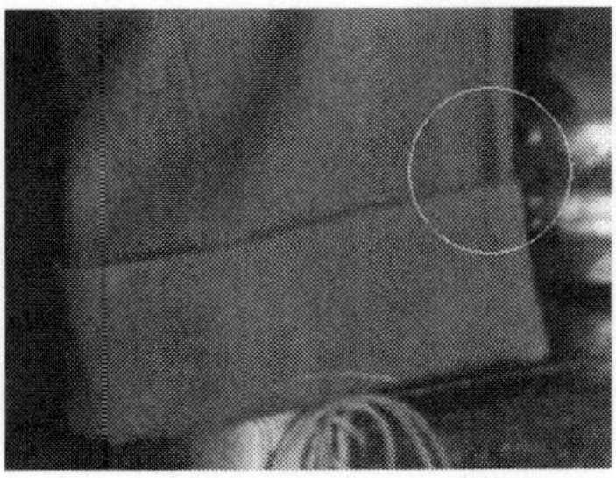

Cuffed pants originate some time ago from men folding the bottom of their pants when they crossed muddy streets; therefore, cuffed pants tend to be short. Many men these days like to wear their pants too long. They have no business to wear cuffed pants as the multi-folds in the cuff are difficult to rest gracefully on top of the shoes.

31-5. What is the proper width of pant cuffs?

Source: private archive of Monteforti family, GNU.

Pant cuffs should be wide enough to make an impact and render a statement.

The majority of American men prefer cuffed pants because they mistakenly think cuffed pants are dressier. Cuffs serve no real purpose. In addition, they have more disadvantages than advantages. If a man insists on wearing a pair of cuffed pants for whatever reason, do you not think the man ought to wear the cuffs correctly? As explained previously, cuffs on modern pants are seldom made correctly because the pant bottom tapers too much. To make the job easier, most manufacturers, including many famous designer brands, would rather construct cuffs that are 1 ¼" or shorter.

Kenneth Karpinski, an image consultant, claimed that the width of the cuff is not a serious issue. Then, what is the reason for wearing cuffed pants if the width of the cuff does not matter? May a man wear 0" cuffs? The gentleman's rule is that the width of the cuff should be 1 $^{5}/_{8}$" if the wearer is shorter than 5'10" and 1 ¾" if the wearer is 5'10" or taller.

Most American men desire cuffed pants, yet few men wear a correct cuff width because the majority of the readymade cuffed slacks have the wrong cuff width. Many men wear tailored slacks but they do not know that cuff width matters. Few tailors or dressmakers will finish a pair of pants with a cuff width of 1 $^{5}/_{8}$" or 1 ¾" unless the customer asks for it.

Everybody knows that the devil is in the detail. How wonderful will it be if you are the only person around wearing the correct cuff width? It is a rare opportunity to distinguish you from the rest of the crowd. For those men who desire cuffed pants, I recommend them to have the cuffs of their pants altered properly.

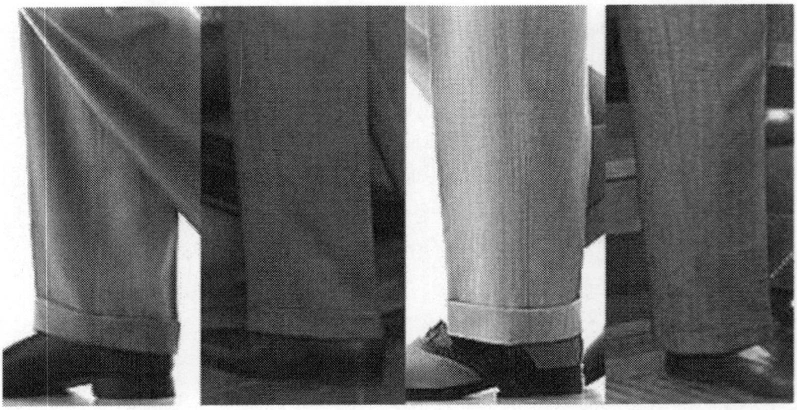

Insufficient cuff width makes the cuffs look insignificant and make the pair of pants look cheap.

Part Five:

What not to wear

Hart Schaffner & Marx

This country can't afford waste in food or clothes— neither can you. Our clothes wear long and save

In an ad during World War I, Hart Schaffner & Marx urged consumers to buy their clothes and save. In truth, people waste their money more on buying the wrong size clothes or wearing the clothes incorrectly than on buying bad quality clothes.

32. What makes an oxymoron?

An oxymoron, according to *Webster's Dictionary*, "is a figure of speech in which apparently contradictory terms are combined to produce an epigrammatic effect, e.g. 'cruel only to be kind.'" In men's apparels, several oxymora have been suggested.

32-1. Formal jackets should have distinct lapels.

Men wear formal dresses to attend formal parties or ceremonies. As fashion trend moves toward more casual setting, many men wear business clothes such as a suit to attend parties. Fashion experts believe that it is an oxymoron to wear formal dresses that look like business clothing. Take dinner jackets or tuxedos for an example. A dinner jacket can either be single- or double-breasted, but should have satin or grosgrain lapels in either peak or shawl style. It is an oxymoron to wear a tuxedo with notched lapels, which are most common in business suit and sport jackets. "Notched lapels on a dinner jacket eviscerate its formal character," said Nicholas Antongiavanni, author of *The Suit: A Machiavellian Approach to Men's Style.*

Critiques put down notch lapels as they point to the side not up, almost like the reverse of two turn signals, (> <). Once emphasized in satin or grosgrain, the notch lapels draw the eye out, not up.

Grosgrain

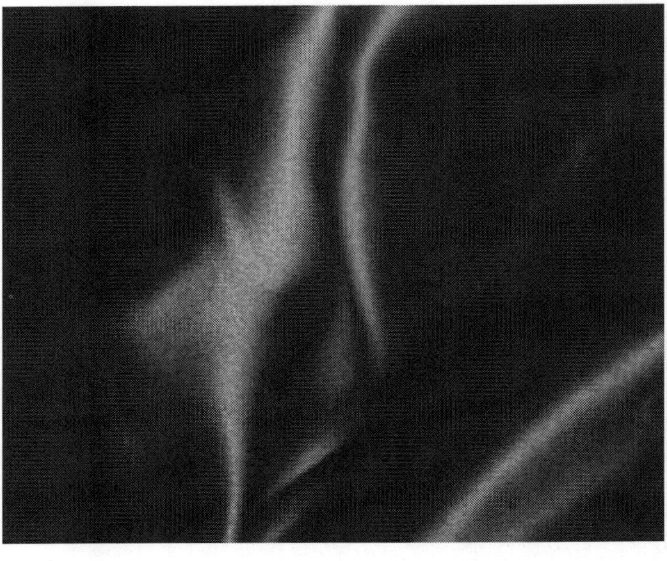

Satin

By Nicolas Esposito, CC-BY 2.0

It is hard to distinguish between a formal and a business jacket without the satin or grosgrain lapels.

Legendary American astronauts, including John Glenn, Neil Armstrong and James Lovell, celebrated NASA's 50th anniversary. Most of them wore dinner jackets with notched lapels.

It is an honor to receive an award on stage. It will be perfect if the recipients wore jackets with correct lapels. Darn it.

Rock Hudson's notched vs. Reagan's peaked lapels.

Dennis Hopper wore shawl, whereas Jack Nicholson wore peak lapels.

By Alan Light

A young man wore a tuxedo made of duck tapes. At least he got the lapels right.

32-2. Wear blazers of intense or vibrant colors.

A key difference between a sport coat and a blazer is that the blazer has metal buttons. Perhaps there is no other jacket that is more versatile and popular than a navy blazer. It goes well with so many different pairs of pants and shirts. It can be worn in the city, in the countryside, and at seas. It is in style 12 months a year. It is suitable to wear for work, at leisure, and to parties. Many men consider the navy blazer classic, authoritative, and indispensable.

Many fashion experts trace the origin of the term, blazer, to the famed battleship, H.M.S. Blazer. A fashion writer, G. Bruce Boyer, disagreed and wrote the following.

> The term "blazer" originates in the late nineteenth-century version of the traditional sports jacket. At first worn for cricket, later for boating, tennis, and other sports, it was a short coat usually boldly colored and accompanied by flannel trousers and straw boater hat. Originally the term had come from the particular jacket worn by the members of the Lady Margaret Boat Club of St. John's College, Cambridge. To distinguish themselves from other college boat clubs, members wore a bright red flannel sports jacket, which undoubtedly led to not a few stares and several remarks along the lines of, "Good Lord, Wilfred, did you see the jacket on that chap? Bit of a blazer, what?" In short, the derivation of the term "blazer" as it applied to sports jackets is found in the bright color, rather than any naval associations.

The original meaning of the term, blazer, was to blaze with vibrant color. If a man wishes to wear a blazer, I suggest that he should choose a colorful one, such as crimson, plum, billiard-table green, and other bright hues. I make my

recommendation not because flamboyant colors fulfill the historical meaning of the blazer, but because dull colors just do not match up with the solid metal buttons, especially the shinning ones. Ironically, the most popular color of all blazers, navy, does not fulfill the original requirement. If a man does not prefer vivid colors, he may choose intense hues. It is pointless to wear blazers in dull or weak colors, such as gray and beige. The above photo shows that President Reagan and the members of 1984 U.S. Olympic team wore bright red blazers (See the colored version of this photo in the back cover of this book). Occasionally, I encountered customers who brought in their suit or sport jackets and wanted to convert them into blazers. The problem is that the jackets are muted colors and are unsuitable for blazers. Oxymora indeed!

Fashion authorities argue about where the blazer originates from. It is undeniable that the blazer has its root or influence from the military uniform. In military, the number of buttons in the uniform often represents the rank of the wearer. Some men like blazers because the solid brass buttons look official. If it is true that wearing a blazer helps a man boost his authoritative image, the man ought to respect the jacket's heritage. I have encountered high school age men, looking for a double-breasted blazer with four or six buttons. It reminds me of Prince Albert's words, "A gentleman will take care that his clothes are of the best quality, well-made and suitable to his rank and position." In a democracy, ranks no longer exist. But, I would encourage younger men to start with a two- or three-button single-breasted jacket. As they grow older and become more mature, they can wear a six- or eight-button blazer if they wish.

Wearing an eight-button naval suit, King George VI of the United Kingdom inspecting the crew of the Norwegian destroyer HNoMS Draug.

In his book, Red Socks Don't Work, Kenneth Karpinski, reported the following.

> Researchers found that when volunteers looked at a series of pictures while answering simple questions they

> had no problem until the picture became more complex--seven points of interest--at which time they had difficulty answering even the simplest questions. Their attention was being drawn to the visual stimuli and they were missing the verbal message.

To avoid distraction, experts promote a "rule of seven," which suggests that a man should not have more than seven points of interest on his body at any time. A point of interest is anything that in and of itself draws attention. The metal buttons, especially the shiny ones, on a blazer are points of interest and can be very distracting. If you wear a blazer, be sure that you take the Rule of Seven under consideration.

The metal buttons on a blazer are points of interest, which distract attention from the face.

You just can't help looking at the large metal button on President Reagan's and Glenn Beck's blazer, can you?

Screenshot, fairuse.

32-3. Prefer a white contrast collar in a spread collar and French cuffs.

Most contrast collars are solid white. Contrast collars in other colors or in patterns are uncommon. If they do exist, they probably belong to sport shirts. Many contrast collar shirts are made with non-matching collar and cuffs. Connoisseurs consider it a bad manner. Some fashion historians traced the origin of contrast collar to the detachable collar in the 19th century. If this is true, a white contrast collar does not require matching white cuffs. Nevertheless, a white contrast collar does appear more authentic and elegant with a pair of contrasting white cuffs.

A matter of etiquette arises when the white contrast collar is involved. Alan Flusser commented that "a straight point contrast collar in white is as much a sartorial oxymoron as button cuffs on a dress shirt with a white contrast spread collar." There are no clear etiquette rules concerning the use of contrast collars. After all, the collar is a novel creation. If you desire one, choose a dressy one. The dressiest combination is the white contrast spread collar with matching white French cuffs.

A spread collar and French cuffs are preferred for a white contrast collar.

Sir Norman Hartnell wore a contrast white collar with a spread collar and French cuffs.

32-4. The bowtie should be worn in front of, not behind or beneath the wing collar.

A bowtie can be worn with a wing or turndown collar. If a wing collar is chosen, the bowtie is always worn in front of the wings, not behind or under the wings. The function of the wings is to push the bowtie forward. Hence, it is an oxymoron indeed to wear a bowtie behind or beneath the wings. Many wing collars sold in the market are poorly designed, making it very difficult to accommodate a bowtie. This explains why many men are unable to tie the bow in front of the wings. If you cannot find the right wing collar, it is better not to wear one.

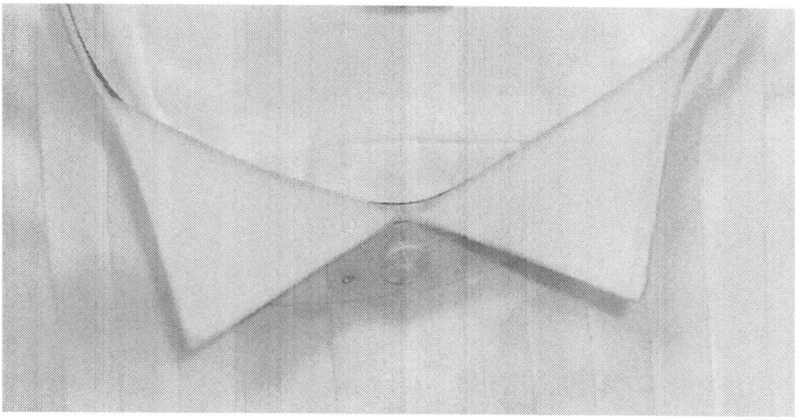

The purpose of the wing collar is to spring the bowtie outward. To achieve this goal, the wings are supposed to stay behind the bowtie in order to give the push. Perhaps because many men have difficulty in keeping the bow in front of the wings, a tuxedo rental company stitches the two wings to the collar stand. The two wings will stand behind the bow for sure, but lose their reason to exist.

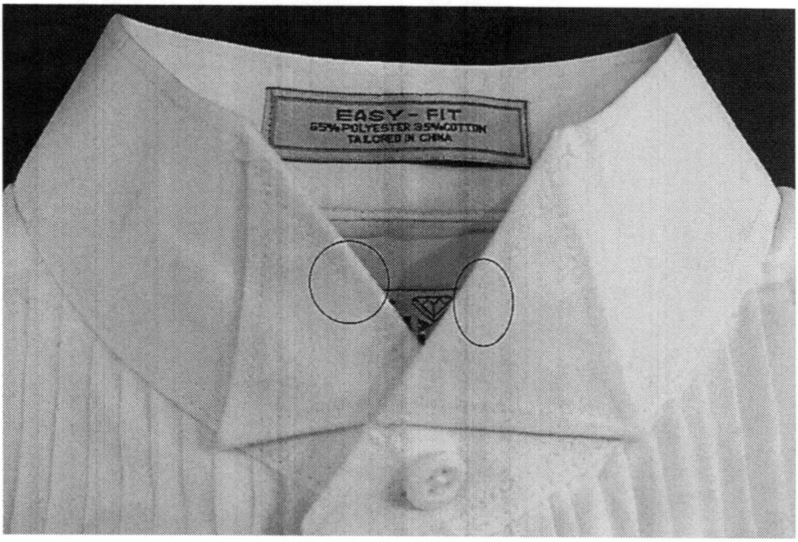

The bowtie should not be worn behind or under the collar wings.

It appears that Kevin Kline should tighten his bowtie. It is impossible to keep the bow above the wings if the tie is sagging.

33. Avoid shirt collars with tie space or no space.

33-1. A collar with tie space looks like a defect.

A dress shirt looks fabulous when it is worn with a necktie. The narrow opening of the point collar does not leave enough space to accommodate the modern tie. The beauty of the tie knot cannot be fully revealed if the collar covers part of the knot. Very often, the tie knot lifts the collar up, preventing the points from touching the shirtfront--which is a no-no in menswear. At the same time, the two wings of the collar push the tie downward, preventing the tie from arching out. To accommodate the tie, many point and button-down shirts are intentionally made with a gap between the two sides of the collar. The gap, called tie space, is generally from ¼" to ¾". A collar with tie space looks like a defect, created by a careless or unskillful shirt maker. It is unflattering at least. You should avoid wearing a collar with tie space.

If you own a shirt with tie space and the collar is too loose for your neck, you can move the top shirt button inward to eliminate the tie space. You may then ask, "How can I show the tie knot?" Answer: Wear a spread collar. A spread collar never comes with tie space--unless it is mistakenly left by poor workmanship of the shirt maker.

The tie knot is the head of the tie. Let it be shown. It is pointless to hide the knot behind the collar.

Manufacturers often intentionally leave a gap between the two wings of a point collar to allow room for a tie knot. The gap, known as the tie space, looks unbecoming and should be avoided.

The tie space is often found in a narrow point or button-down collar. A spread collar has a wide space between the two points; therefore, it does not need and should not have a tie space.

Bill Moyers and British Prime Minister, Gordon Brown, wore a spread collar with tie space. It is unclear that Mr. Brown fastened the top button of his shirt.

33-2. *Wear a collar opening with sufficient room to show the tie knot.*

The Guido or Tony collar made by Guido Fashions has little or no opening room to show the tie knot. Although the collar was once popularized in the *Goodfellas* movie and HBO's *the Sopranos*, the style has no merit and should be avoided for business dress.

The Guido or Tony Collar

The Guido collar was once popularized in the move, Goodfellas.

Screenshots, fair use.

34. *Waistcoats stay on the waist.*

The conventional wisdom is that a waistcoat or vest should reach the waistband of the trousers. To achieve this goal, many men have to wear a longer vest because they hang their pants a few inches below the waist. This does not create a problem until the man wears a tail coat. It is considered a sartorial terrorism if a man allows the sight of the waistcoat to show beneath the front of the tailcoat. To correct this mistake, the man should either lengthen the front of the coat, or move up the trousers and wear a shorter vest.

The vest should be long enough to reach the waistband of the pants, or the waistband should be high enough to be touched by the vest.

Fair use.

Billy Chrystal hosted the Academy Award. Shouldn't he know it is embarrassing to show the vest beneath the front of the tailcoat?

Fair use.

This photo appeared on December 12, 2011's Kansas City Star, showing members of Kansas City Chorale. It is disturbing that everyman in the photo wears formal dress to impress and pay respect to the audience. Yet, everyman dresses improperly.

If the President of the strongest county on earth could not make the simple thing right, what do you think other ordinary men will do?

35. Tie the bowtie straight

35-1. Why do so many men wear a crooked bowtie?

Photo of David Lynch, Jerry Seinfeld, Don DeFore, Rob Morrow, John Corbett, Michael Jeter and Tim Curry by Alan Light. Photo of James Marsters by Raven Underwood, CC-BY 2.0.

Many men are afraid of wearing a bowtie because they think it is too complicated to tie a bowtie. So, they give up the idea of wearing one, or buy pre-knotted bowties. Alan Flusser wrote, "There is no point in sporting the bow tie unless you plan on tying it yourself. Place a mathematically perfect pre-tied bow under your chin and you forsake all individuality. The hand-tied bow's moody loops and unpredictable swirls give you that subtle insouciance, that desired aplomb."

Flusser observed that the bowtie was once considered "a garment that combines confident flourish with absolute respectability." There is nothing to show respect if the bowtie is worn incorrectly.

In truth, it is easy to tie a bowtie. You tie the bowtie the same way you tie your shoes. The difference is that you cannot see what you are doing when you are tying a bow on your neck. Many men tie a bowtie in front of a mirror. This may create more confusion for a beginner because everything you do appears in the opposite direction in the mirror. For a beginner, it is probably easier to practice a few times on the upper leg. Tie the bow and go to a mirror for adjustment. To get the right size bow, you may have to try several times. Many men wear pre-knotted bowties, which are often sloppy, not "mathematically perfect" as described by Flusser. One serious drawback of using a pre-knotted bowtie is that the width of the bow may not go well with the wearer's face. If this is the case, I suggest the wearer re-knot the bow. The width of the bow should finish within the outer edges of the eyes and the outside lines of the face or shirt collar.

33-2. Vertical vs. horizontal bow

Why do so many men wear a crooked bowtie if it is easy to tie a bowtie? One possible cause is that they wear a wrong bow. Many men tie their shoes with a vertical bow instead of a horizontal bow. The residual twisting force, created by using the wrong knotting method, pulls the tie in the vertical direction, resulting in a crooked bowtie.

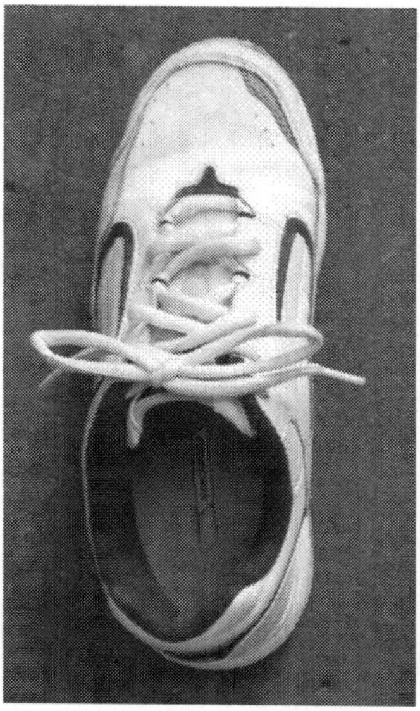

horizontal bow

vertical bow

The problem with a pre-knotted bowtie is that the width of the bow may not correspond to the wearer's face. If this is the case, the bow should be re-tied.

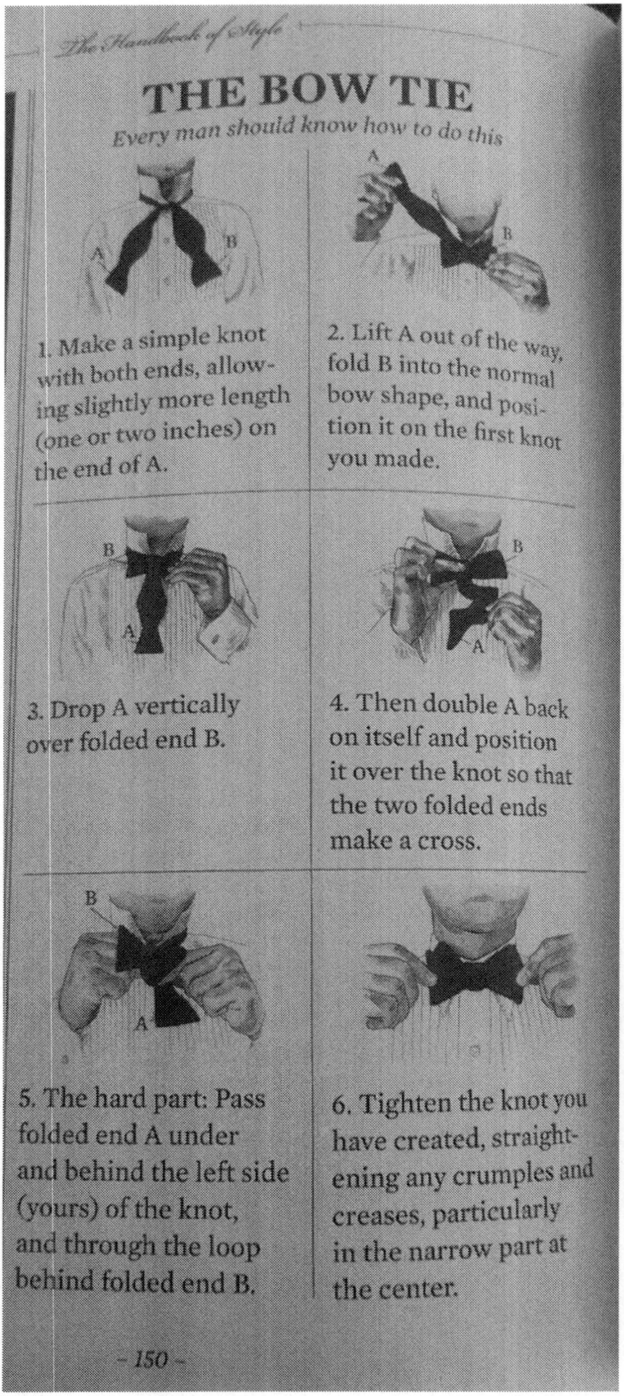
The Handbook of Style

THE BOW TIE

Every man should know how to do this

1. Make a simple knot with both ends, allowing slightly more length (one or two inches) on the end of A.

2. Lift A out of the way, fold B into the normal bow shape, and position it on the first knot you made.

3. Drop A vertically over folded end B.

4. Then double A back on itself and position it over the knot so that the two folded ends make a cross.

5. The hard part: Pass folded end A under and behind the left side (yours) of the knot, and through the loop behind folded end B.

6. Tighten the knot you have created, straightening any crumples and creases, particularly in the narrow part at the center.

– 150 –

In Esquire's The Handbook of Style, the subtitle reads "Every man should know how to do this." The handbook then illustrates the wrong method of tying a bowtie—the vertical instead of the horizontal bow. It seems that the correct subtitle should read "Every man should not do this."

Despite the plea from fashion experts that gentlemen should tie their own ties, Spencer Tracy had his bowtie knotted by his maid. The result was a crooked bow.

(Screenshots from *Cass Timberlane*, fair use)

Two Methods to Tie a Horizontal Bow

Method One

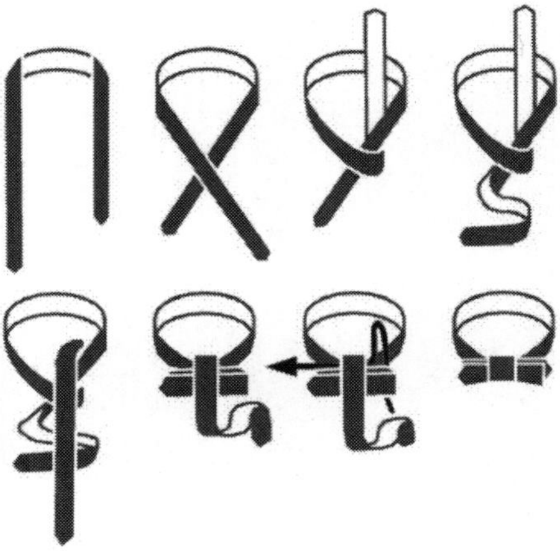

by Chris 73, CC-BY 2.5.

Method Two

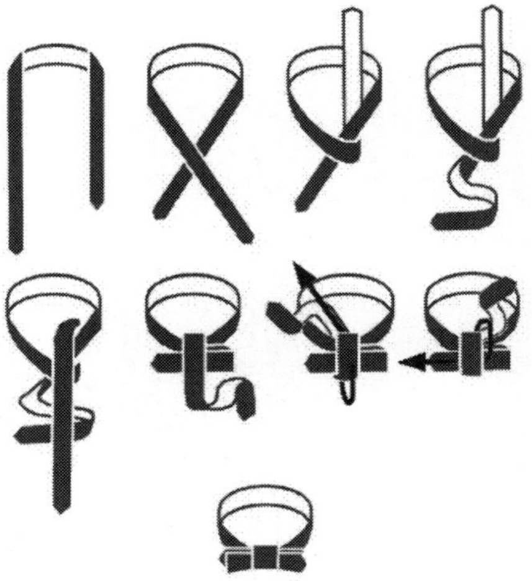

by Chris 73, Creative Commons Attribution ShareAlike (CC-BY-SA) 3.0.

How a Vertical Bow Is Created?

When tying a tie, only one end is moving around. The moving end is called the active end, and the other passive end. If the active end of the tie wraps the passive end from the wrong side, a vertical instead of a horizontal bow is created. The following procedures explain how a vertical bow is produced.

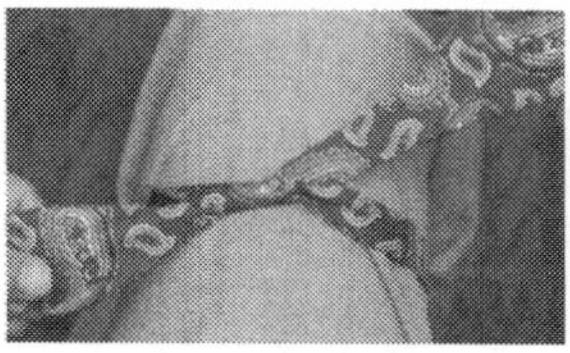

If the active end is on the upper side of the loop

and you begin the knot by wrapping the passive end from the lower side,

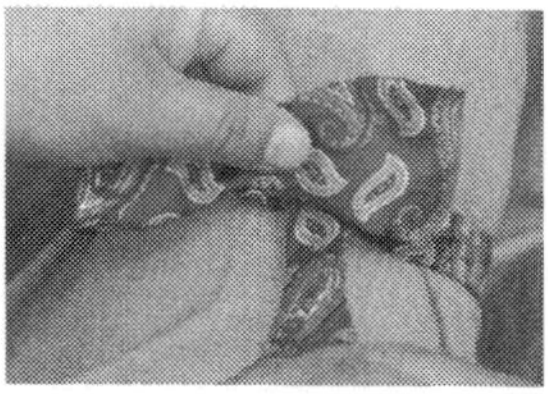

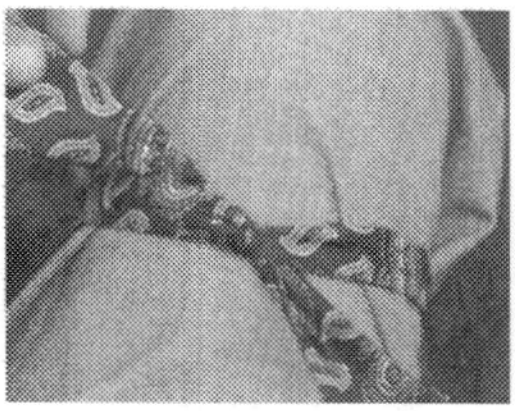

or if the active end is on the lower side of the loop

and you begin the knot by wrapping the passive end from the upper side,

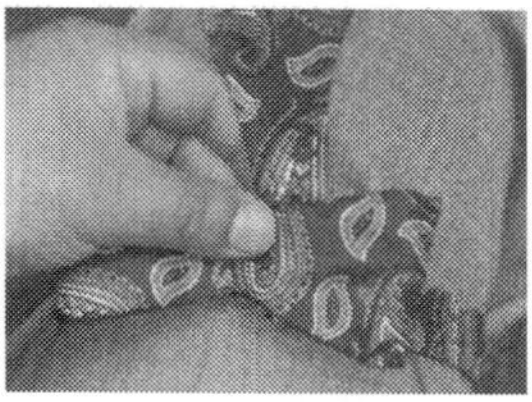

you will create a vertical bow.

How to Knot a Horizontal Bow

The following procedures demonstrate the correct way to tie a horizontal bow using Method One.

Version One:
Presume that the two ends are crossed in such a manner that the active end is on the upper side of the loop.

Start the knotting process by placing the active end on top of the passive end from above.

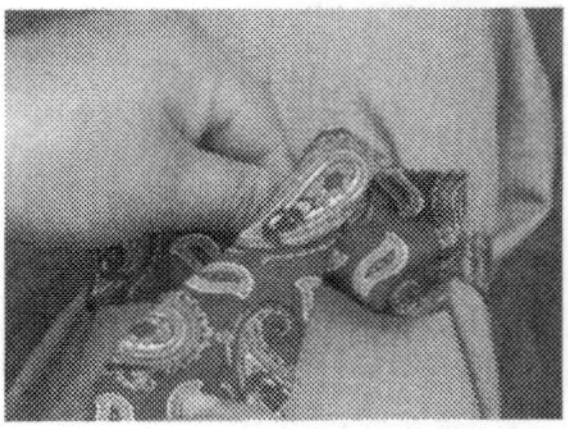

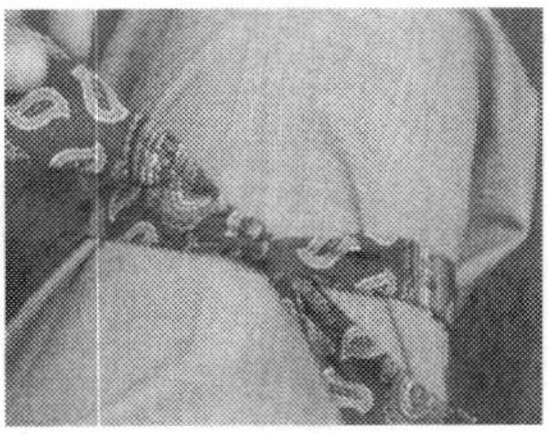

Version Two:
Presume that the two ends are crossed in such a manner that the active end is on the lower side of the loop.

Start the knotting process by placing the active end on top of the passive end from below.

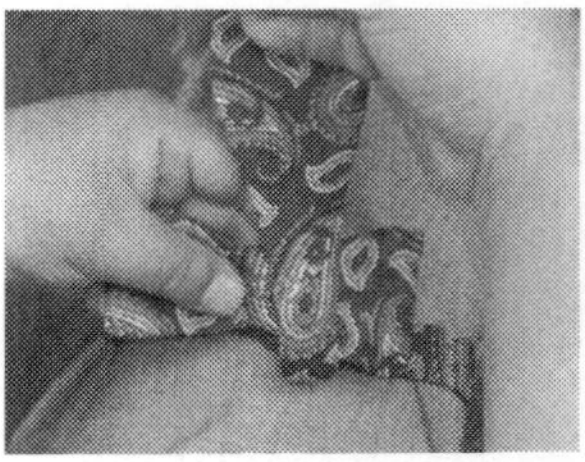

Both versions will produce a horizontal bow.

36. Do not tuck ties inside the pants.

What should you do if your tie is too long? Fashion experts, including Alan Flusser, suggest a man can tuck his tie inside his trousers in the style of Fred Astaire or the Duke of Windsor. I do not know why all of the experts with a brilliant mind would come out with such a bizarre idea. The tie belongs to the neck, not the pants. The tie should never be put inside the pants. Tucking the tie inside the trousers not only will damage the tie but also will affect the movement of your top body. What is more, a tucked tie looks tacky and objectionable.

An important question: How can any tie be too long? A man can always adjust the length of the tie by knotting the tie at any place he desires. It is impossible for a tie to be too long unless the man wants it to be long. Men wear a long tie because they have a wrong presumption that is the small end (back piece) of the tie should never extend beyond the large end (front blade) of the tie. Indeed, the back piece of the tie should be covered by the front piece. So, why not hide the back piece? A man should hang the front blade of his tie to his navel. If the small end of the tie exceeds the length of the large end, he has several options. 1) He can cut the offending excess off. 2) He can hang the extra length over the tie tag. 3) He can fold the small end a few inches up and secure the fold with a safety pin or with a few stitches of thread. Or, 4) he can use the military style by inserting the small end between any two buttons of the shirtfront, as done by the Duke of Windsor. No one will notice what the man has done as long as the small back piece is hidden behind the large front piece.

Jack Benny, Andy Warhol, and President Ford tucked their ties inside the pants.

You can hide the extra-length of small end by folding the back piece or inserting the back piece inside the shirt. If you decide to fold the small end, you can fold it through the label loop or self-loop to provide a lift for an arched tie.

An image consultant, JoAnna Nicholson, posted a question, "When is the short end of your tie too short?" She suggested that a man can move up the bar tack or self-loop as much as 4" if the small end of his tie is too short to fit through the bar tack or loop. This is a bad advice. If the small end becomes too short to fit through the loop, it is likely that the man knots his tie in the wrong section of the tie. He ties his tie too close to the narrowest part of the tie. There is insufficient width of fabric to form a decent knot. The man should tie his tie shorter or use a longer tie.

37. Shirt etiquettes

Not every dress shirt has the same appearance of dressiness. How dressy a particular shirt is can be determined by dressiness scale in a few details. Some men and women are searching for French cuff shirts in button-down collar or in oxford cloth. They will be disappointed. Being ignorant about shirt details, many men embarrass themselves by committing social blunders. Here are some examples.

1) Wear a bowtie with a button-down or tab collar.

Theoretically, a bowtie can be worn with any type of shirt collars except the wide spread collars. Even so, I recommend a man not to wear a bowtie on a button-down collar. Cary Grant wore a bowtie on a button-down collar in some of his movies. The two collar buttons beneath the bowtie are very distracting and look silly. Moreover, the button-down collar is usually made with soft interlining or without interlining. The collar is too soft to provide a firm support for the bowtie. The button-down collar ranks at the bottom of the dressiness scale. How does it look good with a dressy bowtie?

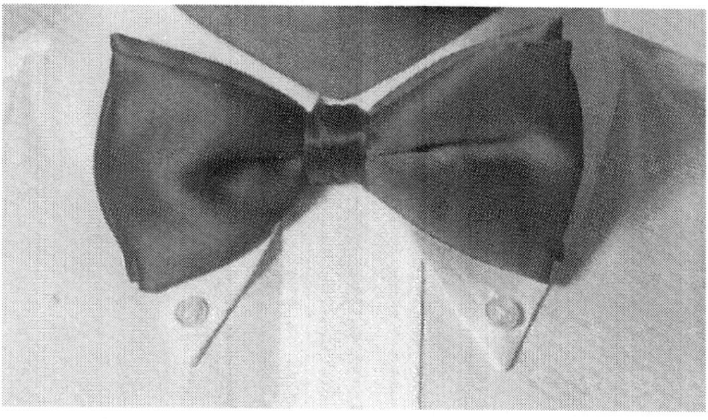

How could any man in his right mind wear a bowtie on a button-down collar? Although there is no rule suggesting that a button-down collar cannot be worn with a bowtie, the two collar buttons beneath the bow look very unbecoming. It is equally silly to show a collar tab under the bowtie.

photo by Clq

by Mark Coggins, CC-BY 2.0

2) *Wear a bowtie with a cutaway collar.*

A bowtie can be worn with a wing collar as well as a turndown point or spread collar. Spread collars are generally considered dressier than point collars. For the purpose of accommodating a bowtie, however, a point collar has its merit. The both sides of the collar wings are closer to each other in the point collar style and provide a firmer support to the bowtie. The two wings help push the bowtie forward just as the wing collar does. If you desire to wear a bowtie with a spread collar, choose a modified or standard one instead of the cutaway style.

Avoid wearing a bowtie with a cutaway collar as it will fall under the collar instead of standing in front of the collar.

A bowtie can be worn with a spread or point collar.

Photos fair use.

3) *Wear a pin collar without the pin or wear a tab collar without a tie.*

Many men are unsatisfied with the way their tie hangs. The tie falls straight down from under the shirt collar and looks lifeless. So, they use a collar pin or tab in a desperate attempt to arch out the tie. The collar pin or tab only works with a point collar. Ironically, the point collar is exactly a major factor that prevents the tie from arching out. The narrow opening of the point collar tends to push the tie downward. The tab pulls both wings of the collar, causing the two sides of the collar to cave in. Moreover, it is difficult to pass a tie through the tiny hole left by the collar pin or tab unless the tie is thin or narrow. Then again, a thin or narrow tie may be unable to produce a substantial knot. A tie is thin because the shell fabric or the lining is light. A thin tie without a substantial body is seldom a good quality tie.

There are several methods to use a collar pin. The simplest way is to use a safety pin that punctures through both wings of the collar. The holes resulted from the piercing tend to disappear after laundering. Nevertheless, repeated piercing in the same location may damage the collar. A better way is to allow the pin to pass through a set of reinforced eyelets. The pin is then secured by a screw nut. Another method is to use a collar bar that clips on both wings of the collar. The bar does not make holes on the collar but is not as secured as the pin.

It is rude to wear an eyeleted pin collar without the pin. It is equally rude to wear a tab collar without the tie. The only purpose of the collar pin or tab is to help pull out the tie. Hence, it is absolutely redundant to wear a collar pin or tab without the tie.

By Yesmen Mike Andy, CC-BY-SA 3.0

A man wore a pin collar without the pin, exposing the two eyelets.

Fashion experts often comment that the pin or tab collar is elegant. To me, the pin or tab collar is redundant. It says that the wearer wishes to do something but does not exactly know what to do with his tie. The wearer ends up sacrificing the look of the collar and forcing the tie to erect with a pin or tab. There are better ways to arch out a tie without using a collar pin or tab.

TV screenshot, Fair use

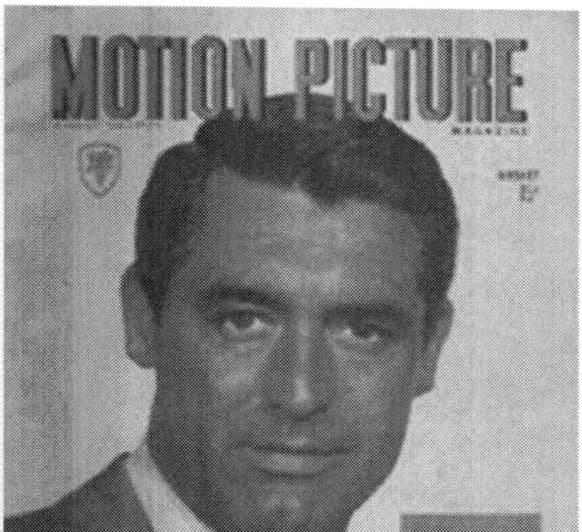

The collar pin or tab does not always work and often creates a wrinkled collar.

4) *Wear a button-down spread collar.*

The button-down collar is the most popular style in America. Most dress shirts and sport shirts are made with this collar style. This style was originally designed to keep shirt collars from fluttering up in the faces of English polo players. John Brooks of the Brooks Brothers brought the idea home to New York and created the button-down shirt in 1900. The button-down shirts are well liked among American businessmen. They become the hallmark of the international executives.

The spread collar is considered dressier than the point collar, which in turn is dressier than the button-down collar. Thus, most button-down collars are also point or modified point collars. The main purpose of the button-down is to hold down the collar wings and ensure that the two points of the collar will touch the shirtfront. Because spread collars tend to be shorter than the point collars and they tend to touch the shirtfront when the top shirt button is fastened, it is unnecessary to wear a spread collar that has two buttons on it. Most spread collars are fused with multiple layers of interlining and tend to be stiff and crisp. In contrast, most button-down collars are bonded with light or no interfacing and tend to be soft and flexible. The two styles are incompatible and do not blend well.

Robert Taylor wore a button-down spread collar, which is uncommon these days.

38. Collar defects

38-1. It is inexcusable to wear a defected shirt collar.

The two collar wings are the most difficult parts of the shirt to produce. Should a tailor or worker make an error, the mistake is likely to occur in the wings. The two collar wings are also the most noticeable part of the shirt. Yet, most consumers do not even bother to take a look at the collar when they purchase a shirt. I have constantly seen men on television, including noted personalities, wearing a shirt with a defected collar.

A. Tie space

The most common defect is the tie space. As explained previously, some shirt designers intended to leave a gap between the two sides of the inverted V to accommodate the tie knot. Tie space is often found in a point or button-down collar with a narrow inverted V opening. Whatever the intention of the shirt designers, most shirts sold in the same group have a different amount of tie space. This inconsistency demonstrates that not every tie space is left intentionally. They are more likely a result of poor workmanship. It is my opinion that a shirt looks better without tie space. If you need the space to accommodate the tie knot, you should choose a spread collar. A spread collar should never have a tie space. If you see one, you know for certain that the space is an unintended defect.

A spread collar should never have tie space.

B. Overlapping

The two sides of the collar wings are supposed to meet or touch at the top to form a sharp inverted V. If the two sides do not meet, a gap (tie space) will emerge. On the other hand, if both sides come too close, an overlapping will occur. Both defects can be fixed by moving the top button outward on the collar stand.

Screenshot photos, fair use.

We frequently see men wear an overlapping collar, in which one wing is higher than the other. The photos of four TV personalities from Fox News indicate how common the defect is.

C. Crooked collar

Another common defect is that the two collar wings do not hang evenly on both sides of the shirt front. In other words, the collar wings are crooked. How ludicrous it is, you may think, for a man to wear a crooked collar. In reality, a great percentage of shirts sold in the market have a slightly uneven pair of collar wings.

D. Uneven wings

Occasionally, you may find a shirt collar with a pair of unequal size wings.

Screenshot, fair use.

Dr. Isadore Rosenfeld wearing a crooked shirt collar.

It is silly to wear an uneven collar with one wing larger or longer than the other wing.

E. Collar stand turning outward

Another common defect is that part of the collar stand turns outward. The problem exists perhaps because the stand is not stiff enough or because the turn-down layer was not attached to the stand correctly. When the outer layer is folded down, it also brings down part of the collar stand. I have seen people often wear shirts with the top portion of the collar stand turning outward above tie space, showing two parallel layers of fabric.

The modern dress shirt collar is called turned-down collar because the collar first stands up from the bottom edge of the neck and then falls down to rest on the shirt. One common defect is that part of the collar stand above the button turns inside out when the collar folds down.

F. *Bubbled or dented collar*

To attain a crisp look, the top layer fabric of a dressy collar is often bonded with a layer or layers of interfacing, called "top fused." Occasionally, the top fused collar bubbles owing to the breakdown of adhesive after repeated laundering and ironing. Dented spots also occur perhaps because uneven or excessive adhesive has been applied. Bubbles and dents can also occur in other fused parts of the shirt, such as sleeve cuffs, front placket, and shoulder, arm or side seams.

Fair use.

screenshot, fair use.

G. Bent collar

Many designers intentionally created bent collar wings to accommodate a thick tie. The collar wings form the shape of a frog, which looks very unbecoming. Even a thick tie will be unable to fill the large space between the collar and the shirtfront. The style may not be considered a defect, but it surely is an ill design,

A pair of bent collar wings.

In order for the two collar buttons to stay flat on top of the shirt front, the button-down collar is often made soft with light or no interlining. The thin collar tends to reveal the unattractive imprint of the tie loop beneath the collar. The buttons are often in the wrong places, making the two wings to bend and pucker.

38-2. Avoid conspicuous or puckered top stitching on the collar of a dress shirt.

Many designers use contrast or bulky hand stitches to give shirts a casual or artistic look. Because the primary function of the top stitching is to secure layers of the shirt fabric and interfacing, the stitching is preferred to be inconspicuous. Except for designing purposes, large or puckered top stitching is the sign of a poorly manufactured dress shirt.

Large or puckered stitches on the collar look unattractive.

38-3. Be aware of unsighted imprints and marks from pressing.

Shirts returned from a cleaner shop often are damaged by improper pressing or starching. It is the man's responsibility not to wear a damaged collar with wrinkles, imprints, scorches or other types of unsighted marks.

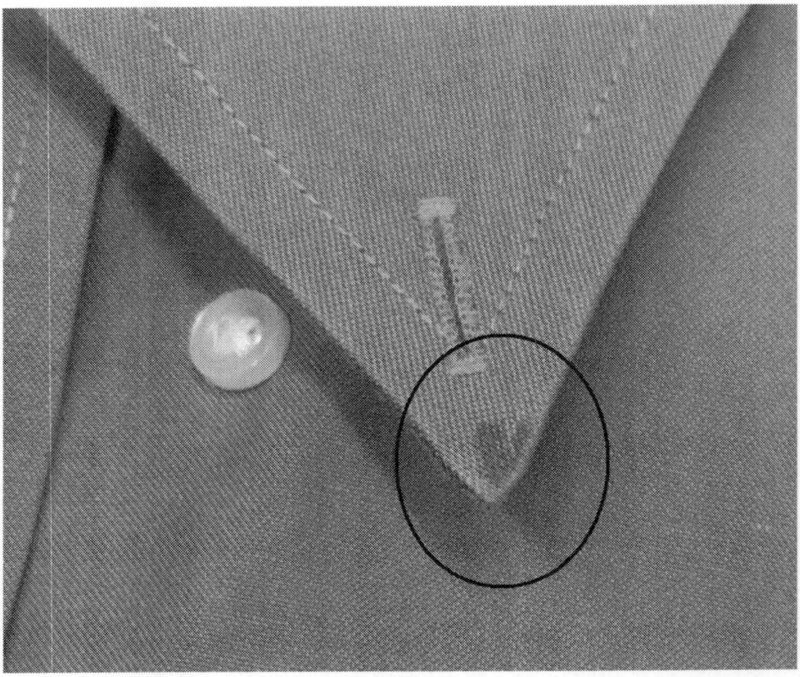

Scorched mark caused by heat from ironing

39. Plain front pants should not have cuffs.

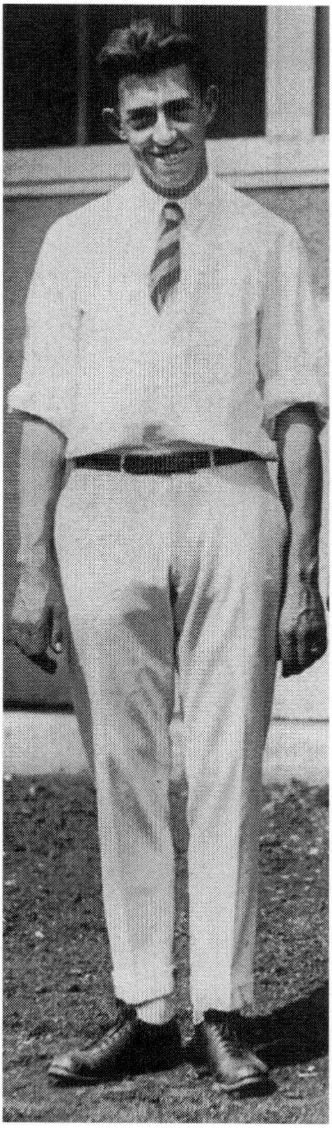

A customer bought a pair of plain-front pants and wanted the pants to be shortened. The salesperson asked the customer whether he wanted his pants to be cuffed. The customer said, "Yes." When the customer returned a week later to pick up his pants, I happened to be around and noticed the problem. I mentioned to the customer that he probably would be the only person in the city who wore a pair of plain-front pants with cuffs. The customer felt embarrassed and asked me to change the bottom finish of the pants. (The left photo shows Francis Quimet, the 1913 U.S. Open golf champion, wore a pair of plain front pants with cuffs.)

Another customer brought back to the store a pair of tailored pants and complained that the cuffs were not done right. There were unwanted creases on one of the cuffs. A salesclerk at the suit department accepted the return. Another associate smoothed out the wrinkles with a steamer. I looked at the pants and found that the pair had a plain front. It amazed me that so many people had handled the same pair of trousers and no one ever told the customer that flat front pants should not be cuffed.

Although making flat front pants with cuffs is an easy task, traditionally men do not wear cuffs with a pair of plain-front pants. Manufacturers make readymade plain-front pants with cuffs for women's slacks but not for men's slacks. Some men do express to me their desire to buy a pair of plain-front pants with cuffs. They will be disappointed for being unable to find any in the market. When a man buys a pair of tailored slacks or wants to alter the bottom of a pair of readymade slacks, he has the opportunity to request the pants to be finished with or without cuffs. If a man is uninformed and if the fitter and the tailor are ignorant about this sartorial blunder, the man may have a rare chance to make such an awkward mistake. I hope someone in the street or in his workplace will stop him immediately.

In the movie, Lord of War, an African dictator used the term, blood of bath, when he spoke with a gunrunner. The arms dealer told the dictator the correct term is "blood bath", not "blood of bath." The dictator said he liked his way. The dictator continued to speak and tried to call the arms dealer "lord of war." The dealer said there is a word for that. It is called "warlord." The dictator replied that he still preferred his way. It is rare to find a person who cares so little about the words he uses, such as this African dictator. Most people would never intentionally use incorrect words and grammars, or use words they do not know or understand. But, they might intentionally wear wrong clothing or accessories. Some people are tyrannical in some ways about their clothing. I recently encountered several customers, who wanted their plain front pants cuffed. When the tailor told them that flat front pants are usually finished with plain bottom, they replied that they are different. These customers did not realize that there are good ways and bad ways to be different. Being rude and ignorant is definitely not the best way to show difference.

The Duke of Windsor sometimes dressed himself in unconventional ways, such as inserting his tie between two buttons on the shirtfront. Fashion critics often comment that the master understood the rules and therefore knew how to break the rules. There are a few customs in men's clothing, such as unfastening the last button of the vest and wearing non-matched set of tie and pocket square. I do not believe it is a big deal if a man disobeys the tradition by fastening the last button of a vest or wearing a matching tie and pocket square set. But, it is intolerable to wear a pair of plain front pants with cuffs. Connoisseurs consider the act a sartorial terrorism. It is extremely rare that a gentleman would intentionally commit such a mistake.

It is unclear whether Lester B. Pearson, former Prime Minister of Canada and Nobel Peace Prize winner, wore a pair of plain front pants with cuffs or rolled up the bottom of his pants.

40. Avoid tight dress pants.

40-1. Dress pants and jeans fit differently.

A pair of jeans is cut tight in the seat area just as a woman's bra must fit tightly to have a lifting effect. A pair of dress pants should not fit like a pair of jeans. The seat should have sufficient amount of fabric to allow movements, and should never show much the curve of the buttocks.

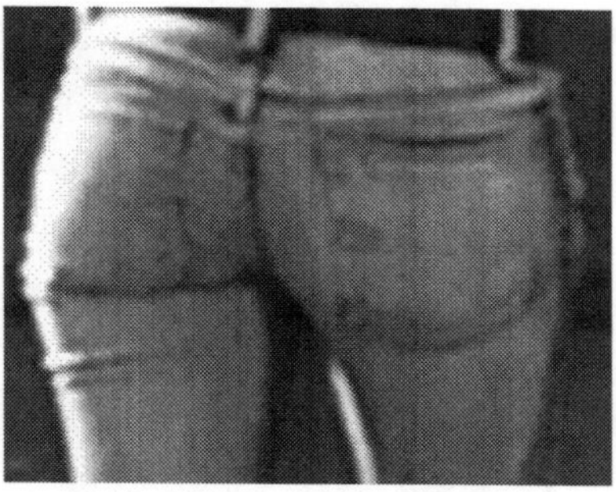

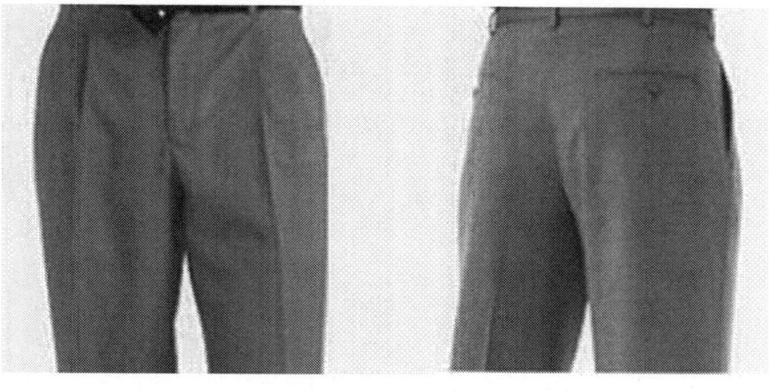

Unlike jeans, dress slacks should have sufficient room in the front and the seat to allow movement.

40-2. *Dress pants are better off roomy in the rise and seat areas.*

A pair of pants should be roomy in the rise and seat areas for three good reasons.

1) If a man wears a jacket, the large gap between the jacket and the pants can be better filled with a pair of loose fitting than a pair of tight fitting pants.

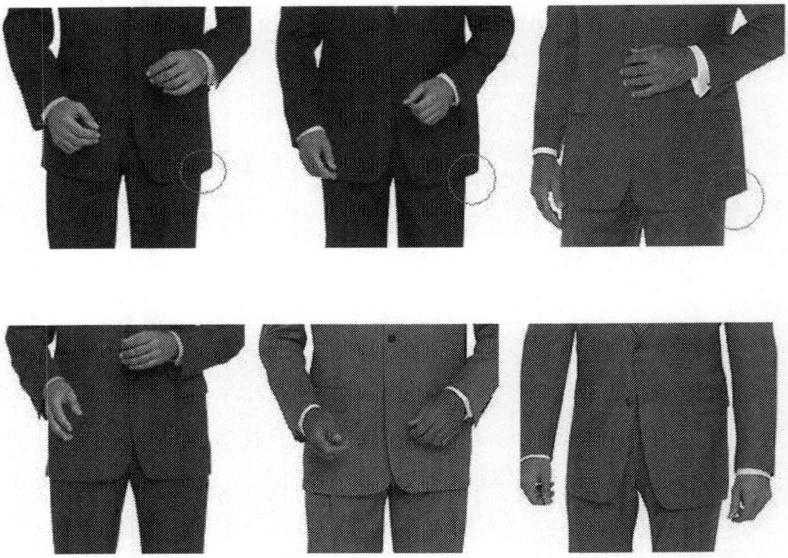

Compare the top row suits that have a large gap between the jacket and the trousers with the bottom row suits that do not have a gap. Which group of suits is more attractive?

by Steve Jurvetson, CC-BY 2.0.

It looks unbecoming to have a large gap between the jacket and the trousers. A pair of full-cut pants not only provides a better transition from the upper- to the lower-body, but also provides a better balance between the volume of the upper- and the volume of the lower body.

Because pant legs are tapered toward the ground, a longer jacket tends to create a larger gap between the jacket and the trousers. Thus, it is wise for a man not to wear too long his jacket or to wear a pair of overly tapered slacks.

2)   Most of the women's slacks are non-pleated and tight fitting to show the curves of the female figure. Men have a relatively large sized reproduction organ, which needs to be concealed. Most men place their organ on the left side of the pants, known as "dress left." President Clinton was asked by a young lady which way he dresses. He replied, "Left." The pleated pants help conceal the male organ. Tight fitting non-pleated pants tend to imprint the shape of the reproduction organ (often called "camel toes"), especially when the man is seated. Tight pants also tend to show the outline of an undergarment or shirt tail when the shirt is tucked inside the pants.

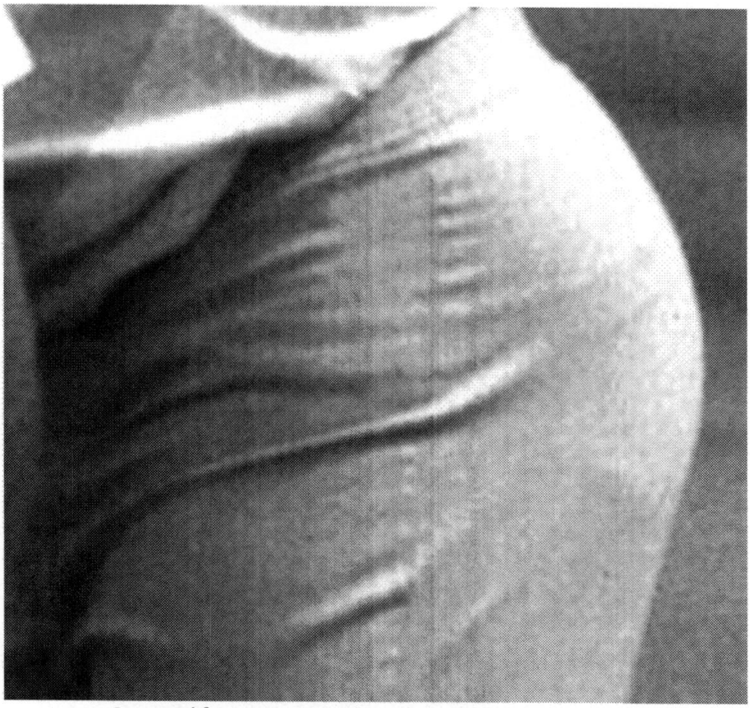

A pair of tight slacks may reveal the outline of the shirt tail and underpants.

George Washington showing camel toes

Irving Kaufman, an early 20th century singer, showing that he was "dressing left."

Screenshots, fair use.

Angie Harmon's tight pants look smooth when she stands still. The pants start to wrinkle as soon as she bends her body or walks.

3) A tight fit in the rise tends to create horizontal lines below the belly and pull the pockets open.

Tight fitting pants tend to create horizontal lines below the belly.

Photo by Alan Light.

Tight fitting pants also pull the pockets open.

40-3. Allow extra fabric in the thighs to seal the space created by a jacket.

Sport pants or jeans usually come in a variety of different cuts, from the skinny to the husky: slim fit, regular or classic fit relaxed fit, loose fit, and baggy fit. Some designers use other terms to designate different cuts. Trim fit, custom fit, tailored fit, modern fit, city fit and "fit to fit" are the same as slim fit, whereas easy fit means relaxed fit. The cuts in dress pants tend to be more standard and uniform. Manufacturers seldom indicate the cut in expensive dress pants, especially tailored clothing. The safest way to know the cut is to try on the pants. Vanguard fashion designers change the style and the cut of their pants based on the fashion of the days. Plain-front pants are usually made trimmer than pleated pants. Pants with deep pleats tend to be cut fuller than pants with shallow pleats.

If a man does not wear a jacket, he has the liberty to choose the style and the cut of the pants. But if he does, he should take the cut of the jacket into consideration. Depending on the cut of the jacket and the body shape of the wearer, the jacket may leave a large space around the thighs. A pair of pants with a fuller cut in the thigh area can fill the gap and provide a better transition from the jacket to the pants.

41. Avoid wearing both belt and suspenders.

41-1. The pant waist should stay horizontal to the ground, all the way around.

Many men wear good quality pants but they wear their pants incorrectly. One of the most common mistakes is to wear the pant waist lower in the front than in the back. A pair of pants looks at its best when the creases are hung straight without any break (left photo). The pants will drape gracefully when the pant length is correct and the pant waist is horizontal to the ground, all the way around. Wearing a pair of pants lower in the front not only will ruin the correct proportion between the head and the torso, but also will cause the pants to sag toward the legs, breaking the crease line.

Many American men, however, have difficulty keeping their pant waist horizontal to the ground because of their large belly. If a man has difficulty keeping his pant front up, he can try a pair of braces or suspenders. Connoisseurs consider braces the best way to hang a pair of pants. Even so, most men dislike braces perhaps because they are not as convenient as belts. The braces should always be covered by a jacket. As the jacket becomes unpopular these days, it is a hard sell to recommend wearing braces without a jacket. It is difficult to determine which sartorial violation is more serious, wearing the pants lower in the front or exposing the suspenders. I am in favor of wearing braces if a man has a prominent middle.

By Michael Pereckas, CC-BY-SA 2.0

Oliver Hardy wore a pair of suspenders to keep his pants up and his pant waist horizontal to the ground.

41-2. Wear loose fitting pants with suspenders.

Occasionally, I encounter customers who come to the store to buy suspenders because their doctors ordered them to wear pants with suspenders. The customers bought the suspenders but wore the suspenders with their old pants. Various medical reports have contributed some stomachaches to tight pants on the waist. The stomachaches mysteriously disappear when the patients wear a larger size pair of pants. When wearing suspenders, the waist of the pants should be large enough so that the pants will fall without the suspenders. When a man sits, his waist expands. A larger size pant waist will accommodate the expansion of the belly; therefore, it helps eliminate the unwanted horizontal lines resulting from the stress in the pant front. A pair of larger sized pants hung by suspenders will drape gracefully and will look much better than a pair of tight-waisted pants worn with a belt.

Suspenders come in two styles: clip-on and leather attachment that fastens to a button. Because most pants are not equipped to accommodate button-on suspenders, many men use clip-on suspenders. The clips often leave unsightly marks on the waistband. Button-on suspenders are more secure and elegant. Hence, a man or his tailor should sew on the buttons if he wants to wear suspenders. The buttons can be sewn inside or outside the pants. Nevertheless, many men do not pay attention to the correct locations of the buttons. The two front strips of the suspenders should line up with the two main pleats so that the pleats will jut out from the pant front, creating a beautiful side view of the crease lines.

The two front strips of the suspenders should line up with the two main pleats or front creases.

41-3. It is redundant to wear both belt and suspenders.

In the movie, *Ace in the Hole*, Kirk Douglas said the following to a newspaper boss, who wore both belt and suspenders.

> I'm a pretty good liar. I have done a lot of lying in my time. I've lied to men who wear belts. I've lied to men who wear suspenders. But, I'd never be so stupid as to lie to a man who wears both belt and suspenders. You strike me as a cautious man, a man who checks and double-checks.

Kirk also wore both belt and suspenders. At the end of the movie, however, he abandoned his suspenders.

Fashion experts often consider it redundant to wear both belt and suspenders. The main purpose of a belt and suspenders is the same. That is to hold up a pair of pants. Why should a man wear both if one is sufficient enough? You may think there is nothing wrong to add extra security by wearing both. The problem is that the pants made for suspenders and the pants made for belts are cut differently. To take full advantage of suspenders, the pant waist should be loose enough to guarantee that the pant waist can be hung high and horizontal to the ground, and to ensure that the pant legs will drape gracefully. On the contrary, the pant waist made for belts should not be too loose to avoid unnecessary puckering when the waist is squeezed by the belt. It is silly either to wear a pair of tight pants with suspenders, or to wear a pair of loose pants with belt. Hence, it is impractical to wear belt and suspenders at the same time because both types of pants are incompatible. In other words, you simply cannot wear a pair of pants that is tight and loose at the same time. Connoisseurs consider it inappropriate to wear suspenders with a pair of pants that has belt loops on it. If a man decides to hang his pants with suspenders regularly, he may want to remove the belt loops. A man who wears both belt and suspenders strikes me as an insecure or suspicious man, not a cautious man. A cautious man, who checks and double checks, does not make such an unnecessary mistake.

It is redundant to wear both belt and suspenders at the same time.

It is silly to wear a pair of tight pants with suspenders or to wear a pair of loose pants with belt. When the pant waist is loose and squeezed by a tight belt, unsightly folds or wrinkles will form.

Peter O'Toole wearing suspenders with a pair of trousers without belt loops.

41-4. It is unnecessary to match the color of tie and the color of suspenders.

Many authors recommend that the color of the suspenders should match the color of the tie. I think this recommendation is redundant. The suspenders are supposed to be covered by a jacket. The color or pattern of the suspenders matters little. As the fashion trend moves toward casual attire, more men these days wear suspenders without a jacket. Even so, the color and pattern of the suspenders should coordinate with but not match the color and pattern of the tie for the same reason that the pocket square does not match the tie. Fashion authorities do not recommend matching between the tie and pocket handkerchief because a matching set lures eyes to look sideways, not vertically. The only function of the suspenders is to hang the pants. It is silly to compete between the tie and the suspenders. A well-attired dresser will allow his tie to dominate by wearing a pair of subtly patterned and colored suspenders.

Showing suspenders is a trade mark of Larry King, which is not an elegant way of self-expression. I use the term, showing, intentionally. A man who sits in front of TV camera all the time does not need a pair of suspenders.

42. What to avoid when wearing a pocket square

42-1. It is unnecessary to match the pocket handkerchief with the tie.

Fashion experts unanimously suggest that the pocket square should not match the tie. They explain that what a man wears should encourage the viewers to look vertically instead of sideways. Hence, a pocket square should relate to the tie as little as possible. To ensure that a pocket square will not overtly relate to the tie, Alan Flusser came out with an idea. He proposed that the texture s of the tie and pocket square should differ. "If the tie has a silken luster, the pocket square should be of a dry material such as linen. If the tie is of a dulled material such as wool, linen or cotton, the pocket square can be shiny, such as a printed solid or foulard." The proposal may be too strict to be practical. Most ties and pocket squares are made of fine silk. It is unreasonable to ask a man not to wear a tie or pocket square made of the best material. Fashion experts often suggest that the texture of the tie should somewhat conform to the texture of the suit or sport jacket, such as a coarse wool tie with a textured jacket. It makes absolutely no sense to wear a shiny satin handkerchief on a nubby tweed jacket only because the smooth surface of the silk square will contradict the rough texture of a wool tie.

The expert's explanation does not sound convincing. It is unclear that a matching tie and pocket square set is more distracting than a non-matching set. If a pocket square will distract the view from the tie, should it be better not to wear one at all?

George Foreman wore a matching tie and pocket square set, made from the same fabric. The practice has been considered a sartorial blunder.

Men's clothing lacks variety and looks uniform. A man only wears few decorative items. Why forsake the opportunity of adding interest and versatility to the ensemble by wearing different tie and pocket square? A matching pair looks pretty much the same and suggests that both items come from the same package.

The shirt serves as the background for the tie whereas the jacket is the backdrop of the pocket handkerchief. Most men wear contrast shirt and jacket, such as a light shirt and a dark jacket. This makes it more difficult to choose a matching tie and square set that goes well with both the shirt and the jacket.

There is no sound reason that a pocket square should not match the tie. At the same time, there is no sound reason that a pocket square should match the tie either. If a man insist on a matching tie and pocket square set, I find no reason to object the practice. What is silly is that many men mistakenly think a pocket square must match the tie. They will not wear one unless it is perfectly matched.

The pocket square and the tie are separate items. It is absolutely unnecessary to relate one to the other. If you enjoy wearing pocket squares, choose those that coordinate well with your jackets. If you bought a tie and a pocket square in a set, this does not mean that you are obligated to wear both in the same outfit. If you insist on matching, match between the minor colors in the tie and pocket handkerchief.

Although the reason for wearing a non-matching tie and pocket square set may be unpersuasive to many men, it is my opinion that a well-attired man is better off to follow the tradition, the same reason that a well-dressed man will unfasten the last button of a vest. There are different stories about the last button of the vest. One story suggests that King George IV forgot to fasten the last button of his vest. His friend,

George Brummell, the legendary dandy, noticed the mistake and immediately followed suit. Another story claims that King Edward VII was so heavy that he could not get the bottom button fastened on his vest, or he simply forgot. The act became a gentlemanly tradition. If you decide to correct the past mistake by fastening the last button of the vest, no one will consider you a smart person. If you leave the last button open, some sophisticate dressers may think you know the history and follow the custom. If you insist on matching your tie and pocket square, you are taking the risk that someone may regard you as an ignorant person. What do you have to lose if you follow the conventional wisdom? "Overtly coordinating, or even worse, matching the tie and handkerchief, is a sure sign of an unsure dresser," observed Alan Flusser.

by PocketSquareZ, CC-BY-SA 3.0

42-2. Choose a pocket square according to the folding method.

To choose a pocket square, you should first know how you will fold it. Most customers worried too much about the color of the fabric. When I asked them which form they intended to use, most of them were stunned. Some of them did not even know how to fold any style. I showed customers the photo in previous page. They were excited to learn that there are many interesting ways to fold a pocket square. Some forms can be presented more effectively with a stiff piece of cloth while other forms are better to be displayed with a piece of soft material.

Most pocket squares are made in a single solid color. If you wish to create multi colors, you can use a handkerchief with patterns or trims in different colors, or combine more than one solid color handkerchief. Some handkerchiefs have a different color on the reverse side. Some have different color arrangements in different sections of the square. This is like several handkerchiefs in one.

In recent years, fake squares are gaining popularity. I have been asked by many customers about where to buy them. Fake ones are made by gluing small pieces of fabric on the top of a cardboard. The cardboard can be inserted into the jacket's chest pocket, showing only the fabric arrangement. I discourage the use of any fake pocket square since it suggests the wearer is either lazy or unintelligent to learn how to fold a simple piece of cloth.

42-3. How to fold a pocket square

There are no golden rules concerning how to fold a pocket square. Here, I am to provide a few samples of popular forms. You can create your own styles. It is just as simple as you fold your napkins on a table top. Some folds, such as the Peaks, the Three Points and the Four Points, appear more studied while some forms, such as the Puff and the Flop, produce a random shape every time you fold it. The choice of the fold should not only accommodate your outfit and the atmosphere of the event, but also reflect your personality and your mood.

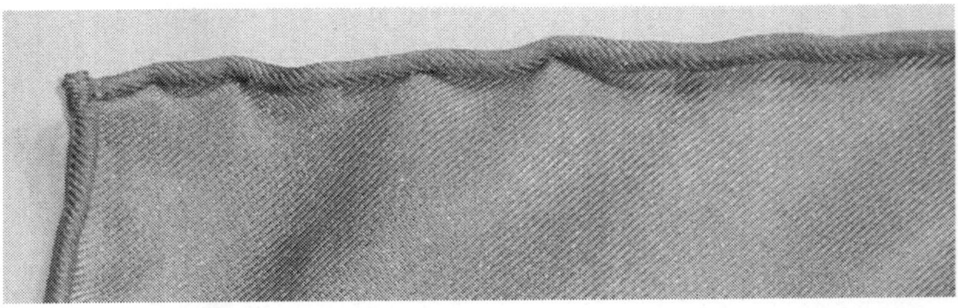

The edges of a fine handkerchief are always hand rolled and stitched.

How to Fold the TV Fold

The TV fold originated in the 1940s and became very popular during the 50s. It is one of the simplest forms and is usually done with a solid stiff handkerchief.

There is no certain way to fold a TV fold. As you fold the hank to about one-eighth its full size, slip the hank into your pocket with the most edges showing about one-half to one inch above the pocket line. Make sure it is razor straight. The fold may be unfeasible for a slanted chest pocket. If you insist on wearing one with a slanted pocket, you may tip the handkerchief so that the edge of the hank parallels the line of the pocket opening.

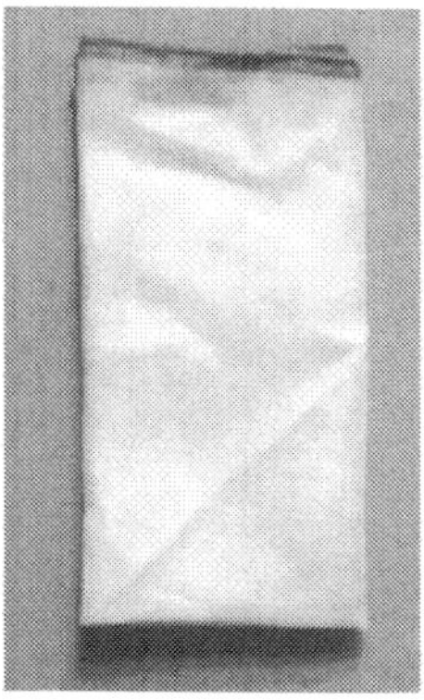

Keep the TV Fold thin and straight.

How to Fold the Puff

The Puff was allegedly invented by Fred Astaire. It is one of the few folds that do not show the edges. Hence, it is best done with a soft silk foulard.

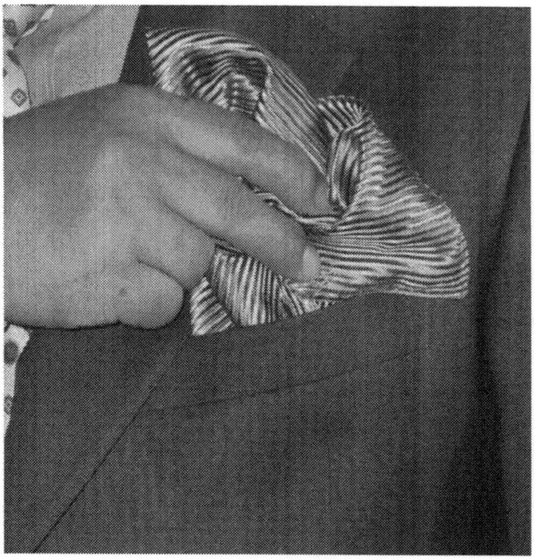

To execute the fold, you grasp the hank by its center and insert the entire hank into the pocket with the points hanging straight down first. You then pull and spread the fabric so it fills the pocket opening with only a "puff" of fabric showing.

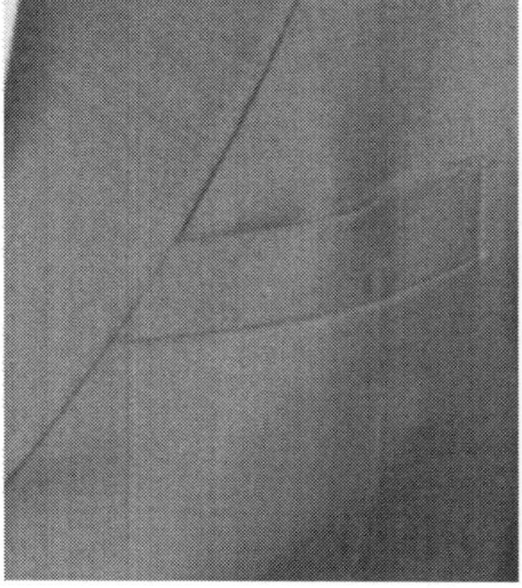

Prince Charles wearing a Puff.

How to Fold the Three Points

Fold the square into a triangle with the points matched perfectly. Have the flat side toward you, the top facing away.

Move the lower right corner to the left of the top by a couple of inches. Then, move the left corner to the right of the top.

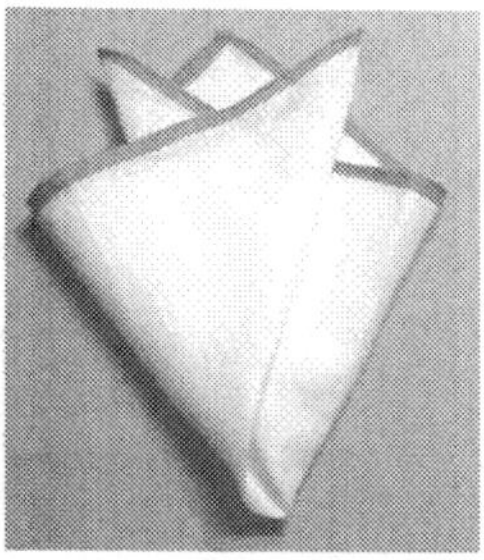

Adjust the points so that they are even in height and spacing. Fold the bottom up. Flip the hank and insert it into the pocket.

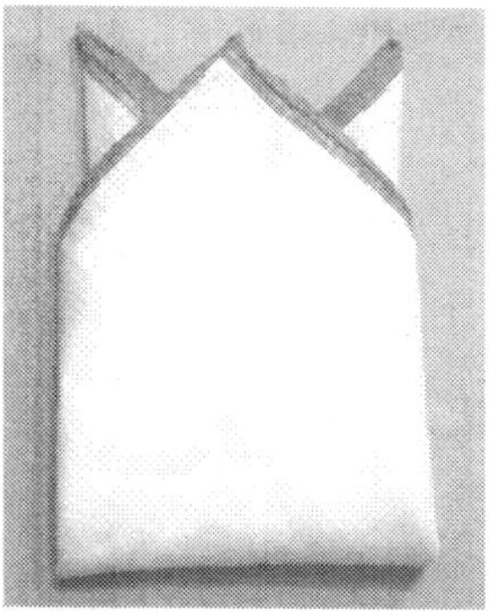

No matter how many points a hank has, keep all points sharp. It is pointless to showcase multi-points while none of the points is pointed.

How to Fold the Four Points

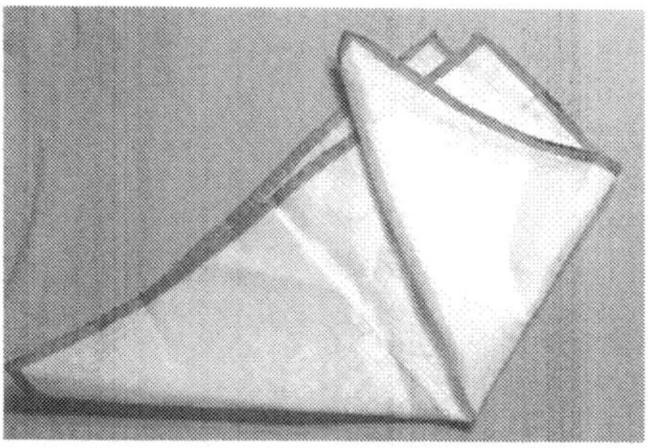

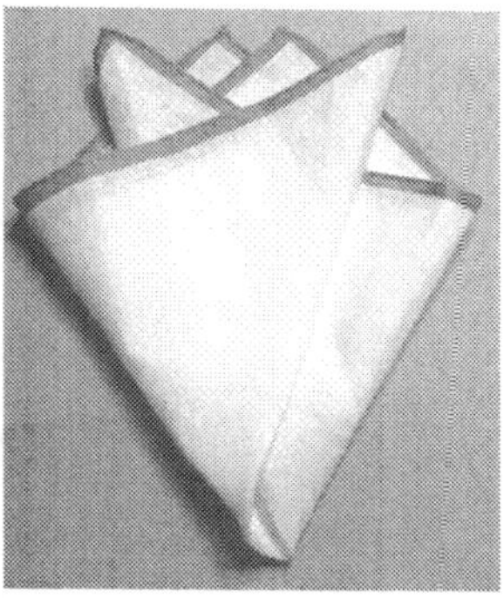

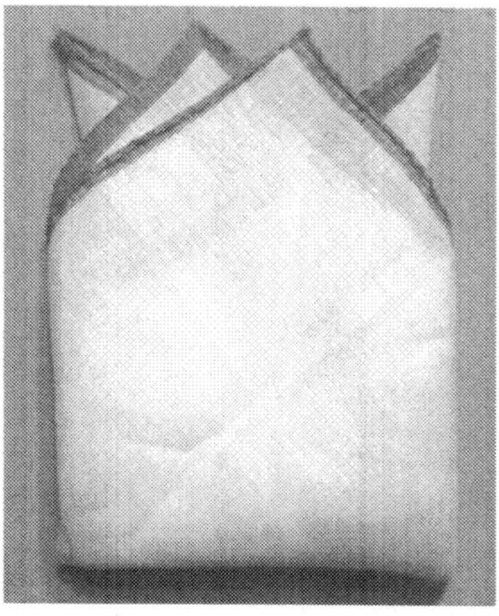

Star by folding the square into an imperfect triangle, showing twin points instead of one point at the top. Follow the same procedure that you fold the Three Points.

TV screenshot, fair use.

I have had difficulty finding a photo showing a man wears a handkerchief with multi-points. The style is less common perhaps because it is more methodical than other folds.

Chris Wallace, Fox News anchor, wore one version of the Four Points.

How to Fold the Peaks

To highlight the sharp points of the Peaks, this fold is best done with a stiff hank such as a piece of starched linen.

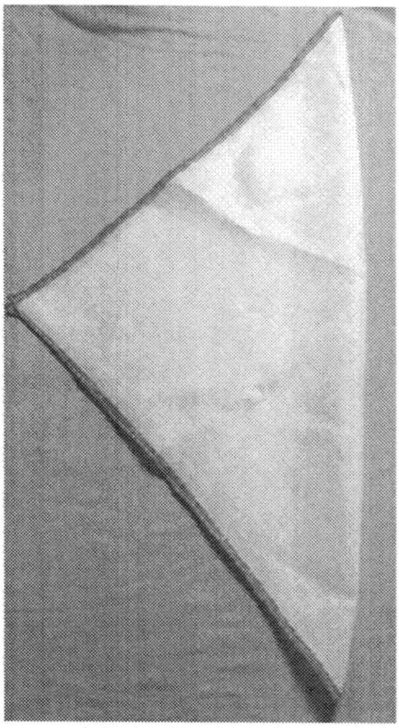

Fold the square into a perfect triangle with the flat side to your right. Move the bottom edge up to the right of the top. Then, move the left hand corner to the right of the two peaks just created. Fold the base up and insert the hank into the pocket.

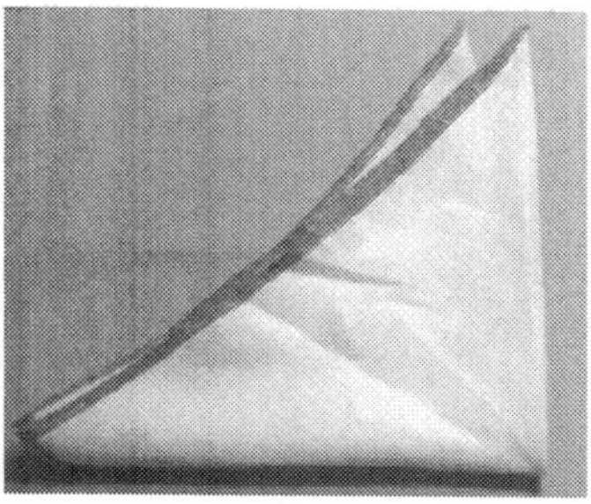

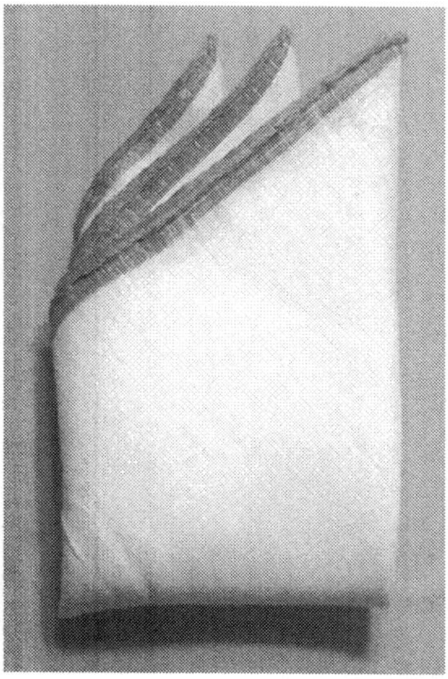

Did Charles Rangel wear his Peaks backward? It is preferred that the slope of the peaks parallels the slant of the jacket lapel.

How to Fold the MTN

This is one of the simple, elegant and popular styles. There is no name for it in literature. I therefore call it MTN, the abbreviation for "Mountain" because of its shape. The MTN is a deviation of the Peaks. Follow the same steps that you fold the Peaks. You fold the handkerchief into half by bringing down the peaks from behind and then turn it around.

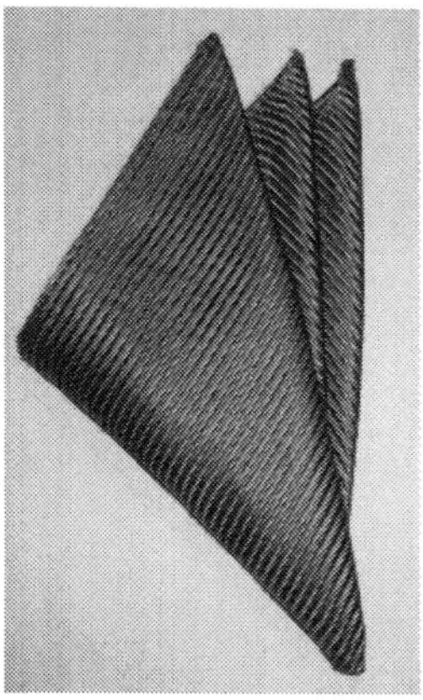

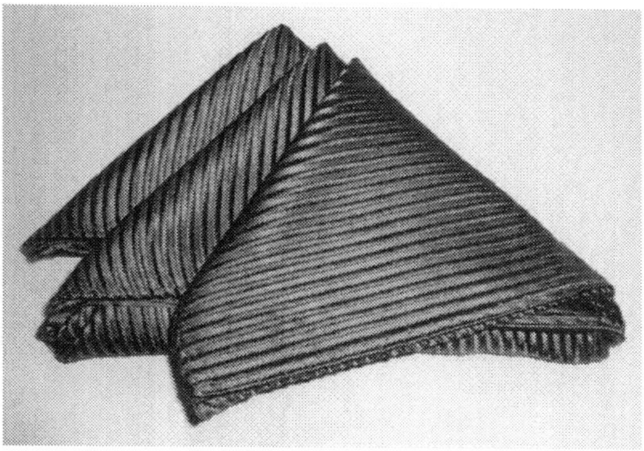

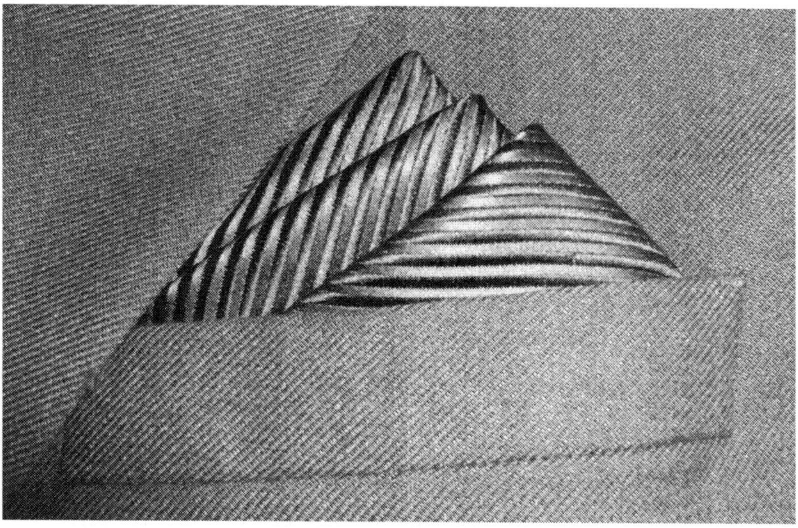

How to Fold the Flop

To create the effect of a flop, this fold is best done with a soft hank. First, you hold the fabric by its center. Use the thumb and forefinger of your other hand to circle the hank as it hangs straight down. Slide your circling thumb and finger down more than half way and insert the center into the pocket, allowing the points to fall freely with a "flop."

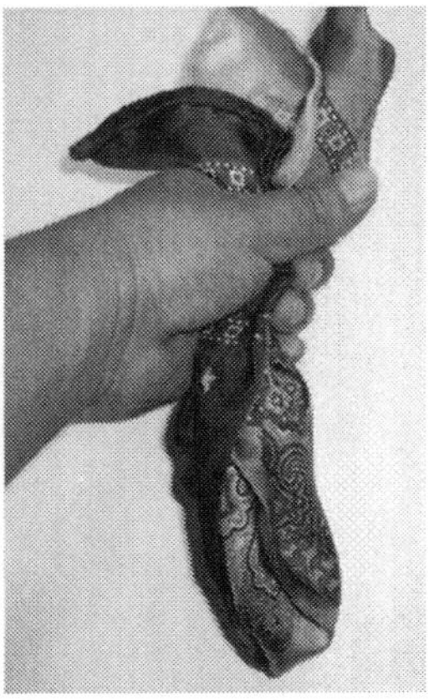

You can also knot the center of the cloth and insert the knot into the pocket. You may angle the points toward the shoulder. "This positioning helps in fostering a degage air, while emphasizing the lapel's diagonal slant and shoulders' breadth," wrote Alan Flusser.

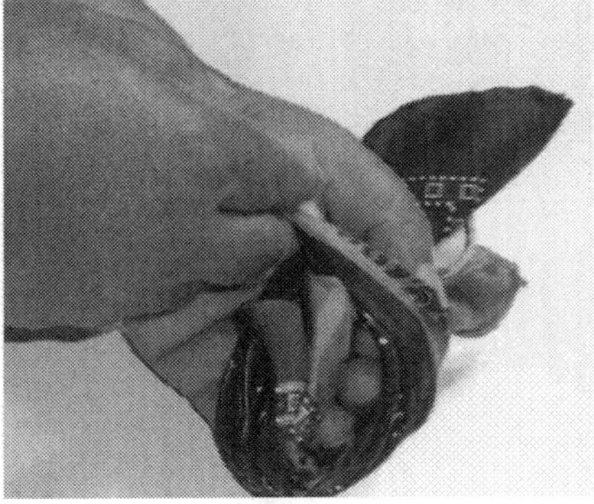

A common problem with the Flop is that it tends to collapse if the hank is pulled up too high.

Photo by Alan Light

The "flop" can be spread out symmetrically or slanted to one side. It the latter is chosen, the points should angle toward the shoulder.

How to Fold the Triangle

This fold is a simple design, recommended by Alan Flusser for a stiff handkerchief. There is no definite name for it. It may be called "One Point" or "Triangle." The point of the fold should be angled toward the shoulder to emphasize the slant of the jacket lapel and the breadth of the shoulder.

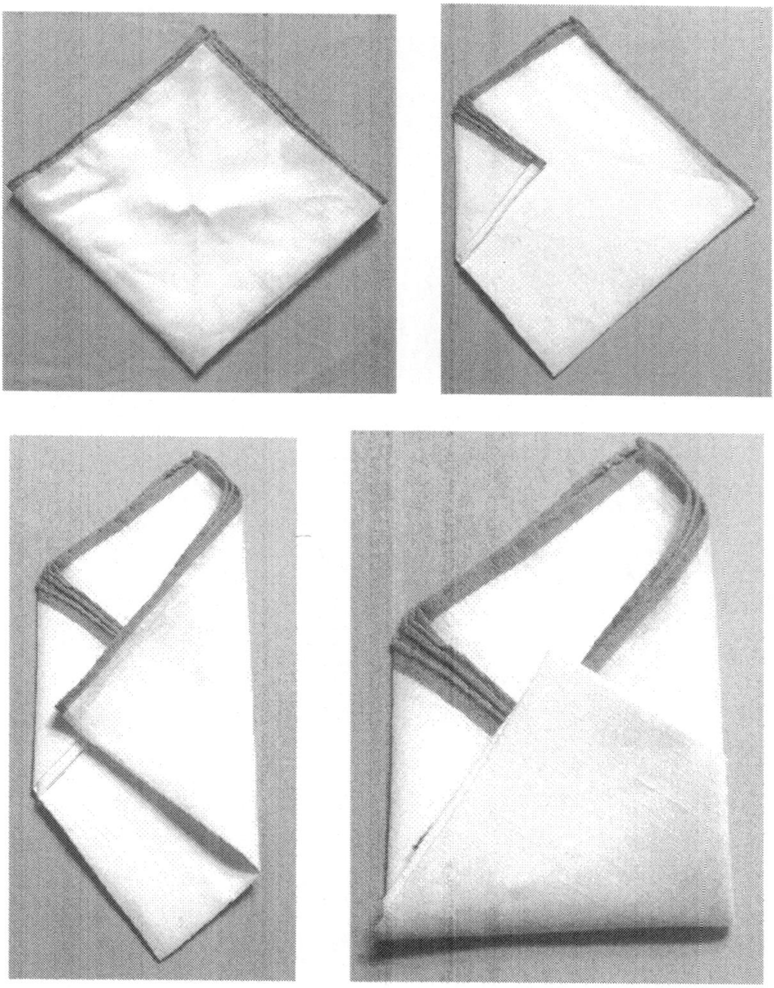

Whenever there are asymmetrical points, they are always angled toward the shoulder. It would be better if President Reagan tilted his handkerchief the same way Nelson Rockefeller tipped his.

How to Fold the Plop

This is my least favored style because the fold tends to be too narrow to fill the pocket opening.

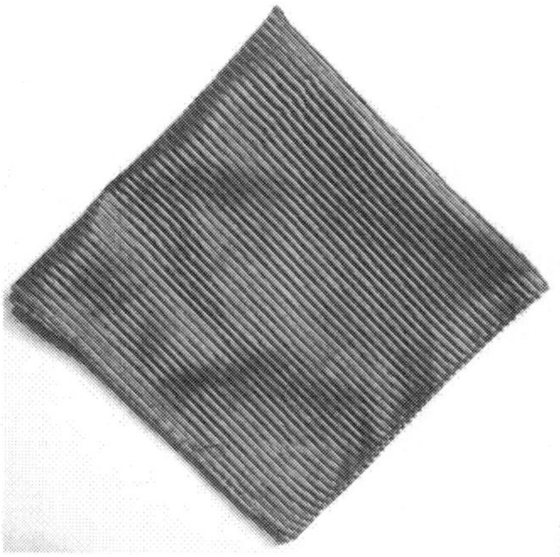

Fold the hank to a smaller square, one-fourth its full size. Pick up this smaller square by its center. Use the other hand to roll all of the loose corners together to form a cone. Insert the hank into the pocket and arrange the pointed top so that a dimple shows in the center.

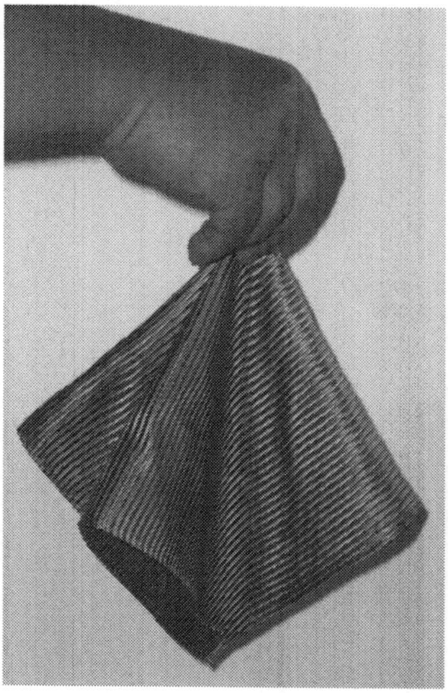

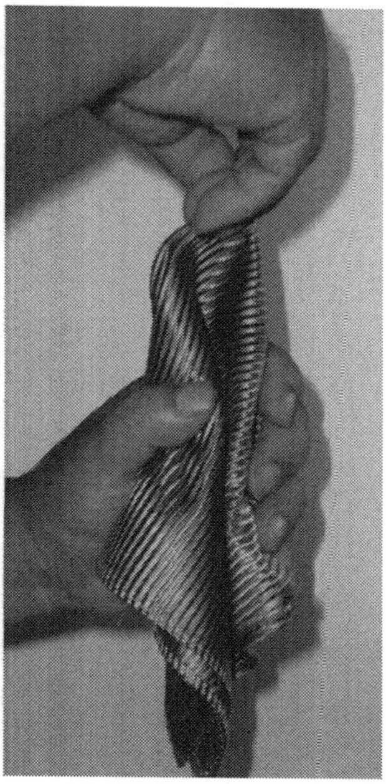

Did Cary Grant and Gary Cooper wear a Plop, or did the hank simply fall down inside the pocket? It is redundant to wear a handkerchief that is too small to be noticed.

TV screenshot, fair use.

Sharron Angle appeared on O'Reilly Factor wearing a well-executed Plop with a nice dimple.

42-4. *What to avoid*

The pocket handkerchief should not be too large that it bulges. Nor should it be too small that the cloth shifts around inside the pocket. The ideal size for a handkerchief is the twelve-to-fourteen-inch square for thick fabrics and sixteen-to-eighteen-inch square for thin materials. Alan Flusser wrote the following.

> Wearing a handkerchief that looks neither affected nor sloppy is akin to developing a discerning palate for good wine or food; it takes some practice. Douglas Fairbanks,

Jr. often reminded me that if you want to dress well, it takes time to look as if it took no time at all.

The following are additional steps that you should avoid when wearing a pocket handkerchief.

A ridiculous display of pocket handkerchief.

I do not believe that any man in his right mind would intentionally fold the handkerchief so small that it falls out of sight. My guess is that the folded hank does not fit the pocket securely. It shifts and falls inside the pocket after the man has moved around a while.

Fashion experts suggest that a pocket square should be displayed in a modest manner. Hence, the square should not peek out of the pocket more than an inch or so. In truth, the height of the handkerchief should base on the style of the fold. For a traditional TV fold, one half inch is sufficient. For fancy patterns, such as the "three points" or "peak," they may require more than an inch.

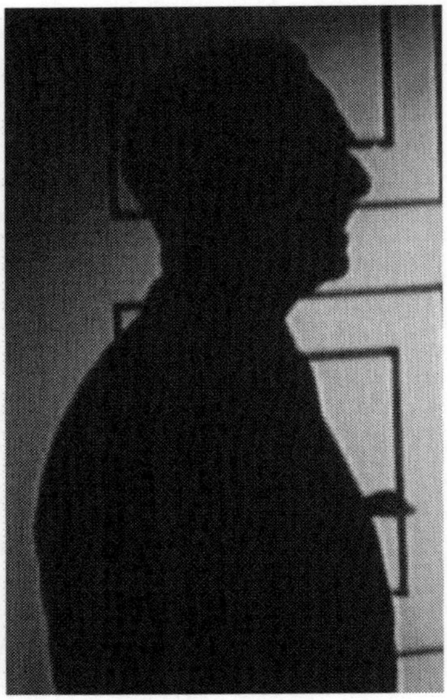

It is undesirable to wear a pocket square so high that it falls and flutters around.

Fashion authorities advise that a pocket square and flower should not be worn together for the combination is distracting. It has been well known that Fred Astaire (top photo) was insecure about the look of his face. He often wore both to distract viewers from looking at his face.

Because the pocket square is folded to reveal its points, the edges need the graceful roll and stitch to convey its refinement. It is preferred that the hand-rolled edges are shown when you fold and place your handkerchief in the pocket. The overly sharp edges and corners look unnatural and suspicious. (screen shots, fair use.)

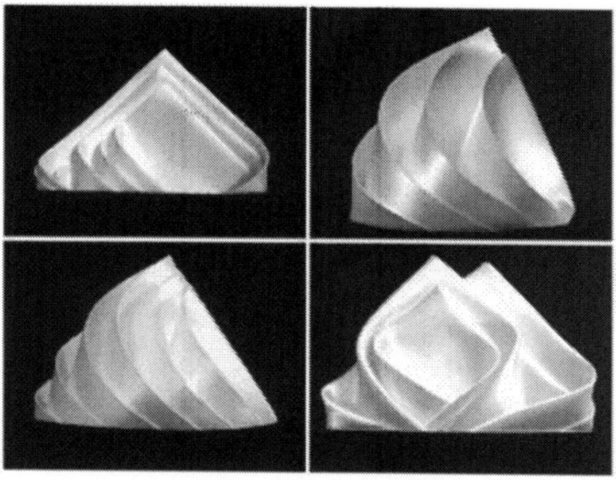

Pre-folded custom pocket squares are sold in the market. Some are stylish with interesting shapes or multiple colors. You can create your own unique style with your origamy skill or by using more than one hankerchief.

Part Six:

Murphy's Law

If anything can go wrong, it will.

George Brummell, the legendary dandy, always had his neck cloth wrapped neatly. His peers could not figure out how he did it, so they spied on him. There was no secret. All he did was spent half a day just trying to wrap his neck cloth gracefully. Once he got it right, he walked out the door.

There are days that you seem unable to dress right. You knot a tie and the tie is either too long or too short. You put on a dress shirt and forgot the collar stay. You buy a non-iron shirt. The shirt is wrinkle-free, but it begins to tear at the crease or seam after just a few wears. You love to wear Khaki pants but they fray terribly at the bottom of the pant legs. You bought a pair of fancy wool pants and had it hemmed at the store. Soon you discover that the two legs are uneven. If anything can go wrong, it will.

43. Make the dimple right.

I once heard Bill Hemmer, the host of Fox News program "America's Newsroom," made a comment in the show to his co-host Megyn Kelly that a well-knotted tie looks like a different tie. To him, a well-knotted tie has a nice dimple. From time to time, I met customers, who commented that they like or dislike certain brands of ties because the ties do or do not produce a good dimple. They talked as if the dimple is the most important part of knotting a tie. One of the major clothing chain stores in the U.S. issues a shopping guide for its customers. One page of the brochure reads "THE SECRET OF THE PERFECTLY EXECUTED TIE IS THE DIMPLE." This is wrong.

When the fabric of the tie permits, a dimple or two smaller dimples can be created by using the index finger to press a slight convex cavity into the tie just below the knot. The dimple or dimples add an elegant touch to the knot. The dimple also strengthens the tie knot and helps provide a forward arch or thrust to the tie knot. In truth, a dimple may be unavoidable if the tie is wide, if the tie is not tapered enough near the knot, or if the knot opening is small. When large amount of tie fabric passes through a small opening of a tie knot, the extra fabric will be squeezed into folds or wrinkles. The wider the cloth and the smaller the knot opening, the larger or more the dimples will be. This explains that it is more difficult to form a dimple with a skinny or narrow tie and with a larger knot. The stiffness of the tie construction will also affect the forming of the dimple.

Most men are frustrated by the uniformity of the tie knots and long for a different look of the knot. Being incapable of creating a unique style of knot, they tackle the problem with the wrong solution. A dimple or dimples in the center of the tie knot can consume the extra fabric and eliminate unwanted folds or wrinkles. Nonetheless, we should not exaggerate the importance of the dimple. Many well-attired men including the legendary Duke of Windsor wear a tie without any dimple. A small dimple or dimples tend to add interest and strength to the knot, but a dimple that is larger or longer than the knot itself may overshadow the tie knot and look pretentious. If a man uses a dimple, he ought to make sure that the dimple is positioned nicely.

Like Bill Hemmer, many men mistakenly think the secret of a well-tied tie is the dimple.

Screen shot, fair use.

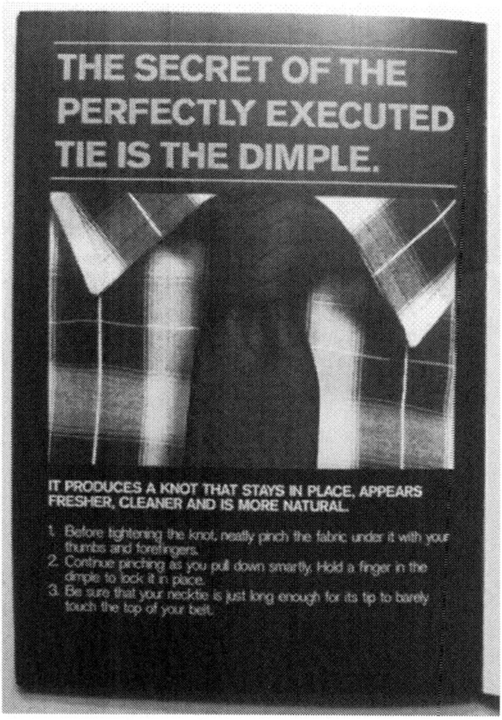

A shopping guide issued by one of the major clothing chain stores in the U.S. falsely Suggests that the secret of the perfectly executed tie is the dimple.

Governor Pawlenty wore a tie with two uneven dimples.

Screenshot, fair us

On August 17, 1998, President Clinton apologized to the nation for his lying about sexual relationship with Ms. Lewinsky. He must have had a bad day; the dimple in his tie knot was crooked.

44. Collar stays—the necessary evil

Robert De Niro must have forgotten his collar stays.

The two points of a turned-down shirt collar should touch the chest front when the top shirt button is fastened. Collar stays are devised to help hold down the collar wings.

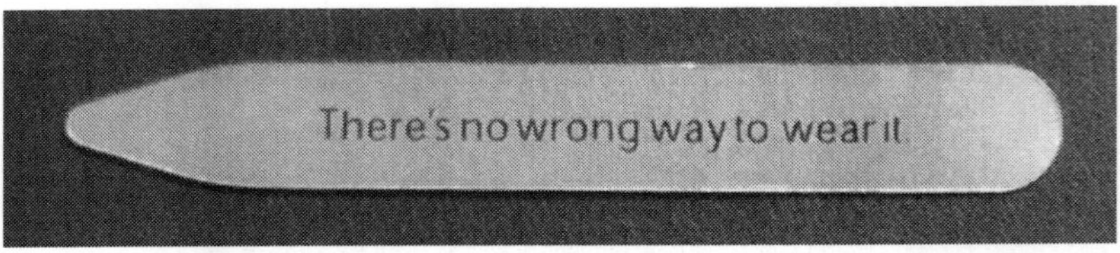

The writing on the collar stay from one of the major clothing chain stores in the U.S., Express, states that "There's no wrong way to wear it." Is that true? If you wear the collar stays incorrectly, complications may occur.

Most point and spread collars are equipped with removable stays. They should be removed before the shirt is laundered and ironed. Pressing over the collar stays can cause damage to the shirt. Perhaps because of this reason, some manufacturers including famous designers often provide thin plastic stays to avoid or reduce the damage in case that the stays are left in the collar when laundered. Then again, thin collar stays are ineffective to hold down the collar. I suggest the thin stays be replaced with thick ones. Or, you may insert two instead of one thin stay for each collar wing.

The photo shows the imprint of the collar stay on a non-iron shirt. The damage could be much worse if the shirt is a regular cotton shirt.

I work in the men's department and frequently meet customers who come to the store to purchase replacement collar stays. It seems common that men lose their collar stays. Currently, there are no standards concerning the size of the stays. The length of the stay is determined by the length of the collar wing. The width and the thickness are subject to shirt manufacturer's interpretation. The most popular width is about $^3/_8$". Some designers may intentionally create stays of a different width just to render a fashion statement. In order to work with all different types of shirts, the universal collar stays tend to be narrower than $^3/_8$". The narrow stays may not work as well as the regular ones.

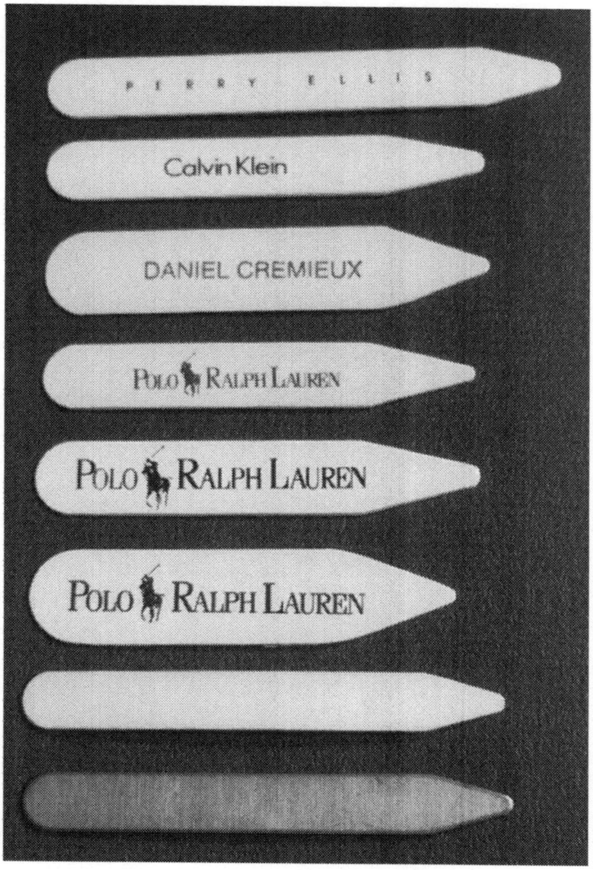

Different shirt makers often provide collar stays with different width. The same designer may give different widths for different shirts (middle three). The bottom two stays, one plastic and one brass, are universal stays, which tend to be narrow in order to fit most shirts.

Dressy shirts tend to have a stiff collar, which may be able to touch the shirt front without a collar stay if the collar fits the neck properly. Casual dress shirts, on the other hand, often have a soft collar, which may be unable to touch the chest front even with a collar stay. You may have to double the number of stays in order for them to work. Whatever you do, make sure that the stays are installed properly. Or, they may leave undesired marks on the collar.

Screenshot, fair use.

The tiny bump on Leonardo DiCaprio's collar is likely caused by a collar stay that is too long for the collar.

Screenshot, fair use.

Collar wings bend at the location where the collar stay resides.

There seems a problem with Mayor Bloomberg's collar stay.

45. Why do some collars bend easily?

The two corners of the collar wings do not have to be angled. They can be rounded. Nevertheless, the great majority of the modern dress shirts have a pair of pointed corners. Another defect is that the two pointed corners do not appear sharp. Many men wear a shirt collar with the two points bent or curved. This is a serious defect, which may be caused by limp collar wings, or by incorrect topstitching.

Screenshot, fair use.

Rounded collar

Occasionally, I meet customers who refuse to buy dress shirts of certain brands because the corners of the collar wings bend easily. These are smart shoppers. Most consumers do not notice the problem even if they wear a bent collar.

Why do the two points of the collar wings curve or bend? Three explanations may be made. First, dress shirt collars are traditionally made stiff so that the collars will not bend or wrinkle as the neck moves around. To make the collar stiff, firm layers of interfacing are used to add thickness to the collar. The layers of interfacing are often glued to the top layer of the shirt fabric, called top fused. Collars of some sportier shirts may have a soft layer of interfacing or no interfacing at all. A thin or soft collar tends to curve or bend, especially when the collar wing is long.

Second, the layers of shirt fabric and interfacing are held together by stitching alongside the edge of the collar, called edge stitching, or by stitching at a quarter inch from the edge, called quarter topstitching. Some designers try to make a fashion statement by topstitching at ⅜" or more from the edge. Collar stays are unable to reach the corners of the collar wings. Consequently, the two points of the collar wings tend to curve or bent. Hence, you should avoid any collar with topstitching at more than ¼" unless the collar is made so stiff that it will not curve. On the other hand, some designers make their shirt collars without interfacing and without edge stitching or topstitching. These collars do not have the sharp edge of a decent shirt. They look swollen and puffy. Smart dressers should avoid this type of shirts.

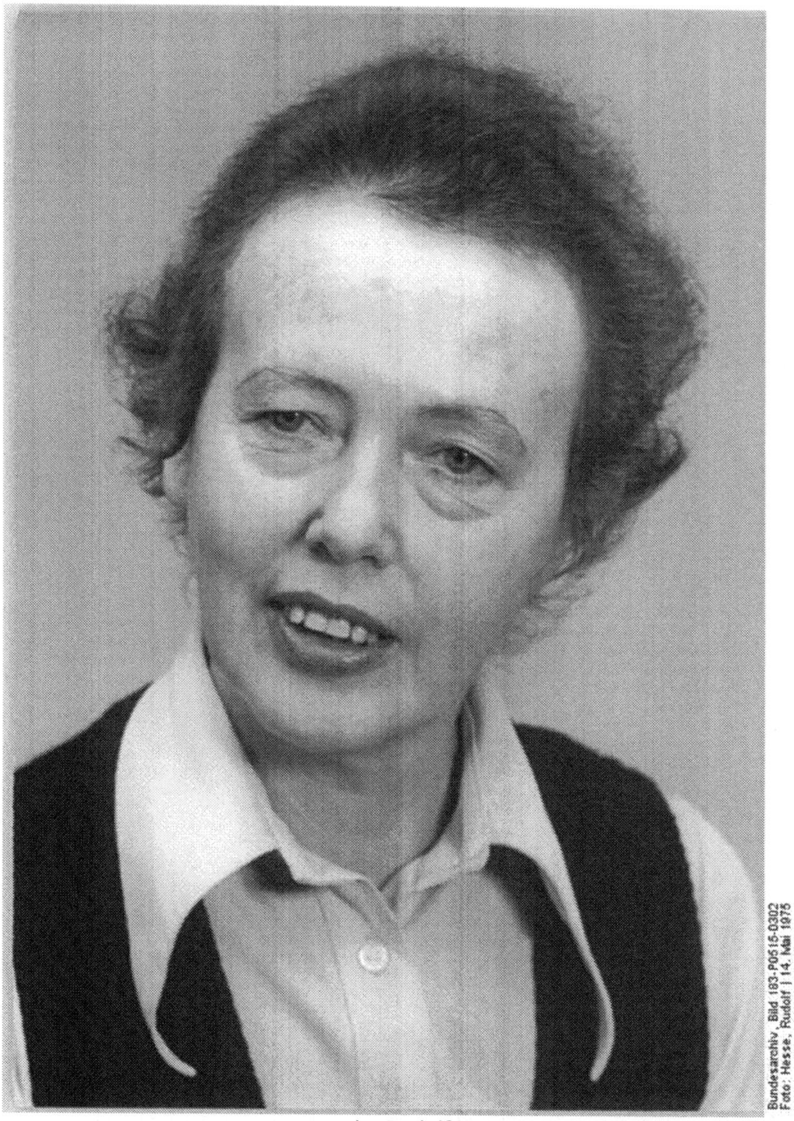

A soft, long collar wing tends to curve or bend easily.

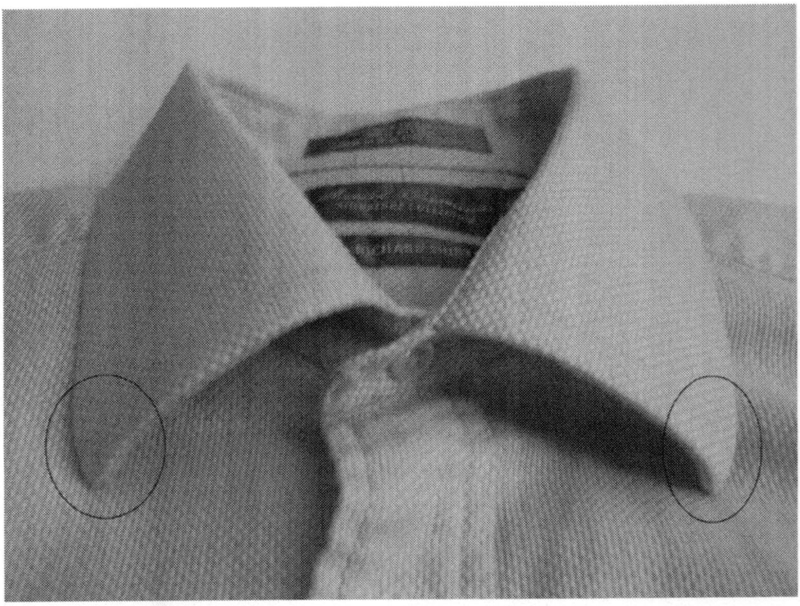

The topstitching is ⅜" away from the edge of the collar, preventing collar stays to reach the tips of the collar points. Consequently, the two points of the collar curve or bend.

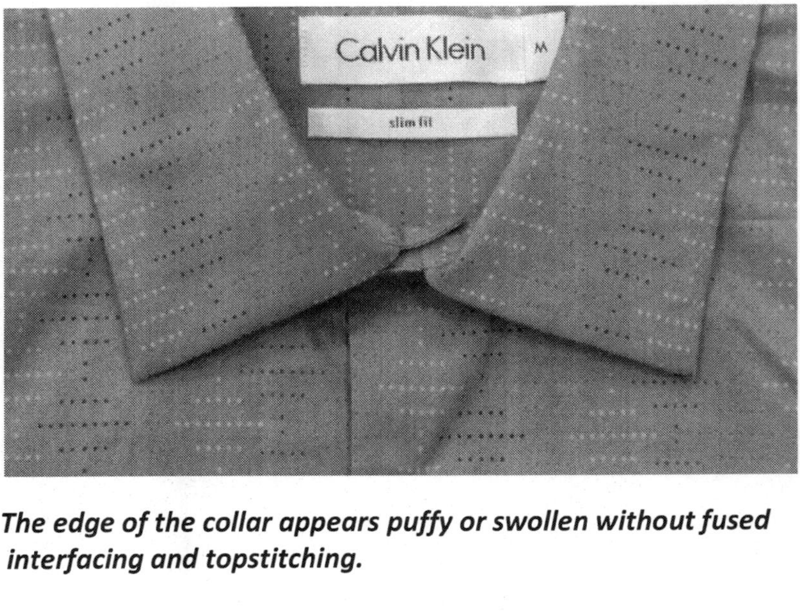

The edge of the collar appears puffy or swollen without fused interfacing and topstitching.

Third, the collar is the most difficult part of the shirt to manufacture. Several layers of shell fabric and interlining are sewn together near the edge with the two layers of shell fabric being placed in the middle. The pile of stitched layers, (a), is then turned inside out to form a pointed corner, (b). The areas A and B, shown in figure (3), contain twice more whereas Area C contains four times more layers of fabric than those in the rest part of the collar. This makes Point f very vulnerable to bending, especially when the two lines of topstitching happen to intersect at Point f. Many shirt collars, including top-quality ones, bend easily because the collars are topstitched along the border of the double-thick area. A bent collar is a serious defect. Many shirt manufacturers, however, seem not to notice the problem and continue to produce defected collars. It is wise for consumers to pay attention to such a detail.

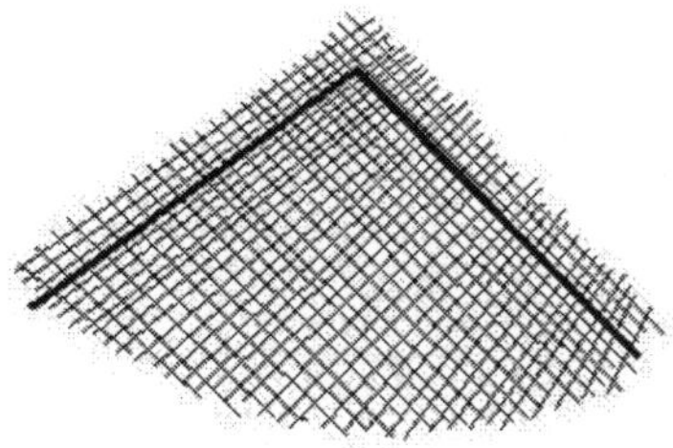

(1)

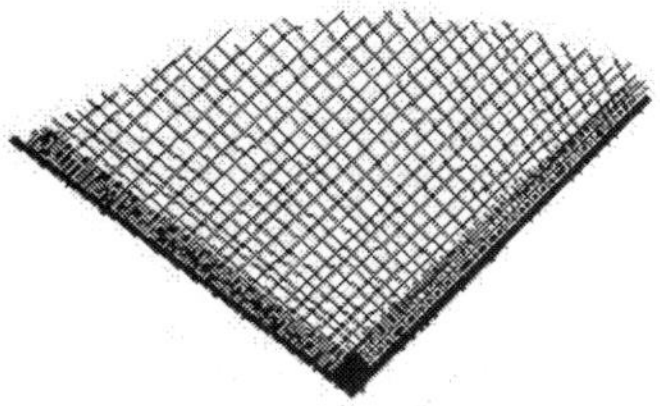

(2)

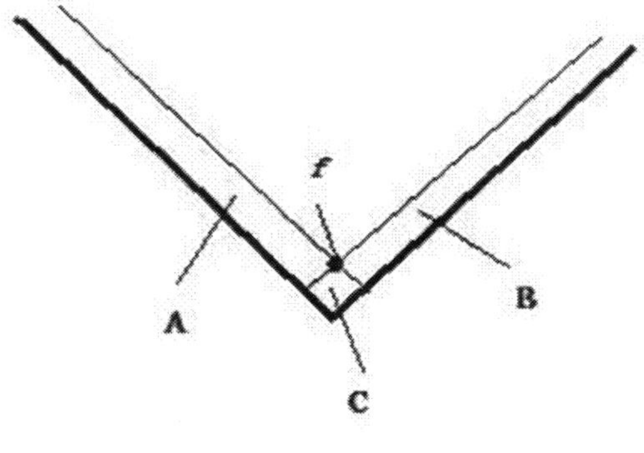

(3)

Button-down collars are usually made with light or no interfacing. They tend not to have a weak spot such as the Point f. In addition, the tip of a button-down collar is fixed to the shirt front by the collar button, reducing its chance to bend. Hence, it is rare to find a button-down collar that bends at the corner.

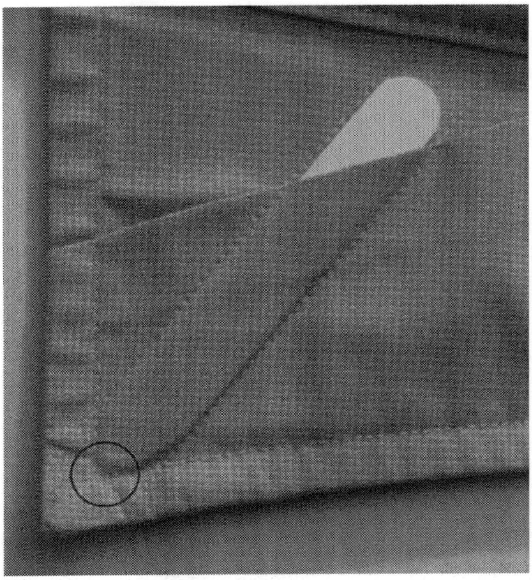

The corner of the quadruple-thick area is vulnerable to bending especially when it is the intersection of the two topstitching lines and the tip of the collar stay.

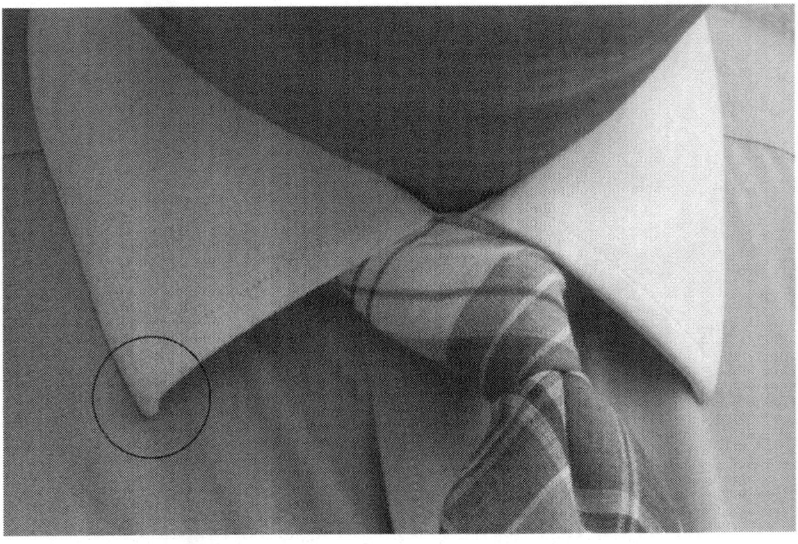

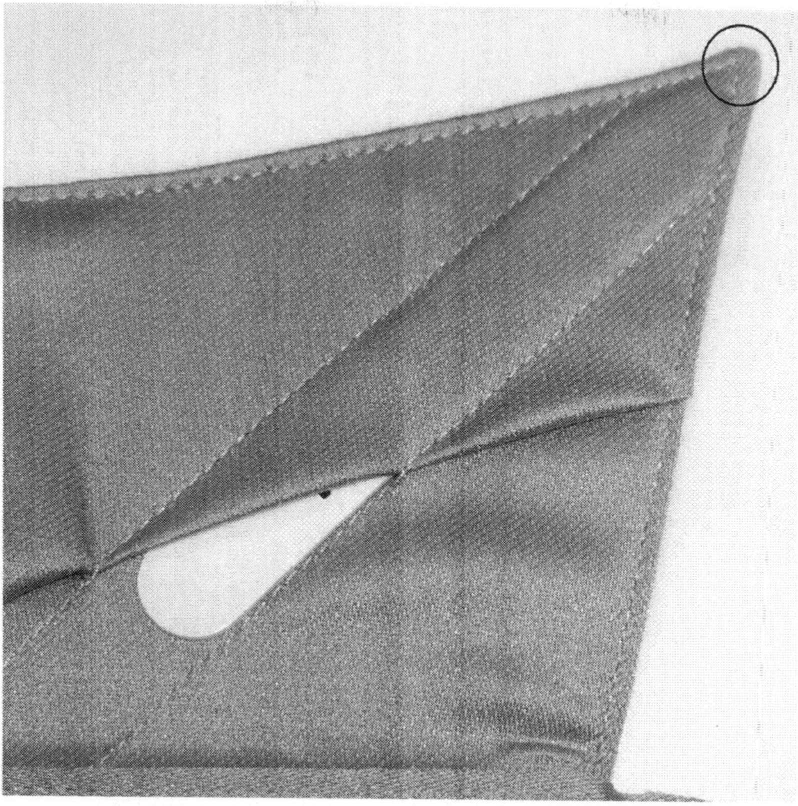

Edge stitching allows the collar stay to reach the tip of collar, preventing the corner from bending.

Screenshot, fair use

Journalist, John Stossel, wore a bent shirt collar.

A crisp collar with sharp edges and angles looks very becoming.

46. Why should a non-iron shirt not be ironed or starched?

46-1. Why does cotton wrinkle?

Cotton is composed of a material called cellulose. The molecules in cellulose contain many thousands of atoms and are shaped like long chains. The long, chainlike shape of the molecules makes cellulose a good fiber. The chainlike cellulose molecules are joined together with cross-linked hydrogen bonds, which make cotton fabrics wrinkle resistant. If you stress a dry cotton fabric slightly by folding it or sitting on it, these hydrogen bonds force the molecules back where it belongs, and no wrinkle will form. When the cotton fabric gets wet, water (including humidity and sweat) tends to interfere with those hydrogen bonds and prevent the fabric from returning to its wrinkle-free state when the fabric is stressed. This is the reason that natural fiber clothes coming out of the washer tend to wrinkle.

46-2. How does the non-iron treatment work?

In the early 1990s, the garment industry began to produce "non-iron" garments using advanced chemicals that provide strong cross-linking bonds between various fiber molecules. It was first thought that cross-linking strengthens cotton fibers and make the fabric wrinkle resistant. Scientists now believe it is the strengthening of the hydrogen bonds, which make cotton fabrics resistant to wrinkling.

While the industry continues to perfect the wrinkle-free technology, it seems that the non-iron treatment at this stage only works well with fabrics made of thicker yarns or stronger weaves. Chemicals can only assist in providing recovery from wrinkles to some degree. Many vendors exaggerate the effect of non-iron treatment. They tend to claim a garment to be wrinkle-free or non-iron as long as the garment has been treated with the non-iron process. For years, I have warned customers that non-iron dress shirts made with thin yarns and soft weaves, such as herringbone, tend to wrinkle more easily. Customers keep returning to the store and confirming what I said is correct.

46-3. Handle non-iron shirts with care.

Despite the effectiveness of the wrinkle-free treatment, you should launder your non-iron shirts carefully. Hand wash, line dry is always the best. If you prefer to use a laundry machine and a dryer, use the delicate cycle and dry the shirt in a small load with medium or low temperature. The advanced dryers these days are featured with a "de-wrinkling cycle", which magically reduces or eliminates wrinkles in the clothes. If for any reason your non-iron shirt appears slightly wrinkled, spray the shirts with water and the wrinkles will smooth out in no time. This method works because moisture such as cool water mist and hot steam can reset the cross-linked hydrogen bonds and smooth out the wrinkles. When spraying, avoid the creases as the moisture may smooth out the creases. Do not stress the damped area while the area is still wet, or the wrinkles will occur.

46-4. Avoid pressing the creases.

Many customers ask me what will happen if they iron a non-iron shirt. There is no reason that the non-iron shirts cannot be ironed. But why would any person want to iron a wrinkle-free shirt? As I have explained in the previous chapter, not every non-iron shirt is wrinkle-free. If you happen to own a bad non-iron shirt or if you mishandle a normal non-iron shirt, the shirt may become wrinkled and need a touch-up. You can remove the wrinkles by spraying the area with water.

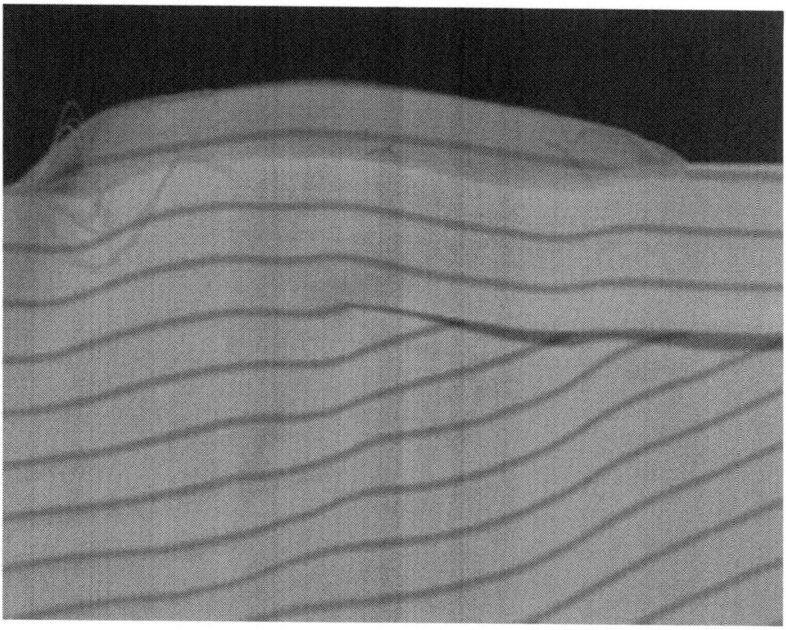

The permanent crease should be left alone. Repeated pressing often causes the crease to tear.

Creases are like wrinkles. The difference is that creases are designed while wrinkles tend to be random. It is difficult to crease a wrinkle-free shirt once the shirt left the factory because the chemicals or synthetic fibers that resist wrinkles also resist creases. As explained in the previous chapter, some, but not all, chemically treated non-iron and wrinkle-free shirts have permanent creases in all of the pleats and sleeve creases. The advanced chemicals used in the non-iron treatment are able to keep creases permanent. If you insist on pressing or ironing a non-iron shirt with permanent creases, you should avoid touching the creases. If you have to re-shape the creases, be sure that you iron the creases at exactly the same place of the original creases. Otherwise, you will create another crease near the permanent crease. It is unsightly to have more than one crease at the same location. Try not to hard press the creases or the creases may break after repeated pressing.

Some customers refuse to buy non-iron shirts because the shirts tend to tear at the creases after repeated ironing. I tease customers by asking the question, "Why did you iron a shirt that tells you 'no-iron'?" Just as you can break a steel rod by bending the rod back and forth at the same spot, you can break a piece of fabric by ironing and pressing the fabric repeatedly at the same location.

46-5. The pros and cons of non-iron shirts

Some consumers like the features of non-iron shirts but hesitate to use the shirts because they send their shirts to the cleaners. Shirts returned from the cleaners are pressed. Why should they spend extra money to buy non-iron shirts? Most drycleaners prefer machine pressing because it is faster. Nevertheless, machine pressing tends to over press seams, vents, pocket flaps, double-thick layers, and other uneven surfaces, causing unsightly impressions. Machine pressing also flattens soft woolens and shines delicate fabrics, especially gabardine, acetate and satin. Machine pressing also create multiple creases at the same location.

If you prefer to send your non-iron shirts to the cleaner, remind your cleaner about the special features of your shirt. Avoid dry cleaning your cotton shirts. Prefer hand ironing or soft press to hard press. The best way is to have your non-iron shirts laundered without hand ironing or machine pressing. If the cleaner cannot fulfill your wish, you should look for another cleaner.

A huge difference between a pressed or starched regular cotton shirt and a non-iron cotton shirt is that the non-iron shirt are 24 hours wrinkle-free whereas a pressed regular cotton shirt may stay pressed for a few hours.

The non-iron treatment weakens the strength of cotton fabrics significantly. Starch is not recommended for non-iron shirts. The application of starch involves high heat, which further damages the cotton fabrics. Repeated pressing and starching also increases the shrinkage rate. Non-iron shirts are not a good choice for those people who like to have their cotton shirts starched.

As the new breed of non-iron fabrics are gaining popularity in the garment industry, many consumers are wondering what makes a cotton shirt or a pair of cotton pants wrinkle-resistant or wrinkle-free. There are different methods to produce wrinkle-free garments. A popular approach is to strengthen the weak hydrogen bonds between adjacent cellulose molecular chains in the cotton fibers. Currently the most common cross-linking agent, DMDHEU, releases a chemical called formaldehyde, which is toxic and can pose health hazards. Hence, additional treatments or alternatives are required to replace, remove or reduce the toxic chemicals. While manufacturers assure that the amount of toxicant in non-iron products will not affect health, the products may be avoided for those people who have a sensitive skin. The various chemicals used in the non-iron process may cause irritation or allergic reaction.

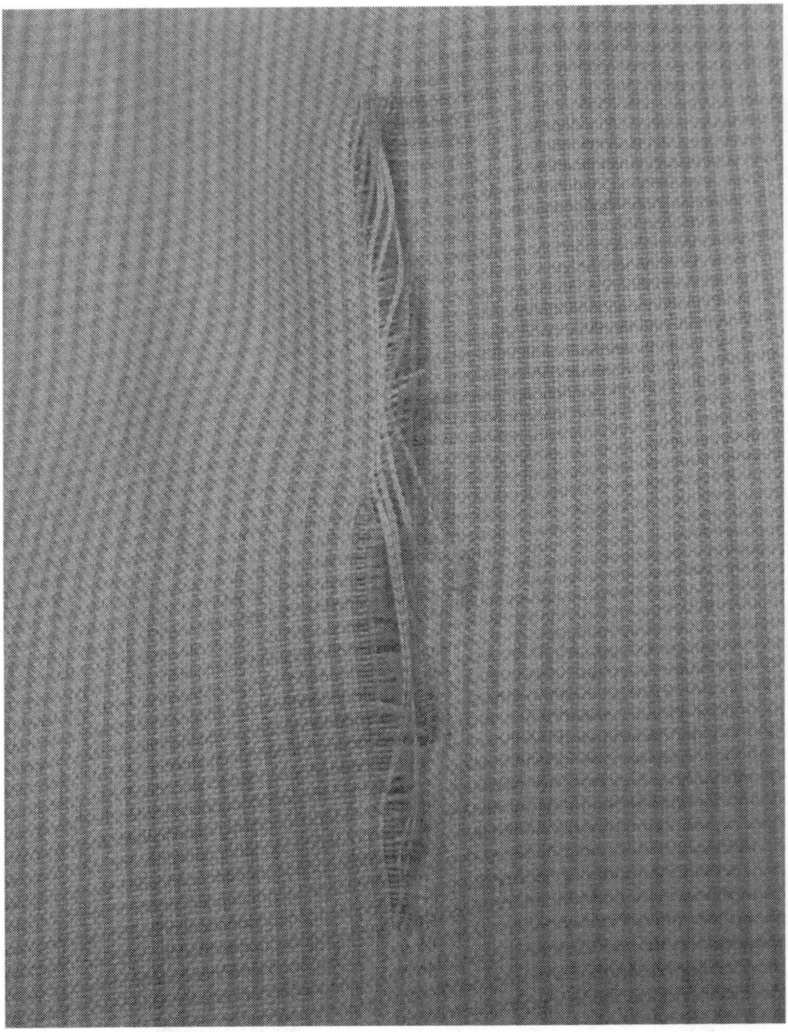

Non-iron treatment weakens the strength of the fabric, reducing the fabric's ability to resist tearing, especially at the seams.

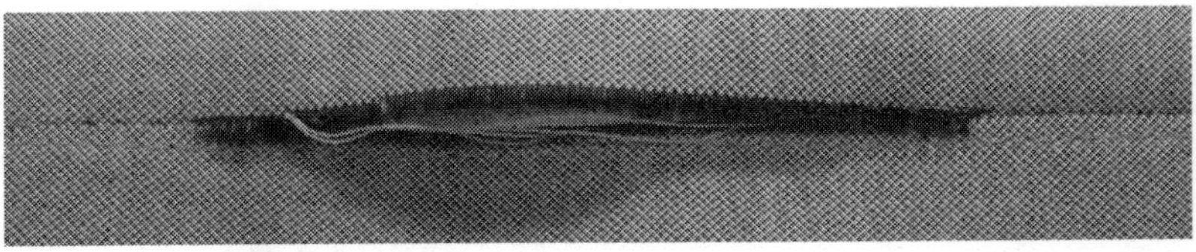

47. Why does the bottom width of the pant legs matter?

I sold a customer a pair of ready-to-wear slacks and recommended him to have the pants shortened since the pants were too long. I was stunned by the price he paid--three times the price of a simple hemming. The customer told me that his tailor insisted on tapering the bottom of the pant legs because the legs were shortened too much. In the past, pant legs are tapered from the waist to the knee and then cut straight down to the leg opening. Today, readymade pants are tapered from the waist to the leg opening. It was a waste of money to taper pant legs that were already narrow.

Like this customer, most men prefer a trimmer cut for pant legs but they never realize the consequences. When pants are cut too short or too narrow, it is easy for the pant legs to be caught inside the shoe or on top of the shoe.

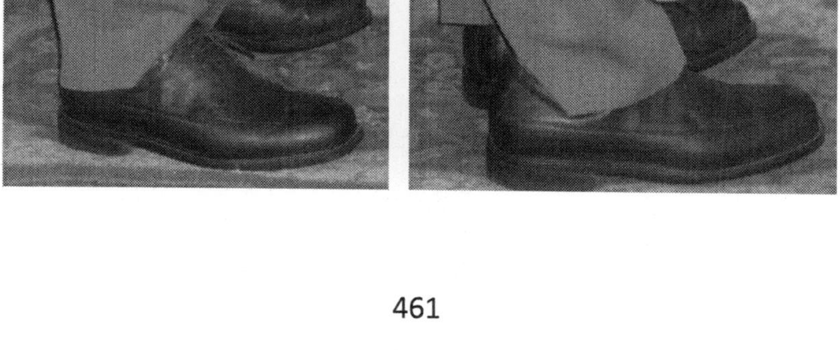

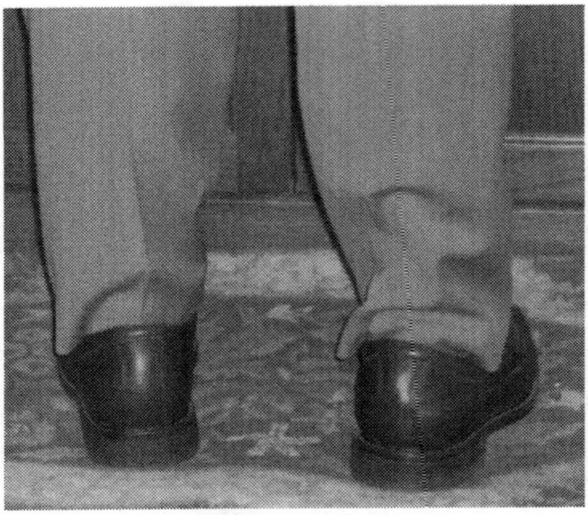

Different fashion experts suggest different bottom widths of the pant leg to cover from ½ to ¾ of the shoe. In truth, it is difficult to determine the proper width of the pant leg solely on the size of the shoe. Foot size varies greatly among different men. I believe the width of the pant legs should correspond to the wearer's body figure and the rest of his ensemble. How large a portion of the shoe should be covered by the pant legs is less important. If everything else is the same, I recommend slacks with a larger leg opening. Slacks with a small leg opening are problematic. They keep falling inside the shoes, create more unwanted break above the shoes, and expose more of the socks especially with loafer shoes. Ideally, the bottom width of the pant leg is to cover about $^{2}/_{3}$ of the shoe.

If you prefer and cannot find readymade pants with a wider leg opening, you may intentionally buy longer pants and have them shortened to the proper length.

48. It is inexcusable to wear a pair of uneven pants.

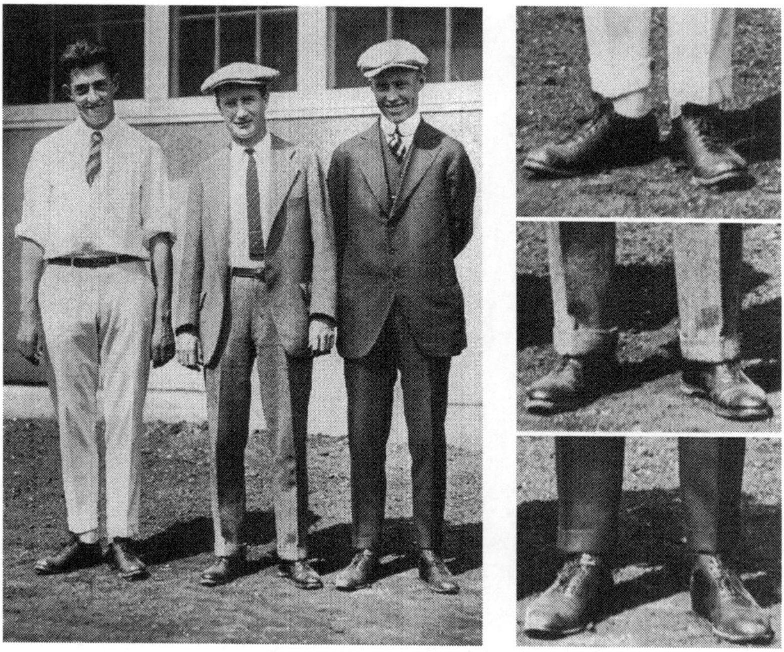

How was it possible that the three of the five amateur golfers who ever won the U.S. Open happened to wear a pair of uneven pants at the same time?

A man can justify his wearing a pair of wrong color, pattern or style of pants by claiming individual taste or preference. But, it is difficult to declare innocence for wearing a pair of uneven pants. Why do many men, including the presidents of the United States, walk around with such a pair of pants?

Many suit departments, alteration shops, or tailors use an upside down "Y" bar to assist in the measurement of pant length. The customer stands on a level platform. The fitter places the one-foot long Y bar upside down on the platform against the back of each leg and makes a mark on the pants at the top of the upside down Y bar. Whoever alters the pair of pants will cut the bottom of pants by lining up the marks on both legs instead of lining up both sides of the pants from the waistband. It is my belief that the Y bar method is responsible for most of the uneven pant legs.

Why do merchants use the Y bar? They use the Y bar to make their alteration jobs easier. Because a pair of pants is hung from the waistband down, it is logic to assume that the pair of pants should be aligned from the top of the waistband. But this will require the tailor to spread out and to line up the entire pants from the waist to the bottom on a large tabletop. It is no wonder that alteration and tailor shops prefer to line up both pant legs at a place near the bottom of the pants. To save a few minutes for each pair of pants can mean a large reduction on the overall work load for a busy shop. In our alteration department, it takes only four minutes to hem a pair of cuffed or non-cuffed pants with a sewing machine.

What is wrong with the Y bar method? How a pair of pants hangs at the waistband will affect the look of the pant bottom. If a man hangs his pants one side higher than the other at the waistband, the two pant legs will appear uneven at the bottom. This happens quite often because every man does not necessarily hang the pair of pants correctly each time they put on one, even if the pair of pants fits perfectly. When a man finds a suit jacket that fits, the suit trousers are often too tight or too loose and require alteration. It is difficult to try on a pair of trousers horizontal to the ground if the waist is either too tight or too loose. The Y bar method works only if a man wears his pants correctly at the waistband, but there is no guarantee that the man will do so during the fitting.

To prove my theory, I sometimes let customers try on the same pair of trousers. The Y bar did yield a different result during each trial. Most customers bought multiple pairs of pants. Frequently, each pair was measured a different length using the same method. In some cases, the measurements generated opposite results. Some pairs indicated the left while other pairs suggested the right leg was longer. This proves how unreliable the Y bar method is.

The supporters of the Y bar method claim that a garment should be tailored according to the way a person wears his clothes. If the wearer hangs his pants higher on one side of his waist, the length of the pant leg should be adjusted accordingly. This is a fallacious thinking because not every man wears his pants at the same location each time he puts on a pair of pants. In truth, most men do not even notice it if they hang their pants uneven on both sides of their waist. If a man cannot show his pant legs even to the ground by wearing a pair of equal length pants, do you think he can do better with a pair of unequal length pants?

The supporters of the Y bar method also claim that the Y bar marks can correct the length difference if a man has a pair of uneven legs. When a man has a pair of uneven legs, he is not going to hang his shorter leg in the air when standing. The uneven legs will result in an uneven waistline. The man is better off to wear a high heel shoe to compensate for the shortage of leg length. Or, the man may wear a pair of specially tailored pants with one side higher on the waistband to conceal the uneven waist. After all, the purpose of a garment is to hide the bad parts and showcase the good parts of the body. If a man has an uneven pair of legs and is unwilling to adopt either remedy, he may have the reason to cut his two pant legs differently. It is inexcusable for a man with a pair of even legs to wear a pair of uneven pant legs.

The photo of the three amateur golfers reflects how common it was some time ago for men to wear a pair of uneven dress pants. It is less common these days to see a man wear a pair of uneven dress pants for two reasons. One is that most men wear readymade instead of tailored slacks. Readymade pants are cut evenly for both pant legs. The other reason is that many men wear their pants too long. It is difficult to tell whether the two pant legs are even if the extra length of pant legs bulges on top of the shoes. No matter if your pants are cut evenly or unevenly, you should make sure that both of your pant legs are equal to the ground when wearing.

49. Why do khaki pants fray easily?

Khaki, chino or twill pants are perhaps the most popular casual slacks. Many men enjoy wearing khaki pants, but they are frustrated by the fact khaki pants fray terribly at the bottom of the pant legs. They wonder why.

49-1. Coarse yarns tend to be loose yarns.

Consumers rarely relate fraying to the size of yarns. Cotton yarns are made by drawing and twisting the cotton staples together. Because a thin yarn contains less cotton than a coarse yarn of the same length, the finer yarn must be twisted more tightly in order to hold the cotton fibers together. Conversely, coarse yarns tend to be loose yarns. Traditionally, the garment industry uses coarse yarns to produce thick fabrics for the purpose of adding strength and reducing the tendency to wrinkle. Oxford cloth and Khaki pants are made of coarse yarns; therefore, they fray and wear out easily.

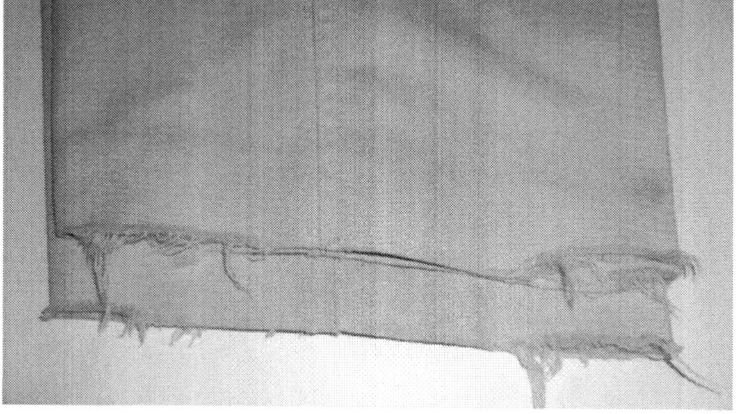

A pair of frayed Khaki pants.

49-2. Twill weave is less stable than plain weave.

Fabrics can be made by weaving, knitting, or simply by pressing the fibers together. Woven fabrics are produced by the interlacing of warp (lengthwise) and weft (filling or crosswise) yarns. There are three basic weaves. They are plain, twill, and satin. Most other types are variations of these three.

a) plain weave:

The simplest of the weave constructions, in which each weft yarn goes alternately over and under each warp yarn. Though the construction is simple, plain weave is the crispest weave.

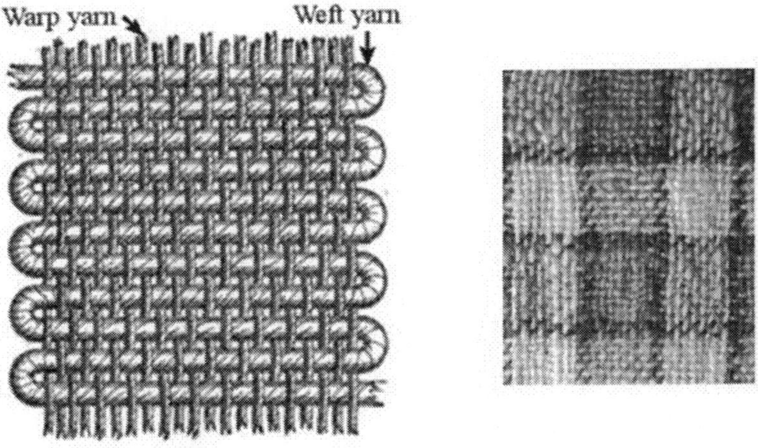

Plain weave

b) twill weave

A basic weave, in which each weft yarn passes over at least two but not more than four warp yarns. On each successive line, the weft moves one step to the right or left, creating a diagonal ridge. As a rule, the steeper the ridge, the stronger the fabric is.

Structure of a 3/1 twill

gabardine

c) satin weave

Another basic structure, in which a warp yarn passes over four to eight weft yarns in a staggered pattern similar to that of twill. Yarns exposed on the surface are called floats, which give satin its characteristic sheen. When the floats are formed by the weft yarns instead of the warp yarns, the weave is called sateen.

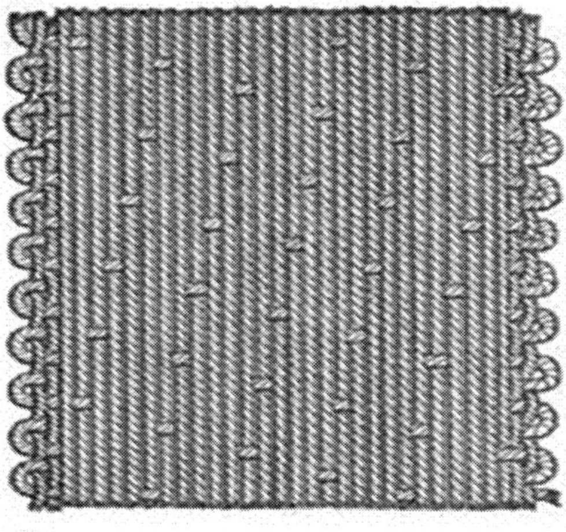

Satin weave with 16 warp yarns floating over each weft yarn.

In addition to the above basic three, patterned weaves, such as jacquard and dobby, are complex structures that require special devices attached to the loom.

A plain weave contains the greatest number of interlacing; therefore, it is considered the most stable weave. One shortcoming of the plain weave is that it tears more easily. The following illustration explains the concept of load bearing during tearing. It is easier to tear a single string of thread (a) than a bunch of threads (b). When a plain weave fabric is torn, only one yarn is present to resist the tear (c). Hence, it is easier to tear a piece of plain weave cloth by breaking the yarns one by one in the same direction.

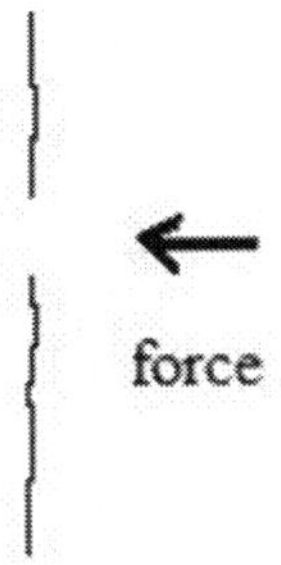

(a)

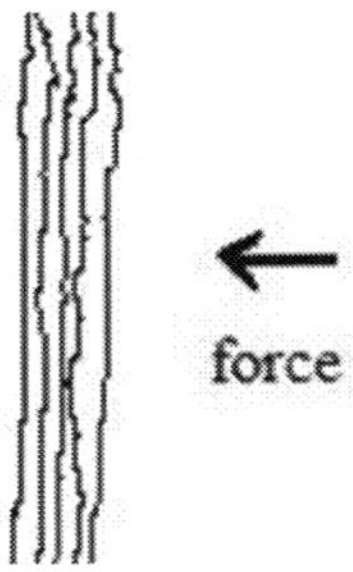

(b)

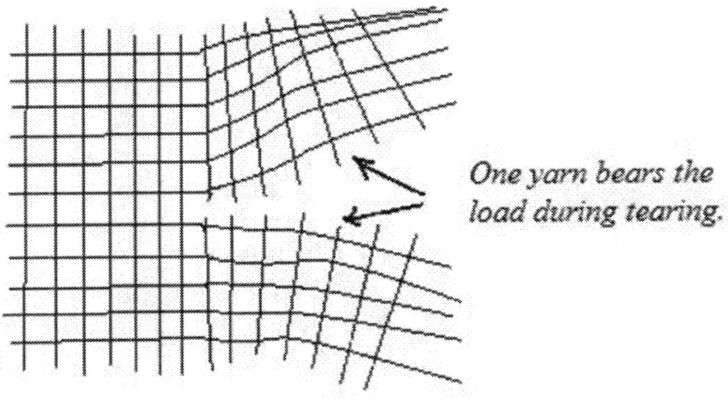

(c)

To reduce the chance of tearing, many casual pants, such as jeans and khakis, are made of twill weave fabrics. Twill weave contains short floats and is less stable than plain weave. When the supporting yarn is broken due to friction, the floating yarns come apart. Thus, khaki and denim pants tend to fray easily. Currently, there is no good solution to this problem. For those men who love Khakis, they just have to replace the worn out pants more frequently. They can switch to pants made of plain weave fabrics, such as canvas and poplin. Or, they can prolong the life of their khakis by adding heel stay, which is a strip of fabric sewn along the bottoms of the pant legs.

50. Restore tailoring details after alteration.

A customer bought three fancy suits and had them altered. He brought one pair of pants back and complained about there was a tear on the top of the back seam. I happened to be around and told him that fancy trousers tend to have a split on back called fish mouth. He said the other two pairs of pants do not have the fish mouth as I described. I asked him if the waist of the other two pairs was altered. He said, "Yes." I told him that tailor skipped the detail when he or she altered the pants. I teased the customer if he wanted to forsake the fish mouth. "Oh, no," he said. He left the store happily, knowing that he owns a pair of good quality pants.

One of the main reasons that one suit is better than other suits is the tailoring. Manufacturers spent more manpower, time and effort to sew pieces together and create a fancy suit. Many men buy luxurious suits and have them altered improperly. Don't you think it is pitiful to pay someone to cheapen or damage your good clothes with unnecessary or improper alterations? If you have fine articles of clothing and have them altered, be sure that they are altered correctly and have the tailoring details such as the fish mouth restored.

A common mistake is that tailors may not restore fused seams after they taper the body of the shirt by altering from the side seams. Consequently, the side seams become puckered after laundry. Wrinkle-free shirts tend to have fused seams. It is ridiculous to wear a shirt that is wrinkle-free throughout the shirt except the seams.

Another common problem concerns the vent of the jacket sleeves. Suit manufacturers tend to produce sleeves that are longer than what an average person needs because it is easier to shorten than to lengthen the sleeves. Most men do not know the proper length of a jacket. They notice the problem right away if the jacket is too short, but they may not recognize the problem if the jacket is too long. Most men these days buy jackets that are longer than they need. Consequently, the sleeves are far too long for some men. If the sleeves are taken in too much, a large portion or entire vent will be lost unless the tailor makes a new vent. Of course, the tailor will not voluntarily take time to make a new vent. The customer has to request it and pay for the service. The problem is that most consumers do not pay attention to details. They may not know they should ask.

Fancy dress pants tend to have a split, called fish mouth, on top of the back seam

Final notes:

Don't sweat the small stuff

Screenshot, fair use.

Consider the source when asking for help. It is risky to rely on a stranger to choose clothes for you.

- Working in a retail store, I have the opportunity to meet all kinds of customers. Through countless conversations with various types of customers, I realize different groups of customers have their different concepts or philosophies about men's clothing and about dressing well. Their concepts or philosophies are often incorrect and are the main reasons that today's men dress poorly. The belief that how a person dresses is his personal choice and there should have no rules about what a person should wear is one of the many erroneous concepts that dissuade many men from dressing properly. Many people will refuse to consider any suggestion that defies their beliefs or ideologies. Unless these erroneous concepts or philosophies are corrected, any talk about dressing well is meaningless or ineffective.

- Men can only wear what they buy and buy what is available to them in the market. The ways they shop have a great deal to do with how they dress.

When shopping, there are only two types of mistakes. One is bought something that you should not buy. The other is did not buy something you should buy. Whereas it is impossible to commit both mistakes at the same time, most consumers, with imperfect information, are making either mistake all the time. Smart shoppers should know which mistake to avoid!

- In his bestselling book, *New Dress for Success*, John T. Molloy suggested five reasons for today's businessmen dressing for failure. The first reason is that "They let their wives or their girlfriends choose their clothing." The second reason is that "They let their favorite sales clerk choose their clothing."

  "The next group that leads men down the path to sartorial slaughter are sales clerks. I mean no offense, and there are certainly some qualified exceptions, but most men's clothing store salesmen come from limited backgrounds and possess limited education, limited personal resources and limited knowledge of the business world. Little or no formal training is required for the job, and even the major stores that do have training programs generally teach their employees how to sell rather than how to serve."

  Most consumers do not believe it is complicated to pick up a clothing item in the store. If they need help, they can always rely on salespersons, they think. Salesclerks in men's clothing stores are generally poorly trained or not trained at all. Over a decade, I have seldom met a customer who dresses correctly. Millions of consumers are given the wrong clothes every day without noticing the problem. What is funny is that they keep thanking salesclerks for selling them the wrong clothes.

  Most consumers are not willing to spend time studying men's clothing. They seek an easy way out by asking assistance from a sales clerk. It is not a bad idea to ask for help as long as the person sought is competent. Most consumers want help but they hardly ever examine what type of help they are getting. Often, customers ask for the right items but the salesperson persuades them to buy the wrong ones. Many consumers did not mind spending money to buy good quality wool slacks but they were scared away by salesclerks, who told them that wool slacks must be dry-cleaned. Each day I hear customers say thanks to salesclerks for their big help. I wonder how these consumers will react if they find out what they have purchased are the wrong merchandise.

- Many men and women mistakenly think the primary goal of men's clothing is to make a man look handsome or pretty. They waste most of their time in searching for garments or accessories that are beautiful, sharp looking or trendy. Upper-middle and lower-middle class men tend to prefer different colors and patterns.

  John T. Molloy did a series of studies in men's clothing in the 1970s. He claimed the American public considers that traditional, conservative and familiar clothes project a look of good taste, of credibility and of upper-middle-class success. He wrote, "In many men's minds tradition and familiarity, not fashion, says sophistication." Familiarity does not breed contempt; it breeds acceptance.

- Many people are conscious about their appearance. They have the right idea to demand quality clothing even though good quality clothing may cost more. Yet, they tend not to have the right idea to distinguish between quality and less quality clothing. Most of them just buy whatever is expensive or whatever famous designers make. Presume that they have found quality clothing. Nevertheless, wearing quality clothes is not the same as dressing well. People will not give a person credit only because he wears quality clothes. They know he does not make the clothes he wears. People will, however, hold a person responsible for how he chooses and how he wears his garments. A quality garment that does not suit its wearer is less useful than a less quality garment that fits its wearer.

- American consumers are obsessed with color matching. They spend considerable amount of time and effort trying to find a tie that matches the color of their shirt, pants, suit or a woman's dress. They want a pocket square that matches their tie and want a pair of socks that match either their pants or shoes. It is absolutely a waste of time and money to match something that is supposed not to be matched.

- Alan Flusser, a prominent fashion designer, believed 90% of all men wear their coat sleeves too long. More men wear a wrong collar width, shirtsleeve, pant length, cuff width, or jacket length.

  Mortimer Levitt, a custom shirt maker, claimed that "Salesmen in the country's best stores do not know how to take a measurement for collar size."

  You can't buy and wear the right size clothing if you are measured incorrectly. But, how can you get measured correctly if the salesmen in the country's best stores do not even know how to measure the collar size? It's time to learn something about the clothes you wear every day.

- Some men bought a fancy suit and have the suit pants cuffed at a wrong width, which is the best way to cheapen a suit. It is puzzling that many consumers search everywhere for some odd sizes that are rare or do not exist while they can acquire the sizes by simple alteration. A garment that is altered to fit the wearer looks like it is worth more than a garment that does not fit.

Most men are between sizes. So, why is it difficult to understand that some alterations may be needed for a better fit?

- Many men prefer to be fitted by a tailor instead of a salesperson. Nevertheless, I have seen countless garments ruined by the tailors as well as salespersons.

  A tailor is like a typist. Stephen King is a popular writer but he does not type well. He uses his two index fingers to type, known as the hunt-and-peck or search-and-peck method. A typist can type fast but may be unable to write a book because it takes intelligence and knowledge to write a book. It is wise to seek a tailor for technical advice such as how to shorten the coat collar and how to hem a pair of pants, but it is silly to ask a tailor for fashion advice unless the tailor happens to be knowledgeable about fashion. I have seen many men stand in front of a three-way mirror and say nothing when the tailor is fitting the garment incorrectly. Most tailors do not know the correct sleeve length and cuff width. I once went to see a tailor to have my jacket sleeves shortened. The tailor argued with me that my sleeves were too short already because they retreated when my hands bent. That is exactly the same reasoning that 90% of all men mistakenly want their sleeves to be long.

  Like other professionals, each tailor has his personal preferences or biases. Some tailors prefer a full-break while some others favor a medium-break for pant length. In truth, the break is the result of pants being too long. Why should any men in their right mind want their pants to be too long? Any rational man should try to reduce or avoid a break in his pants. All the salesperson or tailor does is to cut the pants short if the customer wants no break, and cut the pants long if the customer wants full break. Do you know you can have your pants cut long without a break? The secret is to cut the bottom of the pants differently. Many tailors do not even know how to slant a pair of pants. Most tailors earn their income by piece work. The more alterations, the more incomes are. Dishonest or ignorant tailors like to perform unnecessary alterations. I couldn't believe that so many men and women wear pants with uneven legs. It is more ridiculous that many tailors allow their clients to cuff the flat-front pants.

- Many shoppers are looking for specific brands of merchandise. There is nothing wrong to buy something that works for them. The problem is that they often refuse to try something better only because they are so attached to the old products. They should always know why the products they are using are good. Be ready to replace the old products with better, innovative new technologies.

Books *by* *Ivan M.C. Chen, Ph.D.*

The Art of Arching out a Tie

ISBN: 978-1438254401

The Rules of Ties

ISBN: 978-1438286600

The Essentials of Dress Shirts

ISBN: 978-1438288369

A Perfect Pair of Dress Pants

ISBN: 978-1438287102

The Etiquette of Suits and Sport Coats

ISBN: 978-1438287102

The Secrets of Men's Clothing

ISBN: 978-1453880043

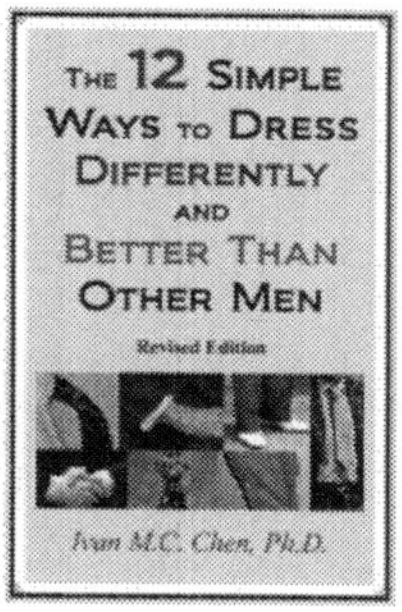

The 12 Simple Ways to Dress Differently and Better Than Other Men

ISBN: 978-1449577056

First Things First in Men's Clothing

ISBN: 978-1460982266

In Menswear Everything Has Two Prices One for the Fool

ISBN: 978-1439298565

The Stupid Things Men Do about Their Clothing

ISBN: 978-1438286136

<u>Learn by Pictures</u>

The Correct Way to Wear Men's Clothing

ISBN: 978-1448651016

What Fashion Experts Teach You Wrong or Did Not Teach You about Fabrics

ISBN: 978-1438269818

Books can be ordered through amazon, createspace.com, target.com, other websites, and any bookseller worldwide.

First Things First in Men's Clothing

Everybody knows that first things come first but few men know what the first things are in men's clothing. Most men waste much of their time and effort buying the wrong articles of clothing because they are looking for the wrong things. Here are examples.

Most consumers believe quality garments wear better and last longer, but they have no clear ideas concerning how to judge the quality of products. So, they buy expensive clothing or buy whatever famous designers make. They do not realize that it is wise to judge the quality of a garment based on industrial standards.

The vast majority of consumers want to buy a tie that looks sharp, beautiful or fun. They also want the tie to match their jacket, shirt and slacks. The tie looks sharp, but the wearer is not.

Most mistakes can be avoided if consumers know how to put the first things first. If a man buys everything he wears according to his face, he will have less to worry about which articles of clothing coordinate well with other clothing items. If a man buys the right size clothing according to current standards in the industry, he will have less to worry about whether his clothing items will wear better and last longer.

This book lists a number of first things that consumers should know when shopping and wearing men's clothing. Once they set their priorities straight, they will find it difficult to buy and wear the wrong articles of clothing. They will also find it easier to buy what they need or want.

The Secrets of Men's Clothing

Mark Twain said, "Clothes make the man. Naked people have little or no influence on society." If you wear clothes, why not wear the right ones correctly? The problem is that most men do not know what the right clothes are or how to wear and care for their clothes properly.

This unique book reveals more than fifty big and small secrets that most men neglect. The secrets have never appeared in previous literature because most fashion experts and writers do not know these secrets either.

- Why do so many men wear a crooked bowtie?
- Why is it smart to hang your necktie according to the length of your face instead of the location of your pant waist?
- Why is it dangerous to wear the Atlantic and Merovingian Knot?
- Why shouldn't you wear shirt sleeves the same length of your arms?
- Why shouldn't you wear the same sleeve length for both barrel and French cuff shirts?
- Why shouldn't you iron or starch a non-iron shirt?
- Why shouldn't you cup your fingers to determine the proper length of a jacket?
- Why is it wise to choose between a two-button and a three-button jacket based on the balance points of your face?
- Why is it better to have the pant legs finished with a slanted bottom?
- Why is it unnecessary to match between the colors of your socks, pants and shoes?
- What are the advantages of mercerized cotton?
- Why should you vary the colors of your clothing for health benefits?
- Where should you wear a tie tack, clip or chain on your tie?
- And much, much more.

The world's first and only book to teach you

The Art of Arching Out a Tie

Many men think fancy clothes help them look good. They do not realize that people are less likely to give a man credit for the quality of his clothes. People know he does not make the clothes he wears. People will, however, give the man credit if he coordinates his outfit nicely and wears his garments correctly. A good-looking tie does not suggest the smartness of the wearer, but a well-arched tie may.

As the fashion trend moves toward more casual and sporty setting, more men are dressing poorly. Many men are searching for ways to dress differently and better than other men. What is a better way to dress differently and elegantly than to arch out a tie? After all, few men in history have ever been able to do so.

There is no other article of men's clothing that requires more skill to execute than the tie. There are about 100 different ways to tie a tie. Every tie book illustrates the methods of tying the three most popular tie knots, the four-in-hand, Windsor, and half Windsor. In truth, these three knots are the main reasons why a man cannot arch out his tie.

The Art of Arching out a Tie is the world's first and only book that teaches men how to arch out a tie without using any artificial device, such as a collar pin, collar tab, or vest. The book will revolutionize the way men tie their ties. Open this book and discover the many factors that help produce an arched tie. You will become one of the few masters who can arch out a tie without the support of any device. The book also provides information, which no other book can offer, concerning the best way to determine the length of a knotted tie and the best location to place a tie tack, tie bar or tie chain.

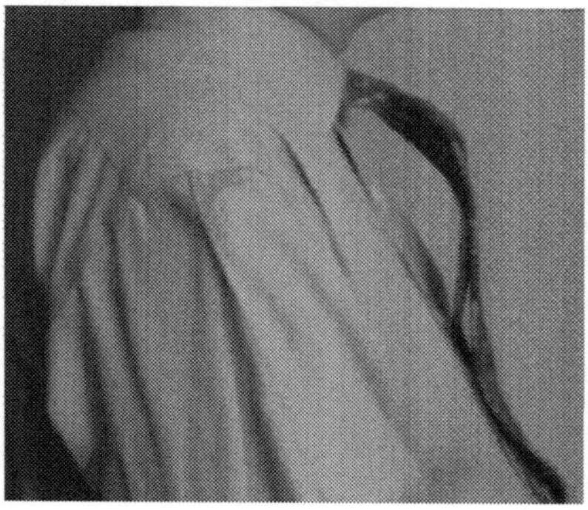

The Rule of Ties *has everything you need to know about ties. The book offers you a paradigm shift and tells you what types of ties are proper for business and social activities.*

The book teaches you how to wear your tie correctly. The ties have been considered the most important status symbols. Many men wear fancy ties but wear the ties with a sloppy knot or at a wrong length.

Tie experts maintain that a well-tied tie should have a forward arch beneath the knot, but no one knows how to accomplish this goal. Every fashion book teaches its readers how to tie the three most popular tie knots, the four-in-hand, Windsor, and half Windsor. If you use one of these knots, you probably will never have a chance to arch out your tie.

The book teaches you the biggest secret in tie history--how to arch out a tie without using any artificial device, such as a collar pin or a vest.

The book teaches you a number of unusual knots such as the diagonal knot. The book also teaches you how to relate the width, length, and patterns of the tie to your face. The book further explains the correct ways of using tie accessories.

The Essentials of Dress Shirts

The great majority of men wear wrong size shirts without noticing the problem. This book is a must read if you commit one or more of the following.

- Do not know what "80's 2-ply" means, or you think the term refers to thread count per square inch.
- Desire a loose collar because it is more comfortable.
- Wear the same sleeve length as your arm length.
- Wear the same sleeve length for both barrel cuff and French cuff shirts.
- Do not know why you should wear a spread collar with a jacket.
- Do not wear a top fused shirt.
- Believe that fabrics made of 2-ply yarns are better.
- Prefer cotton and polyester blend shirts for wrinkle-resistance.
- Wear a collar pin or a tab collar to arch out the tie.
- Wear a shirt collar with tie space.
- Do not know that broadcloth is dressier than oxford cloth.
- Do not know the aesthetic balance between the collar style and the head shape.
- Mix fabrics and styles without matching up the dressiness scales, such as wearing a spread collar made of oxford cloth, or a button-down collar made of broadcloth.
- Do not know that not every non-iron shirt performs in the same way.
- Wear a shirt that has no crease at the pleats or folds.
- Wear a shirt with puckered seams.

Dr. Ivan Chen provides an insider's trade secrets and wisdom that no other fashion book can offer.

A Perfect Pair of Dress Pants

--The most misunderstood topic in men's clothing--

Dr. Ivan Chen has sold men's clothing for more than a decade. He has been disturbed by how American men buy and wear their dress pants. Clothing stores nationwide carry a variety of good quality dress shirts but stock inferior quality dress pants. Merchants do so because consumers keep buying the wrong pants.

Most men want to wear wrinkle-free and machine washable pants, so they choose synthetic or synthetic blend slacks. They are unaware that good quality wool pants are virtually wrinkle-free and can be machine-washed in water. Wool contains lanolin, a natural deodorizer, which prevents wool from absorbing odors. Hence, pants made of worsted wool require minimum care. Unless a man sweats heavily, he really has no need to clean his wool slacks. All he has to do is to air out and brush the slacks regularly, and steam them occasionally. Many men buy fancy wool pants but sent them to the dry cleaner regularly to have their expensive pants damaged quickly.

Most men do not even know how to wear a pair of pants correctly. They wear their pants a few inches below the waistline. They wear their pants too long, leaving multiple breaks in the bottom back of the pant legs. Many men mistakenly think cuffed are dressier than non-cuffed pants. They wear cuffed pants with a wrong cuff width, which is the best way to cheapen a pair of pants. Most men, including fashion experts, are indecisive about cuffs. In truth, whether a pair of pants is cuffed is insignificant. What is important is to finish the pants with a slanted bottom.

A Perfect Pair of Dress Pants tells everything you need to know about dress pants. With the secrets that no other fashion book can offer, you can now wear a perfect pair of dress pants.

The Etiquette of Suits and Sport Coats

Alan Flusser, a prominent fashion designer, claims that 90% of all men wear their jacket sleeves too long. Do you think the rest 10% of men do everything else right about their suits and sport jackets?

After buying a suit, many men have their suit pants cuffed at the wrong width, which is the best way to cheapen a new suit. Other men send their brand new suit directly to a drycleaner and have the suit damaged by over-pressing or by washing with harsh chemicals.

Most men rely on their spouse, girlfriend or salesclerks to select their suits. This is the main reason that today's men dress for failure according to John T. Molloy. Few men ever realize they need to learn something about men's clothing. This book is a must read if you commit one of the following.

- Cup your fingers to determine the length of the jacket.
- Desire longer jacket sleeves for fear that the sleeves may retreat too much when the arms bend.
- Do not know how long a jacket should be.
- Wear long size jackets because you think you are tall.
- Do not know why dress pants should not have a break in the back of the pants.
- Believe that cuffed pants are dressier than non-cuffed pants.
- Do not know why dress pants are better finished with a slanted bottom.
- Do not know that worsted wool garments require little care.
- Send your suits or jackets to drycleaners regularly.
- Do not know wool garments can be washed in water, called wet-cleaning.

The 12 Simple Ways to Dress Differently and Better Than Other Men

As the fashion trend moves toward more casual and sporty setting, more men are dressing indifferently. Dressing normally becomes an exception. Some men want to dress differently from the rest of the crowd, but they often choose the wrong approach. They wear garments of luxurious fabrics in flashy styles to boost their image.

Dr. Ivan Chen believes that any man who can wear a simple article of clothing correctly will look different from most men. The methods included in this book appear simple, yet different and better.

Open The 12 Simple Ways and discover why and how to dress differently and better than other men without additional cost.

- Arch out a tie without the support of a collar pin or a vest.
- Hang a tie that is shorter than two head lengths.
- Wear collars that fit the neck snuggly.
- Wear spread collars, especially with a jacket.
- Wear a jacket just long enough to cover the seat.
- Reduce the break on pants to a minimum.
- Finish pants with a slanted leg bottom.
- Wear the correct cuff width on pants.
- Keep creases sharp on shirts and pants.
- Wear a correct shirt sleeve length.
- Wear a correct coat sleeve length.
- Hang the pants from the waist.
- Wear top fused dress shirts.

In Menswear Everything Has Two Prices One for the Fool

Men can only wear what they buy and buy what are available to them. The way men or their loved ones shop have a great deal to do with how men dress. Alan Flusser, author of *Style and the Man*, says that during the past two decades, men have spent more money on clothing for themselves than in any other period of modern history. Most men buy the wrong clothing, which is one of the main reasons that today's men dress poorly.

Clothing stores nationwide are stocked with mediocre products because consumers keep buying them. To avoid paying a fool's price, consumers either pay the same price for better merchandise, or buy the same quality merchandise at a lower price. Nevertheless, consumers must first know how to detect the quality of merchandise. The fashion industry has often deceived or misled consumers.

Dr. Ivan Chen has sold men's clothing for more than a decade. He understands and explains many phenomena in men's clothing better than any fashion expert. Dr. Chen examines why consumers keep buying the wrong clothing and teaches consumers how to find the best buys in different categories of men's clothing. Dr. Chen often provides surprising, yet convincing explanations. Many of his answers are thought provoking and are contrary to common beliefs.

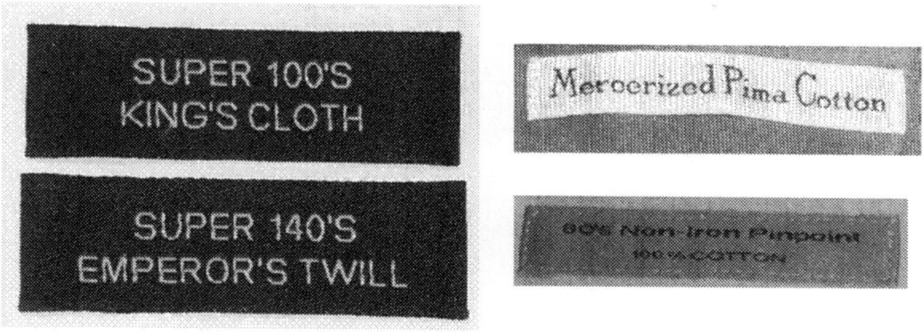

Manufacturers spend millions of dollars each year to put important product information on labels but they never educate consumers about the technical terms. Consumers often buy the wrong products because they have been misinformed or have not been informed.

The Stupid Things Men Do
about Their Clothing

Alan Flusser, a prominent fashion designer and author of many books, believes that 90% of all men wear their jacket sleeves too long. The jacket sleeve is one of the most obvious areas. If a man can make a mistake in the sleeve length, he probably will make mistakes in other areas of his clothing. The majority of men dress poorly these days. Most men do not even know they dress improperly.

Dr. Ivan Chen has sold men's clothing for more than a decade. He has spoken with tens of thousands of customers and has been amazed by the many foolish things men do about their clothing.

- Many men buy fancy dress pants and have the pants cuffed at the wrong length, which is the best way to cheapen a pair of pants. Some men want to buy flat-front pants with cuffs or have their flat-front pants cuffed.
- Many men wear oversized shirts and ask for fitted ones.
- Many men wear their pants several inches below the waistline and still wear longer pants, leaving multiple breaks at the bottom of the pants.
- The vast majority of men tie their ties using one of the most popular three knots, the four-in-hand, half Windsor, and Windsor. They do not realize these three knots are the wrong knots, which prevent the tie from arching out.
- Most men wear their dress shirt sleeves the same length as their arms. Few men know that the sleeve length of a French cuff shirt should be different from that of a barrel cuff shirt.

Dr. Chen collects some of the most common mistakes and offers solutions. He has been able to understand and explain many phenomena in men's clothing better than any fashion expert. Dr. Chen often provides surprising, yet convincing explanations. Many of his answers are thought provoking and are contrary to common beliefs.

Learn by Pictures

The Correct Way to Wear Men's Clothing

In an ad during WWI, Hart Schaffner & Marks urged consumers to buy the company's products and save. In truth, people waste their money more on buying the wrong size clothes or wearing the clothes incorrectly than on buying bad quality clothes.

Dr. Ivan Chen has served tens of thousands of consumers in a men's department store. He has discovered that not every man has the time or is interested in reading a substantial amount of text. This book uses an effective and efficient new approach to learn how to master men's clothing by showing pictures of men wearing correct and incorrect articles of clothing. The photos in this book have impressed and changed the mind of tens of thousands of customers.

A right picture is worth a thousand words. This book will help you learn and learn very fast, and will not let you forget what you have just learned about men's clothing. Read this book in a couple of hours and save money for a lifetime by buying and wearing the right clothes.

What Fashion Experts Teach You Wrong or Did Not Teach You about Fabrics

Manufacturers spend millions of dollars each year to put important product information, such as "80's 2-ply" and "Super 120's", on labels, but they seldom educate consumers the meaning of these designations. Merchants are facing a dilemma. They wish to brag about the quality of their better-made products. But if they do so, how will they be able to sell other less quality merchandise? Clothing stores nationwide are filled with mediocre products. These products must be sold also. This dilemma may explain why merchants are not enthusiastic to educate consumers how to detect quality products. In their language, mediocre garments are made of "fine" fabrics whereas better garments are made of "finer" or the "finest" fabrics.

Fashion experts often boast of their terrific ideas on how to coordinate a set of outfit, how to fit a particular body shape or skin tone, and so forth. They rarely talk about basic technical terms perhaps because they know little about technologies. Some fashion writers, including famous ones, dare to take on this task only to give false information. They often mistake yarn size for thread count. The Federal Trade Commission recently warned that consumers "could be deceived or misled" by thread count information put out by vendors. What a surprise! Fashion experts and manufacturers have misled consumers for some time.

Dr. Ivan Chen has sold men's clothing for more than a decade. He has been disappointed with the inaccuracy of many contemporary writings on men's clothing. Dr. Chen wrote this book to correct some of the common fallacies about fibers and fabrics.

Index

Q

R

S

V

W

Y

2837008R00274

Printed in Great Britain
by Amazon.co.uk, Ltd.,
Marston Gate.